MW00560047

"With *Walkable City*, Jeff Speck demonstrated that he is th[e] thinker of his generation on the subject of city planning. W[ith Walkable] *City Rules*, he establishes himself as the most helpful. There i[s] to have a greater positive impact on our communities and on the practice of urban planning than this comprehensive and engaging text."

—**RON BOGLE**, President and CEO,
The American Architectural Foundation

"Jeff Speck is a total rock star to me. He is a great planner, but his real gift is empowering people to reshape their own communities. There is a huge wave of us out there saying, 'Yes, I DO want to make my town more livable, walkable, equal, and fun.' *Walkable City Rules* is THE super-user-friendly resource to help us spring into action, wherever we are."

—**DAR WILLIAMS**, singer-songwriter and author
of *What I Found in a Thousand Towns*

"If you want to make your city safer, healthier, greener, wealthier, and more equitable, then you need to make it more walkable. *Walkable City Rules* is a must-read for urbanists, city-builders, and everyone who lives in cities."

—**RICHARD FLORIDA**, author of
Rise of the Creative Class

"Jeff Speck, more than any city planner I know, writes about walking in such a common-sense and useful way that he makes you crave a good walk. He not only defines what it is, he eloquently shows us how to achieve it. Another great read, one that gives any city the necessary tools to create a good walk."

—**MAURICE COX**, Director, Planning
& Development Department, City of Detroit

"Jeff Speck has written the book our cities need right now; a practical guide for building the great places of tomorrow. This is essential reading for anyone wanting to make their place better."

—**CHARLES MAROHN**, Founder and President,
Strong Towns

"I am a big fan of the phrase, 'walk before you run' and have applied it figuratively as a framework in business and government. In his influential practice, Jeff Speck applies it literally: places will never be truly great unless they are walkable, no matter what you layer on top, including technology. In this essential volume, Jeff lays out a comprehensive and interconnected set of 'Walkable City Rules' that, if followed by every city and town, would create a nation of happy citizens and superlative outcomes."

—**GABE KLEIN**, Cofounder, CityFi and author of
Start-Up City

"Jeff Speck was the first to introduce me to the concept of a walkable city. With his help, Oklahoma City completely changed its outlook on the built environment and has now transformed itself into a completely different place. How we did it—and how you can do it, too—can be found in this important and compelling book."

—**MICK CORNETT**, Former Mayor of Oklahoma
City and President of the US Conference of Mayors

"In *Walkable City,* Jeff Speck outlined the many compelling social, economic, and environmental benefits that come from designing our communities for people rather than cars. With *Walkable City Rules,* he translates those principles into a concrete plan of action. From zoning changes to public transit investments and road repurposing to saving existing small-scale fabric, this timely and necessary book offers clear, concise, and step-by-step instructions for urban planners and leaders to transform neighborhoods for the better and reimagine their cities at a human scale."

—**STEPHANIE MEEKS**, President and CEO,
National Trust for Historic Preservation

"America's car-focused evolution has accelerated epidemics of injury, inactivity, depression, and isolation. We must transform disease-promoting places into ones that are human- and health-friendly. Speck confronts this task and makes acrobatic what could be pedantic. He writes with humor and verve, but with substance from deep experience. A beautiful book, with superb organization, layout, photos, and writing, *Walkable City Rules* should be assigned reading for every elected official and every health and planning class in America."

—**RICHARD JACKSON**, Former Director, CDC
National Center for Environmental Health

Praise for *Walkable City* (2012)

"*Walkable City* is timely and important, a delightful, insightful, irreverent work—a book designed to knock us out of complacency and make us aware of the simple but real possibilities. It should be required reading. . ."

—RICHARD HORAN, *The Christian Science Monitor*

". . . a recipe for vibrant street life."

—DAVID L. ULIN, *The Los Angeles Times*

"*Walkable City* is very good indeed, a worthy addition to the canon of urban thinking. . . it will change the way you see cities."

—KAID BENFIELD, *Atlantic Cities*

Praise for *Suburban Nation* (2000)

"*Suburban Nation* dissects the design of the suburbs brilliantly. . . [the authors] set forth more clearly than anyone has done in our time the elements of good town planning."

—PAUL GOLDBERGER, *The New Yorker*

"The bible of urbanists is *Suburban Nation.*"

—FRED BARNES, *The Wall Street Journal*

"A book of luminous intelligence and wit. The fiasco of suburbia has never been so clearly described. This is not just a manifesto on architecture and civic design, but a major literary event."

—JAMES HOWARD KUNSTLER, author of *The Geography of Nowhere* and *Home from Nowhere*

About Island Press

Since 1984, the nonprofit organization Island Press has been stimulating, shaping, and communicating ideas that are essential for solving environmental problems worldwide. With more than 1,000 titles in print and some 30 new releases each year, we are the nation's leading publisher on environmental issues. We identify innovative thinkers and emerging trends in the environmental field. We work with world-renowned experts and authors to develop cross-disciplinary solutions to environmental challenges.

Island Press designs and executes educational campaigns, in conjunction with our authors, to communicate their critical messages in print, in person, and online using the latest technologies, innovative programs, and the media. Our goal is to reach targeted audiences—scientists, policy makers, environmental advocates, urban planners, the media, and concerned citizens—with information that can be used to create the framework for long-term ecological health and human well-being.

Island Press gratefully acknowledges major support from The Bobolink Foundation, Caldera Foundation, The Curtis and Edith Munson Foundation, The Forrest C. and Frances H. Lattner Foundation, The JPB Foundation, The Kresge Foundation, The Summit Charitable Foundation, Inc., and many other generous organizations and individuals.

The opinions expressed in this book are those of the author(s) and do not necessarily reflect the views of our supporters.

WALKABLE CITY RULES

WALKABLE CITY RULES

101 Steps to Making Better Places

JEFF SPECK

ISLANDPRESS Washington | Covelo | London

Copyright © 2018 Jeff Speck

All rights reserved under International and Pan-American Copyright Conventions. No part of this book may be reproduced in any form or by any means without permission in writing from the publisher: Island Press, 2000 M Street, NW, Suite 650, Washington, DC 20036.

Island Press is a trademark of The Center for Resource Economics.

Library of Congress Control Number: 2018946755

All Island Press books are printed on environmentally responsible materials.

Manufactured in the United States of America
10 9 8 7 6 5 4 3

Keywords: ADU, affordable housing, autonomous vehicles, bicycle boulevard, bicycle network, bikeshare, bus network, climate change, community, congestion pricing, cycle track, displacement, equity, gentrification, granny flats, highway teardown, Level of Service, local parks, local schools, mass transit, neckdown, parking, parklet, pedestrian zone, public health, red-light camera, slow-flow street, Smart Codes, speed camera, street safety, street tree, streetcar, transit and land use, road diet, sticky edges, traffic study, two-way street, Vancouver urbanism, Vision Zero, walkability study, yield-flow street

COVER PHOTOS

Courtesty of Getty Images:
Aerial View of Busy Crosswalk with People, Seoul, Korea, Lee Kyung Jun/Imazins

Courtesty of Shutterstock.com:
Overhead view of a cyclist on a mountain bike with a white t-shirt and blue helmet, by Wally Stemberger

Overhead shot of a three lane road on a bridge, by Silken Photography

Top view of Copacabana beach with mosaic of sidewalk in Rio de Janeiro, Brazil, by ESB Professional

Top View of Street with Palm Trees in a Beach, by Gustavo Frazao

Street Pedestrians, by Marc Swim

Young couple relaxing outdoors, overhead view: tourism concept, by GagliardiImages

For Milo and Roman

CONTENTS

AUTHOR'S NOTE

"As no better man advances to take this matter in hand, I hereupon offer my own endeavors. I offer nothing complete, because any human thing supposed to be complete, must for that reason infallibly be faulty."

—Herman Melville, *Moby Dick*

THIS VOLUME IS NOT COMPREHENSIVE, but it tries to be. The "101" in the title is an artifice; it could have been half or twice as many. But the book's 200-plus central pages do contain everything that I want you to know—that is, everything that people tend to get wrong these days when designing pieces of cities. Tomorrow, there will be more.

You should read this whole book—not because you need to, but because doing so will cause you to understand more about the practical aspects of city planning than 90 percent of the people currently engaged in that work. Read it twice, and you will be qualified for planning commission. Three times: open your own urban design consultancy.

But, while you're struggling to find the time, feel free to flip around. Start with the items that address the challenges you are facing this week. Like most efforts by New Urban authors, this document runs from the macro to the micro, starting at the scale of the region and ending at the scale of the building. By all means, settle in around your sweet spot, but understand that it is all connected. As Leon Battista Alberti noted, "A city, according to the opinion of philosophers, be no more than a great house, and, on the other hand, a house be a little city."[1]

No doubt, you know a lot of this already, but you don't know all of it. (Even I do not know all of it, as I have forgotten a bunch of what I wrote just yesterday.) Some of the book—especially the first section—may be a bit familiar, as a few lines were cribbed lock, stock, and barrel from *Walkable City*, by necessity; once you figure out the best way to communicate an idea, to sell it to wary residents and skeptical council members, you stick with it. For example, there are a hundred ways to explain the value of parallel parking, but "an essential barrier of steel that protects the sidewalk from moving vehicles" is simply the best. Politicians learn the most effective ways to shape their message, for better or for worse, and then repeat them at every whistle stop; so must planners.

If I can get autobiographical for a moment, here is a synopsis of my professional life since 1992: I spent twenty years listening to the best planners explain their best ideas the best way they knew how. I then wrote those ideas down in *Walkable City*, improving them if at all possible. Next, I recorded the Audible version of the book, which I then bought, and began listening to on airplanes. (Hearing my own voice calmly say familiar things seems to help me sleep.) Eventually, I memorized it. This has really been a great help, both in my lectures and in my work with cities and towns across North America.

I plan to do the same with *Walkable City Rules*. I hope you will too—all of you. In my dreams, I imagine that this book is as familiar to you as it is to me. We are like the lifers in that old prison gag, telling jokes to each other by the number. Instead of asking a public works official to do a road diet, we just say "46!" Instead of admonishing a developer to hide a parking structure, it's "92!" And they all understand what we mean: in my dream prison, nobody tells the joke wrong.

Why are these *Rules?* I considered calling the book *Walkable City Patterns,* as a tribute to Christopher Alexander and a continuation of his technique of presenting a collection of co-dependent design principles across the full range of scales. But, as Alexander has himself admitted, today's built environment is more than anything else the outcome of rules, an octopus-like litany of codes and ordinances that more often than not produce unfortunate if not unintended outcomes. You can't fight rules with patterns, so *Rules* it is.

As a final note, please keep in mind that one important thing in this book will prove to be completely wrong; it's just impossible today to tell which thing. As Yogi Berra said, it's tough to make predictions, especially about the future.

Jeff Speck
Brookline, Massachusetts
28 August 2018

INTRODUCTION

NORTH AMERICA, along with much of the world, has been building and rebuilding its cities and towns quite badly for more than half a century. To do it properly would have been easy; we used to be great at it. But, like voting for president, just because something is easy to do does not mean that it will be done, or done well.

The happy news is that the trends are positive. Cities have been on the upswing for two decades. To the degree that it is practiced in American communities, city planning is now doing more good than harm. But the results are incredibly spotty. Lacking information, city leaders are still repeating mistakes that were widely discredited years ago—among those who were paying attention.

To rectify the sporadic spread of city planning best practices, I published *Walkable City* in 2012. The timing was fortunate: while the term was not often used before 2010, *walkability* now seems to be the special sauce that every community wants. It took a while, but many of our leaders have realized that establishing walkability as a central goal can be an expeditious path to making our cities better in a whole host of ways.

Packaged as *literary nonfiction* and *current affairs*, *Walkable City* was effective at finding readers, armchair urbanists curious about what makes cities tick. It made its way into mayors' offices, council chambers, and town meetings, held aloft by people demanding change. Sometimes, change was

There is room for improvement in current walkability planning.

begun. . . and that's when the problems started. While the book does a decent job of inspiring change, it doesn't exactly tell you how to create it.

Hence this new book, an effort to weaponize *Walkable City* for deployment in the field. Organized for easy access, worded for arguments at the planning commission, illustrated for clarity, and packed with not just data but specifications, *Walkable City Rules* is designed to be the most comprehensive tool available for bringing the latest and most impactful city planning practices to bear in your community. It is hoped that the format, as well as the information it holds, will allow it to be a force multiplier for place-makers and change-makers everywhere.

And if you haven't read *Walkable City*, you should. It may be the best document available for winning converts to the cause. But, in the end, *Walkable City* is for readers. *Walkable City Rules* is for doers—like you.

I. SELL WALKABILITY

1. Sell Walkability on Wealth

2. Sell Walkability on Health

3. Sell Walkability on Climate Change

4. Sell Walkability on Equity

5. Sell Walkability on Community

Part I

SELL WALKABILITY

SELLING WALKABILITY as a community goal is not as hard as it used to be, but there is always opposition, typically from *the usual suspects:* the automotive hordes, tinfoil-hat-wearing Agenda-21 conspiracy theorists, tea-baggers, and the like. Somehow, while a central government investing in highways and subsidizing oil companies constitutes *freedom,* any local investment in sidewalks and bike lanes smacks of a communist takeover.

The inevitability of some pushback, however ill-informed, means that walkability proponents need to be armed with the best arguments in its support. Five stand out: Economics, Health, Climate, Equity, and Community. The first three are discussed at great length in Walkable City; the last two are recent additions for more sophisticated audiences. All are helpful at winning converts.

1 Sell Walkability on Wealth

There are powerful economic reasons to invest in walkability.

IMPROVING WALKABILITY costs money, and budgets are tight. The first step in convincing community leaders to invest in walkability is to demonstrate that such investments pay off. Evidence abounds and can be mustered in support of a handful of powerful arguments.

Walkability powers property values. One of the clearest correlations in real estate is between walkability and home value. As a typical example, homes in Denver's walkable neighborhoods sell at a 150% premium over those in drivable sprawl.[2] In Charlotte, each Walk Score point (on a scale of 100) translates into about a $2,000 increase in home value.[3] Home values determine local property-tax revenue, justifying investments in walkability. Additionally, office space in walkable zip codes has a considerable leasing rate premium over suburban locations, and much lower vacancy rates.[4]

Walkability attracts talent. Educated millennials value walkability, and are moving to more walkable places. 64% of them choose first where they want to live, and only then do they look for work;[5] 77% say they plan to live in an urban core.[6] According to a recent study, a full 63% of millennials (and 42% of baby boomers) want to live in a place where they don't need a car.[7] Companies and cities that wish to attract young talent need to provide the walkable urban lifestyle they desire.

Investments in walkability create more, and better, jobs. A study of transportation projects in Baltimore found that, compared to highway investments, each dollar spent on pedestrian facilities created 57% more jobs, and each dollar spent on bicycle facilities created 100% more jobs.[8] Once built, walkable places

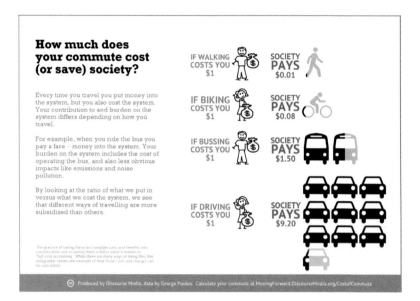

How much does your commute cost (or save) society?

Every time you travel you put money into the system, but you also cost the system. Your contribution to and burden on the system differs depending on how you travel.

For example, when you ride the bus you pay a fare - money into the system. Your burden on the system includes the cost of operating the bus, and also less obvious impacts like emissions and noise pollution.

By looking at the ratio of what we put in versus what we cost the system, we see that different ways of travelling are more subsidized than others.

The practice of taking these less tangible costs and benefits into consideration and assigning them a dollar value is known as "full-cost accounting." While there are many ways of doing this, this infographic shows one example of how those costs and charges can be calculated.

IF WALKING COSTS YOU $1   SOCIETY PAYS $0.01
IF BIKING COSTS YOU $1   SOCIETY PAYS $0.08
IF BUSSING COSTS YOU $1   SOCIETY PAYS $1.50
IF DRIVING COSTS YOU $1   SOCIETY PAYS $9.20

Produced by Discourse Media, data by George Poulos. Calculate your commute at MovingForward.DiscourseMedia.org/CostofCommute

Car-dependent cities make their citizens poorer. . . but they also make themselves poorer through the large hidden subsidies that automobiles require.

have stronger economies. One recent study documents that America's most walkable metros generate 49% more GDP per capita than its least walkable metros.[9]

Car culture doesn't pay. It has been estimated that, between 1970 and 2010, we have doubled the amount of roadway in America. Over the same years, the typical American family has doubled the percentage of its income spent on transportation—from 10% to 20%.[10] By burdening most Americans with mandatory car ownership, our suburban landscape has contributed markedly to the cash-strapped condition of contemporary life.

Walking creates positive externalities. All transportation is subsidized—the question is, *how much?* Walking and biking require sidewalks and bike lanes, but these represent little more than a rounding error when compared to the cost of our roads. Meanwhile, the externalities of driving are clear and huge, including the costs of policing, ambulances, hospitals, time wasted in traffic, and climate change. The externalities of walking and biking are principally those that come from a healthier population. The City of Copenhagen calculates that every mile driven by car costs the city 20 cents, while each mile biked earns the city 42 cents.[11] While not all externalities can be monetized, their substantial long-term impacts—like sea-level rise—represent an economic future that cities ignore at their peril.

RULE 1: When advocating for walkability, use the arguments of property value, talent attraction, job creation, transportation costs, and subsidies/externalities.

2 Sell Walkability on Health

There are powerful health reasons to invest in walkability.

THE BEST DAY TO BE A CITY PLANNER IN AMERICA was July 9, 2004, when Howard Frumkin, Lawrence Frank, and Richard Jackson came out with their book, *Urban Sprawl and Public Health*. In it, the authors made it clear that so much of American morbidity was a result of the fact that, in much of this country, we have designed out of existence the *useful walk*. That important book, and others that have been published since, document how the American health care crisis is largely an urban design crisis, with walkability at the heart of the cure.

The health benefits of having a more walkable community are measurable and huge, and include the following:[12]

Americans are almost four times as likely to die in a car crash than Britons or Swedes.

Walkable communities are slimmer communities. America faces an obesity epidemic that can be linked directly to suburban sprawl. The lower a community's Walk Score, the more likely its residents are to be overweight.[13] Any investment that makes a city more walkable is likely to make it less obese as well.

Slimmer communities have lower health care costs. While a concern in its own right, obesity is most costly due to the diseases that it causes or makes worse. These include diabetes, coronary disease, hypertension, gallstones, osteoarthritis, and a variety of cancers. Treating these maladies is extraordinarily expensive, and

The fact that we don't think twice about taking the car to the parking lot to the escalator to the treadmill in order to walk is one reason why we now have the first generation of Americans expected to live shorter lives than their parents.

most of these costs are borne by society and by municipalities themselves. When cities become more walkable, we all benefit.

Walkable communities save lives. Car crashes kill a remarkable 1.25 million humans each year. In 2017, more than 40,000 of these were Americans—a new record. While most of us take such deaths for granted, it is eye-opening to compare the United States to other developed nations that are less car-dependent. Americans are almost four times as likely to die in a car crash as Britons or Swedes.[14] This is due principally to the design of our cities: the more walkable, the fewer deaths. For this same reason, you are almost four times as likely to die on the road in Memphis or Orlando as in New York or Portland.[15] Year after year, the evidence shows us that it is the cities shaped around automobiles that are the most effective at smashing them into each other.

Air pollution deaths are also an outcome of community design. Approximately 40 million Americans—13% of us—suffer from asthma, and its economic cost is estimated at $56 billion in the United States alone.[16] But asthma is responsible for only a fraction of the 200,000 annual "premature deaths" that are attributed to air pollution. One M.I.T. study found that the leading cause of these deaths was vehicle emissions.[17] Unlike a generation ago, most air pollution now comes not from factories, but from driving.[18] To the lives potentially saved by reducing car crashes, we can add even a larger number saved by reducing auto exhaust. Both are outcomes of making more walkable cities.

RULE 2: When advocating for walkability, use public health arguments including those related to obesity, health care costs, and the death rates from car crashes and air pollution.

3 Sell Walkability on Climate Change

There are powerful environmental reasons

to invest in walkability.

AS LOVERS OF CITIES, most urban planners have had their challenges dealing with environmentalists, because, in America, the environmental movement has historically been an anti-city movement. From Thomas Jefferson, who called cities "pestilential to the health, the morals, and the liberties of man," through much of the history of the Sierra Club, being green in the United States has often meant regarding cities as the principal villains in the despoilment of our planet.[19]

Torontans use one quarter the gasoline of Atlantans,

and five times as much as Hong Kongers.

This anti-city message only became more shrill with the rising awareness of climate change and the popularization of carbon mapping. For many years, the typical carbon map of the United States looked like a night-sky satellite photo: hot around the cities, cooler in the suburbs, and coolest in the countryside. Wherever there are lots of people, there is lots of pollution, after all.

It took a while for a few smart people to realize that these maps were based on an unconsidered assumption, which is that the most meaningful way to measure carbon is by the square mile. It isn't.

The best way to measure carbon is per person. Places should be judged not by how much carbon they emit, but by how much carbon they cause us to emit. There are only so many people in the United States at any given time, and they

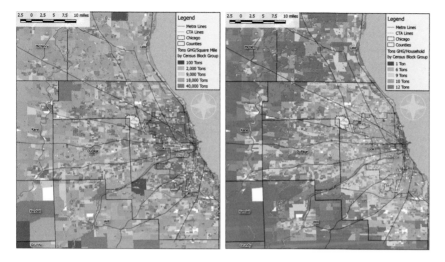

These maps of Chicago, produced by Peter Haas at the Center for Neighborhood Technology, show how measuring greenhouse gases per household sends the opposite message of measuring per square mile.

can be encouraged to live where they have the smallest environmental footprint. That place turns out to be the city—the denser the better.

When you replace carbon-per-square-mile maps with carbon-per-household maps, surprisingly, the colors simply flip. The coolest areas become the hottest, and vice versa, with the greenest part of every city finding itself smack-dab in the center of town. The EPA calls this "location efficiency."

As might be expected, most of the red in these images comes from tailpipe emissions. This is appropriate, since, for most of us, driving is by far the largest contributor to our personal carbon footprint. The more walkable we make our cities, the less they make us pollute. Torontans use one quarter the gasoline of Atlantans, and five times as much as Hong Kongers.[20]

This circumstance would lead us to believe that electric vehicles present a happy solution, but the data so far are not encouraging, for several reasons. First, in much of the United States and the world, an electric car is basically a coal-powered car. Second, as the suburbs have taught us, all of our other, non-automotive consumption patterns expand when we drive. As David Owen notes in *Green Metropolis*:

> The critical energy drain in a typical American suburb is not the Hummer in the driveway; it's everything else the Hummer makes possible—the oversized houses and irrigated yards, the network of new feeder roads and residential streets, the costly and inefficient outward expansion of the power grid, the duplicated stores and schools, the two-hour solo commutes.[21]

The first thing one learns in city-planning school is that how we move determines how we live. If our society is going to slow climate change, it will be by reorienting our cities around transit, biking, and walking.

RULE 3: When advocating for walkability, use climate change arguments and stress location efficiency.

4 Sell Walkability on Equity

There are powerful equity reasons to invest in walkability.

BECAUSE IT FAVORS URBANISM, walkability is prey to charges of elitism. Such claims gain momentum as our nation's limited number of walkable neighborhoods, desired by more and more people, become increasingly unaffordable to all but the wealthy. In the face of these sentiments, it pays to be armed with the most persuasive arguments about why walkability and bikeability are among the most effective tools available for helping to level the playing field in our increasingly inequitable society.

Remarkably, cities with more transit choice demonstrate less income inequality and less overspending on rent.

One third of Americans can't drive. As of 2015, more than 103 million of America's 321 million people did not possess a driver's license. Many more had licenses, but did not feel comfortable driving. When faced with unwalkable environments—the majority of the American landscape—these people have only two choices: to burden others who drive, or to stay home.

Walkability gives the elderly a new lease on life. In unwalkable places, the elderly lose independence much earlier, and end up warehoused in institutions. When they can satisfy most of their daily needs on foot, seniors remain self-sufficient many years beyond the age at which they should no longer drive.

Walkability gives children independence. Most of us would like our children to exercise independence well before they turn sixteen. Walkable environments give children almost a decade of increased self-sufficiency and liberate the soccer mom (or dad) that much sooner.

Transit disproportionally serves the poor and minorities. Almost two thirds of transit riders have a household income of less than $50,000. For more than 20%, that number is less than $15,000. Transit riders are 60% nonwhite.[22] Remarkably, cities with more transit choice demonstrate less income inequality and less overspending on rent.[23]

Walking and bicycling disproportionally serve the poor and minorities. There is a misperception that bike lanes serve principally elite intellectual workers. In reality, a bicyclist (or pedestrian) is more likely to be a minimum-wage laborer than a well-off professional.

Walking and Bicycling to Work by Household Income: 2008–2012

(Data based on sample. For information on confidentiality protection, sampling error, nonsampling error, and definitions, see www.census.gov/acs/www/)

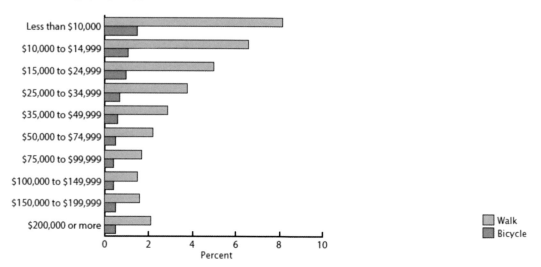

Yes, the rich do walk and bike a little bit more than the not-so-rich. But the real news is at the top of this chart. *Source: U.S. Census Bureau, American Community Survey, 2008–2012.*

Poor, elderly, and non-white pedestrians are disproportionally killed in traffic. African Americans and Native Americans make up 12.9% of the population, but they represent 22% of pedestrian deaths. In all, people of color (including Latinos) are 54% more likely to be struck and killed while walking in the United States.[24] Pedestrians over seventy-five are 68% more likely to be killed than those under sixty-five. And pedestrian deaths are much more common in low-income areas.[25] For these reasons, investments in pedestrian safety are investments in social equity.[26]

Walkability improvements disproportionately help the differently abled. Most visually impaired people can move independently only while walking, and they are effectively disabled by communities that mandate cars for getting around. And every investment in walkability is also an investment in rollability; wheelchair users are among those who benefit most when sidewalks become safer.

RULE 4: When advocating for walkability, use data to prove its social equity benefits.

5 Sell Walkability on Community

There are powerful community reasons to invest in walkability.

ANY PLANNER WHO HAS SPENT TIME surveying a range of communities can tell you the difference between more traditional walkable neighborhoods and automotive sprawl: In walkable places, it is impossible to spend more than a few minutes sneaking around without being approached by an inquisitive resident. In a modern suburbia of cul-de-sacs and garage-fronted snout-houses, a planner can measure streets all day and not elicit a single interaction. Where nobody walks, nobody supervises the public realm, and nobody gets to know their neighbors.

It is only when we are outside of vehicles, and relatively safe from them, that the bonds of community can form.

When we walk we are called pedestrians, and when we drive we are called motorists. Based on the way these two characters behave, it is hard to believe that the same people can be both of them, or even that they belong to the same species. Most pedestrians are by nature ready to engage others, or at least to acknowledge them in some way. Even looking away from another person as you pass is a form of acknowledgement, a behavior caused specifically by the other's presence. Our paths on the sidewalk are a subtle dance of communication and accommodation.

In contrast, most motorists are profoundly antisocial, and often even sociopathic. We are at our most selfish while driving, and often at our most aggressive. Only behind the wheel do we see Sunday school teachers and church deacons flipping each other the bird. Why is this?

The answer is no mystery. To be a motorist is to pilot a private space in deadly competition with other private spaces. Every other motorist on the road has only two roles: competing for asphalt, and endangering your life. Because you are in competition, you are adversaries. Because they might, with one mistake, kill you (and perhaps your entire family), you are enemies.

It is only when we are outside of vehicles, and relatively safe from them, that the bonds of community can form. This point was probably best made by Donald Appleyard's now classic book, *Livable Streets,* which compiled his research in San Francisco about the relationship between social capital and traffic.[27] Comparing streets that were essentially identical but for the number of cars they carried, Appleyard found that most people living on light-traffic streets considered their entire street to be their "home territory," while most people on heavy-traffic streets only felt at home within their own buildings or apartments. More remarkably, while people on light-traveled streets counted on average 3.0 friends, people on busy streets averaged only 0.9 friends.

That's hardly the best ad copy: "Heavy traffic: for those times when you want to have slightly less than one friend."

The impact of traffic is clear. But what about development patterns? In his landmark book, *Bowling Alone,* Robert Putnam set out to determine what was causing a measurable decline in social capital in the United States. He found that suburbanization, and its long commutes, were the most predictive measure he could find. He noted that "each ten additional minutes in daily commuting time cuts involvement in community affairs by ten percent—fewer public meetings attended, fewer committees chaired, fewer petitions signed, fewer church services attended, and so on."[28]

Finally, we even have social capital studies that look at walkability directly. In one of these, researchers at the University of New Hampshire surveyed 700 residents of 20 neighborhoods, split between more and less walkable locations in Manchester and Portsmouth, NH. They found that "those living in more walkable neighborhoods trusted their neighbors more; participated in community projects, clubs and volunteering more; and described television as their major form of entertainment less than survey participants living in less walkable neighborhoods."[29]

LIGHT TRAFFIC

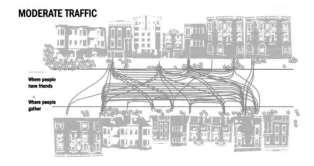

MODERATE TRAFFIC

HEAVY TRAFFIC

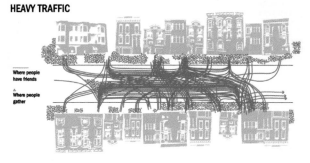

In Livable Streets, Donald Appleyard illustrated how car traffic impedes the formation of social capital.

RULE 5: When advocating for walkability, don't forget the compelling data surrounding its impact on social capital.

Part II

MIX THE USES

PEOPLE WILL NOT WALK unless the walk serves some purpose. The best way for a walk to be useful is if it takes you to something that is different from what is currently in front of you. When walking does this, life is much more efficient, since time is not wasted in transit. . . or traffic.

One wonders what collective synaptic hemorrhage allowed this simple fact to be forgotten. It is head-scratching to read the key texts of the modern movement as they address this topic. The promotional film introducing Futurama, Norman Bel Geddes' "world of tomorrow," at the 1939 World's Fair was viewed by tens of millions of visitors. Here's what it advocated: "Residential, commercial, and industrial areas have been separated for greater efficiency and greater convenience."[30]

What were the authors of these words thinking? How can that statement, which was swallowed whole-hog by a nation and a planet, and unquestioned for a quarter century, even be explained? "You see, we're separating all the aspects of your life by great distances to make your day more convenient." Say again?

It would take many chapters to fully address all of the ways that our daily lives, so badly disassociated by modernist planning, need to be brought back together. This section focuses on the four subjects in need of the most attention—downtown housing, local schools, local parks, land-use laws rejecting sprawl—and ends with an economic framework for making good decisions at the local level.

6 | Invest in Attainable Housing Downtown

Dense housing is central to walkability.

AN IDEAL MIXED-USE COMMUNITY has something approaching a jobs/housing balance. Since most places in America are either mostly residential or mostly commercial, the path to mixed use must logically take one of two directions: either adding commercial uses to residential neighborhoods, or adding residential uses to commercial neighborhoods. Of those two, the former is what we professionals call a *theoretical possibility.* It never happens.

If you want to understand why it never happens, just try building a corner store in a cul-de-sac; you will quickly be escorted over the county line. As starved as suburban pod-dwellers are for walkable retail, nobody wants it near their house. For this reason, almost all efforts at creating more mixed-use places have been focused on bringing more housing to principally commercial areas, especially downtowns, main streets, and those other locations where shops and offices already line sidewalks. These are also the places where walkability is most possible, since they were built at a time when walking mattered.

The value of bringing more housing to these places, which we will collectively (and inaccurately but usefully) label "downtown," is more than just convenience. More housing is what makes a downtown great. Jane Jacobs made this point in 1961, when she observed that New York's Wall Street, with 400,000 workers in very close quarters, was still "miserable at providing services and amenities,"[31] because it lacked what she called *time spread:* activity around the clock. Why were there no great restaurants or gyms on Wall Street? Because a great restaurant or gym needs both daytime and evening clientele, which only exists in places where people both work and live.

Most American cities have very low residential density in their downtown cores. Detroit, for example, has 4.3 people per acre. Tulsa has about 3. These are low-density suburban numbers, in locations where people want to live. Whatever non-luxury rental housing gets built is immediately occupied. Yet developers can't—or won't—build it fast enough. Instead, those few developers active in the downtown are putting up small numbers of luxury condos, which they often can't sell because the downtown, lacking *time spread,* is not yet good enough.

Why this mismatch between supply and demand? Because attainable downtown rentals usually don't make

Restored with the help of State and Federal historic tax credits as well as City subsidies, the Randolph adds 56 market-rate housing units to downtown Des Moines.

money. Building in urban areas is expensive, and, in most cities, only luxury rents can support it. But very few would-be urbanites can afford those rents. Most of the people who are ready to move downtown, in America's less-developed cities, are recent graduates, young entrepreneurs, and childless professionals who don't yet command high incomes. Developers go where the profits are, and they will limit their activity to the suburbs unless some other entity—typically the city—finds a way to make standard downtown apartments profitable.

Some cities, recognizing that developers need a bit of a push to come downtown—and understanding the great value of *time spread*—have taken the leap to investing in new attainable urban rentals. This can be done in a variety of ways. Kansas City waves *ad valorem* taxes on such developments. Des Moines offers a ten-year 100% tax abatement, sometimes in combination with Tax Increment Financing covering the next ten years. It is working: in the year 2000, there were only 2,500 housing units in downtown Des Moines; that number is expected to reach almost 10,000 by 2020. The skyline is now full of cranes, as recent downtown housing developments have topped $450 million in investment.

In addition to money, cities can invest time and skill in downtown housing, particularly when it comes to locating and procuring state and federal subsidies. Lowell, MA, managed to double its supply of downtown housing between 2000 and 2010 by offering expedited special permits for the construction of new apartments in its many abandoned loft buildings, and then hand-holding developers through the process of winning Historic Preservation Tax Credits and Community Renewal block grants.[32] Cities like Des Moines and Lowell that are truly committed to a thriving center realize that city government must identify downtown housing as a key objective warranting investment and care.

RULE 6: Cities should actively invest both money and staff time in the creation of more attainable housing downtown.

7 Push for Local Schools

Size and locate schools with walkability in mind.

PERHAPS NOTHING HAS BEEN STUDIED as much as study, and the outcomes are unequivocal: small schools are better for learning. In one study, schools with fewer than four hundred students were shown to have better attendance rates, fewer disciplinary problems and dropouts, and often higher test scores. So why do we keep making our schools bigger? Between 2000 and 2010, despite this knowledge, the average American high school grew by 14%,[33] and many a school district can still be heard boasting of a big, beautiful new school that is going to cause the closure of several others. School consolidation is still sold as a way to reduce costs while increasing curricular and extracurricular offerings for students.

In all of these studies, little attention is paid to school location and its role in community building. It is forgotten that, when you consolidate, you separate. The larger a school is, the farther away from you it is likely to be, and the less likely students are to walk to it. Meanwhile, walking to school has also been shown to improve both academic performance and psychological well-being, as well as public health.[34] And busing a student to school costs approximately $1,000 per year, adding almost 9% to the cost of public education.[35] Yet, surprisingly, a quick survey of literature covering school size and consolidation does not turn up a single mention of either the cost of busing or its disadvantages.

The typical suburban high school now must dedicate more land area to parking than to schooling. A typical land-use regulation might require that a public high school build roughly 400 square feet of surface parking for every 100 square feet of classroom space. The good news: fewer students are being bussed! Instead, the seniors and juniors are driving the freshmen and sophomores, with the death rates to prove it.

In the 1960s, roughly half of all American children walked or biked to school. Currently, that number is below 13%.[36] Meanwhile, in the Netherlands, two-thirds of children under twelve, and 80% of high-schoolers, walk or bike to school.[37] This stark difference is the result of many factors, including overblown fears of "stranger danger," but none has exerted a stronger influence than community design, and a complete abandonment of walkable local schools as a legitimate goal. For the sake of our children's education and their well-being, this has to change.

The size of the parking lot makes it clear: the kids are driving to this school.

A final factor complicating this discussion is the rise of charter schools, magnet schools, and other district-wide alternatives intended to provide greater choice and opportunity for families. Others with more relevant experience can assess whether the charter school movement is living up to its goals. (Perhaps not: charter schools are more segregated than traditional schools.[38]) But here we should consider them strictly from the perspective of city planning. In that regard, they have been an unmitigated disaster, for two reasons.

First, in cities like Washington, DC, where large segments of the student population attend charters, it is easy to know when school is on holiday: those are the only days when the morning commute is not hopelessly choked by parents driving their kids to cross-town charters, some as far as an hour away (in traffic). Children are often placed in charter schools with little attention to location, and the sad outcome is a generation of kids who begin their miserable commuting patterns at age three, and never stop. This is a bad outcome for everyone: kids, parents, and all the people just trying to get to work by car or bus.

The second problem with charter schools is what they mean for community. Anyone who has sent a child to a traditional neighborhood school can tell you about its role in the creation of social capital. The school is not just for education; it's also a playground and a community center. It is the primary vehicle through which families get to know each other and form a circle of friends. When you send your child to a charter school, that circle is far flung, and your entire social life becomes another experience in commuting. Even worse, neighbors remain strangers, and place-based community is less likely to form.

School facilities policy, which should be based on a wide range of criteria, has recently focused on too few, and not even served those few particularly well. A more holistic approach to determining school size and location points in a clear direction: small, local, and walkable.

RULE 7: Understanding that schools belong in neighborhoods, locate them to be walkable, and resist the urge to consolidate them into large facilities.

8 Push for Local Parks

Size and locate recreational facilities with walkability in mind.

WHERE WERE THE SOCCER MOMS in the 1970s? Those of us who grew up then remember that they didn't exist. In fact, the term *soccer mom* wasn't coined until 1982.[39] It is ironic that, during an era when most mothers didn't work, most kids didn't need them to get around.

Since then, what changed? Even as more and more parents joined the workforce, more and more children lost independent access to parks and playgrounds. This outcome can be blamed generally on the design of our communities, and specifically on the size and location of our sports fields.

As with schools, there has been a strong trend toward the enlargement and consolidation of sports facilities. As with schools, the larger a sports facility is, the farther away it is likely to be, and the more likely that you will be able to reach it only by automobile.

The reasons behind this trend are many. Certainly, economies of scale apply. It is cheaper to mow five soccer fields when they are all in the same place and the grounds-keeper has to get the lawnmower off the truck only once.[40] It is also easier to host tournaments at huge facilities, and one or two giant facilities are no doubt necessary in each

In Weston, Fl: the apotheosis of sports facilities in an automotive age.

metropolis to perform this function. But this fact does not justify the proliferation of mega-fields that is occurring nationwide.

Case in point is the new town of Weston, FL, Fort Lauderdale's attempt to colonize the Everglades. Certainly the town fathers and mothers are proud of their eight soccer fields, eight baseball diamonds, eight basketball courts, and eight-lane Olympic-size pool. But one look at the facility's 1,725 parking spaces and its four-lane access road makes it clear that no child has ever walked there, and few have biked. Indeed, thanks to Weston's looping suburban street network, the adjacent houses are actually a 2.5-mile drive away.

It's a good guess that, in the 1970s, no child had access to such an abundant collection of sports facilities. Most of us had access to one or two soccer fields, baseball diamonds, and basketball courts. But they were in our neighborhood, and we could walk to them on our own. Given the exertion of a typical baseball game, that walk was sometimes half the exercise we got. More important, it allowed both us and our parents the space to do our own thing and grow as individuals in the world.

Communities that want children who are both truly active and growing in independence will keep their sports facilities small and local. For younger children, another mandate is needed, which is to locate playgrounds and tot-lots within a short walk of every household. In well-designed neighborhoods, the most convenient playground is no more than a five-minute walk away, and not across any major thoroughfares.

The perfect tot lot, Washington, DC's Westminster Playground takes the space of three rowhouses.

RULE 8: Understanding that recreational facilities belong in neighborhoods, locate them to be walkable, and resist the urge to consolidate them into large facilities. Locate playgrounds within a quarter-mile of all households.

9 Fix Your Codes

Eliminate legal barriers to mixed use.

ANDRES DUANY USED TO GIVE A LECTURE called "The Story of Planning." In it, he would recount the formative victory of the planning profession. It happened in the nineteenth century, when people were choking on the soot from Europe's "dark, satanic mills." The planners, who were not yet called planners, said, "Hey, why don't we move the housing away from the factories." They did it, and life spans increased immediately and dramatically. The planners were hailed as heroes, and, as we like to say, they have been trying to repeat that experience ever since.[41]

This story is admittedly an oversimplification, but at its heart it is true. Modern city planning began with the intention of separating incompatible uses from each other, and evolved somewhat mindlessly into separating all uses from each other.

By the mid-twentieth century, planners seemed to have gone berserk. Having witnessed the life-changing benefits of zoning, they became zone-happy, introducing more and more categories and more and more rules about what should be separated from what else, until the city of neighborhoods was replaced by the city of zones. The planner Paul Crawford used to point out how the typical mid-twentieth-century zoning code spelled out literally hundreds of separate zone-able property uses, in one case (a small California city) including both "19. Baths, Turkish," and "135. Turkish Baths." This same code permitted the manufacture of potato chips but not corn chips, and allowed chinchillas to be sold retail but not wholesale.[42]

We planners now know that this was wrong. The city of zones is no longer taught in planning school. The leadership of the city planning, urban design, and real estate professions all agree that single-use zoning is a recipe for economical, environmental, and social disaster. Yet, nationwide, the old-school zoning maps still exist, sitting

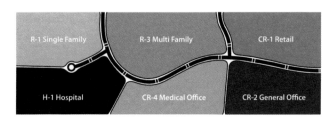

A typical American land-use map ruthlessly separates uses into large zones.

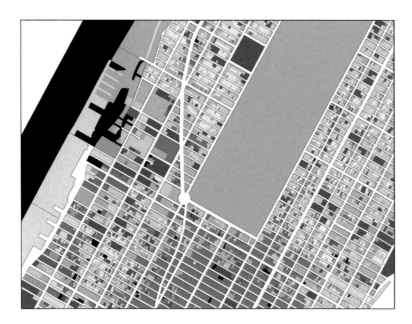

In New York City, flexible zoning allows for a fine-grain mix of uses, including vertically mixed use, shown here in red.

on acre after acre of undeveloped property, directly in the path of progress. When a planner arrives, just about anywhere, to create a layout for a parcel of land, chances are that a plan already exists for that land, and it looks like the image at left. That plan has to be undone before anything good can happen.

It is clear why the city of zones is the exact opposite of the walkable city. If nothing is close to anything different, and the only connection is a single fat roadway, then the population is automatically conscripted into driving. When a walkable city is mapped by land use, the image is remarkably different. If the picture at left is a Rothko, the one above is a Seurat—he was the pointillist. Uses are still separate, but at a much finer grain, like confetti. And a large section of this plan,

shown in dark red, contains buildings holding multiple uses, mixed vertically.

If they are to once again achieve walkable outcomes, cities must replace their use-based zoning codes with something different. There are many ways to do this, but the most comprehensive and effective is to enact a form-based code instead. Form-based codes, pioneered in the 1980s, still address land use—keeping incompatible uses apart—but focus more attention on those physical aspects of private buildings that impact the quality of the public realm, such as height, placement, and where the parking goes. They also replace our current dangerous street standards with designs that encourage walking and biking. Based on the design of livable places, they result in more of them.

As of this writing, 387 form-based codes have been adopted by cities including Atlanta, Baltimore, Cincinnati, Dallas, Denver, Los Angeles, Miami, Memphis, Philadelphia, and Portland.[43] The most widely used generic version, DPZ's SmartCode, can be downloaded for free from smartcodecentral.com.

RULE 9: Eliminate single-use zoning from your ordinances and work toward replacing your use-based codes with form-based codes.

10 Do the Math

Compare apples to apples when making public investments.

THIS RULE is really about urban economics and municipal solvency rather than walkability, but it belongs here because it aligns almost perfectly with the goal of making more walkable cities. Communities that fund infrastructure with an eye to long-term return will invest in compact, mixed-use development—especially in historic districts—and not in sprawl.

with new growth for long-term financial obligations associated with the maintenance of infrastructure."[44] This presents suburban cities with an untenable choice: grow or die.

The underlying problem is that single-use, low-density suburban sprawl simply does not pay for itself. Marohn presents the case study of a typical suburban road. Resurfacing the road cost the city $354,000. Based on all the

Minicozzi found that a traditional downtown midrise building generates more than thirteen times the tax revenue per acre than the city's Walmart supercenter, and twelve times the jobs.

In the book *Thoughts on Building Strong Towns,* and on the *Strong Towns* website (strongtowns.org), Charles Marohn Jr. illustrates how much suburban growth in the United States has effectively been a Ponzi scheme in which each round of unsustainable investment creates a long-term cash flow liability that is only prevented from tanking the city's finances by the development fees generated by the next round of unsustainable investment. He observes that "cities routinely trade near-term cash advantages associated

property taxes collected from residents along that road, it will take seventy-nine years to recoup that cost. But the road is likely to need repaving again in twenty years. *Strong Towns* is chock full of examples of this type, which were easy for Marohn to collect, as they are the standard. They are so common because, as Marohn notes, "None of our public officials has ever asked the question: will this public project generate enough tax revenue to sustain its maintenance over multiple life cycles?"

Operating Expense Ratio
Lafayette Parish, LA

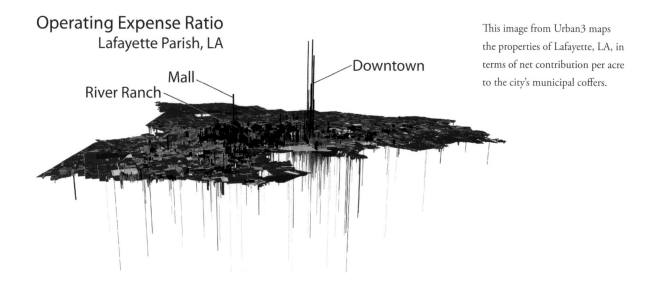

River Ranch — Mall — Downtown

This image from Urban3 maps the properties of Lafayette, LA, in terms of net contribution per acre to the city's municipal coffers.

Asking that question would inevitably lead cities to invest differently. What these investments can yield has been best documented by a colleague of Marohn's, Joe Minicozzi, whose firm Urban3 produces trenchant analyses of how cities misallocate their principal asset, land. In his work, Minicozzi insists that we look at each of our land allocations not as a standalone, and not just in comparison to each other, but in comparison to each other *by acre*. When you do this, the inefficiency of auto-centric development becomes painfully apparent. Studying Asheville, NC, Minicozzi found that a traditional downtown midrise building generates more than thirteen times the tax revenue per acre than the city's Walmart supercenter, and twelve times the jobs.

Recognizing that Asheville is a hopping tourist destination, Marohn applied the same analysis to the "blighted" main street of his home town, Brainerd, MN. He found that, per acre, ugly old stores downtown were generating 41% more tax revenue than a new auto-oriented Taco John's restaurant whose construction the city had just subsidized.[45]

Minicozzi has found similar results nationwide, and illustrates them graphically as in the image above. In almost all cities, revenue-positive downtowns are footing the bill for subsidized sprawl. He sums up his conclusions:

"The urban environment, and downtowns in particular, are the breadwinners for successful communities. If you aren't facilitating that type of walkable urban environment, you are essentially losing your wealth."[46]

RULE 10: Make zoning decisions and municipal investments with an eye to net revenue over time from each acre of land; doing so inevitably leads to more walkable urbanism.

III. MAKE HOUSING ATTAINABLE AND INTEGRATED

PART III

MAKE HOUSING ATTAINABLE AND INTEGRATED

THERE ARE TWO PRINCIPAL PROBLEMS with housing in the United States: Too few people can afford it, and too much of it is segregated by type and income.

In this nation, the affordable housing problem is really an affordable living problem. While government housing assistance programs are needed—and need to grow—housing unaffordability is principally the outcome of two factors: first, a federal tax structure that since the 1980s has redistributed income radically upward to the top 1% of earners (a topic, sadly, beyond the scope of this book); and second, the proliferation of an urban framework—sprawl—that mandates universal automobile ownership, such that working class Americans now pay more for transportation than for housing.[47]

Within this stark landscape, a limited number of tools are currently available to increase the supply of attainable housing, especially in more walkable, transit-served places where residents can perhaps be spared the burden of mandatory car ownership. The best of these also address America's other housing problem, which is that is has been so ruthlessly segregated by both cost and building type, so that society is broken up not just by income, but also by age, lifestyle, and race. Such segregation undermines our social fabric, weakens human empathy, and also limits our potential. As Jane Jacobs asked, "Does anyone suppose that, in real life, answers to any of the great questions that worry us today are going to come out of homogeneous settlements?"[48]

Three techniques for integrating more attainable housing into our communities are described ahead: inclusionary zoning, backyard apartments, and leveraging existing parking lots to improve affordability. In this context, it is also essential to discuss the dark side of gentrification, as well as a remarkably effective tool for reducing homelessness.

11 Mandate Smart Inclusionary Zoning

Take advantage of this important tool for creating more diverse neighborhoods.

COMMUNITIES need both inclusionary zoning and Inclusionary Zoning. The former refers to the fact that most zoning practice is actually exclusionary, and needs to be changed if we want better integrated neighborhoods—as addressed in Rules 6 and 9. The latter refers to the now well-established practice of requiring developers to include below-market-rate units in their market-rate projects. While not the most powerful tool for creating affordability—compared to housing vouchers or low-income housing tax credits—Inclusionary Zoning (IZ) has demonstrated itself both to increase the supply of attainable housing and to limit the displacement of current residents in neighborhoods experiencing development.

Hundreds of IZ programs have been implemented at both the county and the local level since the 1970s. Some of the more prominent ones include Montgomery and Frederick Counties in Maryland and the cities of New York, Boulder, San Francisco, and Los Angeles. Any new local programs should be carefully modeled on these successful examples, but a few rules of thumb need mentioning.

Mandatory, not voluntary: Compared to mandatory statutes, voluntary IZ programs have been relatively ineffective. Orange County, CA, switched in 1983 from mandatory to voluntary and production dropped from about 1,600 units per year to fewer than 90. Mandatory programs are also more predictable than voluntary ones, and much better at serving people with very low incomes.[49]

Experience has shown that market-rate developments are quite resilient when it comes to integrating families of lesser income.

10% to 30%: Most IZ programs require that between 10% and 30% of new units be significantly below market rate. Experience has shown that market-rate developments are quite resilient when it comes to integrating families of lesser income. (It is generally not income diversity but the concentration of poverty that leads to social pathologies.)

Good incentives: Even when it is mandatory, the production of income-integrated housing should be rewarded.

Ten percent of the units in DC's new Park Van Ness Building are qualified as affordable by the District's Inclusionary Zoning standards.

Most IZ programs offer density bonuses in exchange for participation. Expedited approval and fee waivers can also be effective when offered in addition.[50]

A good mix: The goals of IZ are best attained by programs that require a wide range of incomes in each development, distributed fairly evenly among income levels.

On site: Some IZ programs allow for below-market units to be provided off site, or for the developer to pay fees in lieu of actually creating affordable housing. These provisions violate the intentions of the practice.

Permanent: One mistake made by some programs has been to allow developers to revert attainable units back to market rate once the initial renter moves out. This practice undermines supply and incentivizes the mistreatment of subsidized tenants.

Invisible and integrated: Some IZ programs require that below-market-rate units be identical to standard units in the same building. This provision makes no sense when a luxury development offers huge spaces and sybaritic finishes like marble countertops. In this case, lower-cost units should be allowed to be smaller and less expensively built, as long as there is no evidence of this condition exterior to the apartment. Below-market units should also be distributed throughout the development, and "poor doors"—separate lobbies—disallowed.

Big and small: Most programs create a minimum project size below which developments need not provide below-market units. If allowed, such a floor must be set very low, or else developers will be prone to break projects up into smaller pieces to sidestep program requirements.

RULE 11: Pass a mandatory Inclusionary Zoning ordinance based on successful models.

12 Encourage Granny Flats

Allow and Incentivize Accessory

Dwelling Units.

SHOULD SINGLE-FAMILY ZONING be allowed at all? It is clearly an inefficient use of land and infrastructure, as well as the principal form of exclusionary zoning in America. Nothing works quite so well as minimum house and yard sizes when it comes to keeping *those people* out. So why is it legal? The answer is that, for many, the neighborhood of freestanding houses remains the American Dream, and there are few jurisdictions in the United States that are likely to rob people of it.

Happily, there is a way to almost invisibly increase density, affordability, and diversity in single-family neighborhoods, both existing and planned. It's called the Accessory Dwelling Unit (ADU), and also known as the Backyard Apartment, Garage Apartment, Mother-in-Law Apartment, or Granny Flat. It can be found in many prewar American neighborhoods and, after having been forgotten for half a century, is making a comeback in a number of cities across North America.

The ADU takes several forms. Sometimes it is a small freestanding cottage. Other times it is a backward extension to the main house. Often it sits atop a garage. Basements and attics can also work. The key is that it has a

Two apartments sit above garages on a rear alley in the new town of Kentlands, MD.

small footprint—usually less than 500 square feet—and its own front door. In car-dependent places, it may also have its own parking space—if there is no room on-street. It is easiest to provide ADUs on lots served by rear alleys, but they can be made to work almost anywhere. An ADU with a bedroom loft under its roof is large enough to house a couple quite comfortably.

But ADUs can be a tough sell in many conventional single family neighborhoods, where NIMBYs take their Back Yard focus quite literally. Snobbery and fears of strangers and overcrowding can rule the day. When proposing an ADU ordinance, therefore, it can be helpful to cite these advantages:

ADUs represent an investment in property and can be expected to increase a lot's property value.

ADUs are naturally supervised by the people living in the main house (typically the landlord), who quickly put the kibosh on loud partying and other unwanted behavior.

ADUs can (and should) be restricted in size and in duration of lease. Eight hundred square feet is a common maximum size. Minimum lease terms of one month (or longer) allow neighborhoods to avoid "AirBnB blight."

The ADU provides rental income that allows empty nesters to stay in their houses when they retire. They can also move into the apartment and rent out the main house. Either way, ADUs make aging in place possible.

The best way to convince people to support ADUs is to help them realize that, someday, they may want one too.

Because most zoning codes outlaw ADUs, a specific ordinance permitting them is necessary. The list of US cities with ADU ordinances is growing rapidly and includes Portland, Seattle, Minneapolis, Portsmouth, NH, and even America's second wealthiest county, Fairfax County, VA. In Barnstable on Cape Cod, the City offers zero-interest loans of up to $20,000 to build them.

The best way to convince people to support ADUs is to help them realize that, someday, they may want one too.

The greatest recent success story has been in California, which in 2016 passed a law outlawing all local ADU ordinances in favor of a more lenient universal standard.[51] With lot-square-foot minimums, parking requirements, and sprinkler provisions lifted, a building boom has begun. Los Angeles, which saw only eighty building permit applications for granny flats in 2016, processed more than two thousand in 2017.[52]

Once ADUs are made legal, residents can often use some help designing and building them properly. A number of cities, including Seattle, have created excellent manuals that should serve as models for programs elsewhere.[53]

RULE 12: Pass an Accessory Dwelling Unit ordinance based on successful models, and create a City program encouraging their construction.

13 Leverage Housing with Parking Lots

Lower the cost of new apartments by assigning them existing parking spaces.

WHETHER A CITY SHOULD BUILD any new downtown parking structures is a good question. The answer should be based on how auto-dependent the city is currently (arguing in favor) and how auto-dependent the city wants to be (arguing against). Given the onset of ride-sharing services and, eventually, autonomous vehicles, the answer in most cases is probably no.

This debate is not an issue everywhere. Many cities face a glut of parking spaces in their downtowns, due typically to overbuilding in the 1980s and '90s. It is not unusual for an American downtown to contain thousands of spaces that are empty overnight, many of which are empty during the day as well.

This was the case in Lowell, MA, where five large parking structures were severely underutilized at the same time as the City was trying to encourage redevelopment of its many abandoned historic loft buildings. The problem was that developers could not deliver market-rate housing at a competitive cost, due in part to their lenders' requirement that each apartment come with a parking spot.

City leaders came up with a plan: "What if we assign unused parking spaces in our City garages to developers?"

Lowell, MA, dedicated empty spaces in its municipal parking structures (top of image) to serve new apartments in rehabilitated buildings (bottom of image).

They changed City rules to allow apartments to locate their parking anywhere within a 1,000-foot radius of the building, and wrote letters that developers could show their lenders.

The results were remarkable, as this unburdening lowered the cost of a typical unit by more than 10%, making renovations profitable. For this reason and others, the City was able to double its supply of downtown housing in a dozen years, and reduce its percentage of subsidized housing from almost 80% to below 50%.

Similar, if smaller, successes have been achieved in Hamilton, OH, and elsewhere, and could become common if more cities would try. Albuquerque has enough empty spaces in its four downtown municipal garages to support more than 500 apartments. Downtown West Palm Beach has enough for more than 900. Downtown Boise, more than 2,000.

In Boise, not all of these spaces are publicly owned, but that need not be a barrier. Cities with the will can broker deals between lot owners (usually big employers) and apartment developers, in which both parties profit. The fact is that a downtown parking space, especially in a structure, is an asset worth tens of thousands of dollars, and that asset is being wasted if empty.

The math is slightly tricky, and there is no established formula, but, to qualify, a parking lot must have a good amount of evening vacancy and a small but significant amount of daytime vacancy. Because office parking sched-ules and apartment parking schedules are almost perfectly complementary—most office workers vacate their spaces before most residents arrive home—only a limited number of daytime spaces must be kept available for residents who don't drive to work. Apartment leases must be written carefully (with parking charged separately, as it always should be) and individual spaces may not be assigned. But the rest is pretty simple.

The fact is that a downtown parking space, especially in a structure, is an asset worth tens of thousands of dollars, and that asset is being wasted if empty.

It is unfortunate that developers and their banks still require nearby parking for new residential construction. That is changing in some places, and may eventually change everywhere. But, until it does, a strategy of matching wasted parking spaces with residential construction is a great way to leverage new housing downtown.

RULE 13: If your city has parking garages with vacancies, create a program assigning empty spaces to new housing construction nearby.

14 Fight Displacement

Use proven tools to limit the negative impacts of gentrification.

NEIGHBORHOODS CHANGE. We can't begin with the assumption that change is bad, especially in poor neighborhoods, where gentrification leads to declines in violent crime. For that reason, gentrification must be distinguished from the displacement that it often causes, and which can be understood as a more universally negative phenomenon.

Gentrification refers mostly to the way that a neighborhood's cost of living and social structure change as a result of an influx of wealthier people. Existing residents are met with higher rents and more expensive (and often less useful) services, as well as a sense that the neighborhood is no longer "theirs:" they must share its streets and other public spaces with new, different people whom they do not know, and who often eye them suspiciously as their greater wealth gives them privileged access to the neighborhood's commercial amenities.

Displacement, in contrast, is the way that the increased cost of living in the neighborhood forces people out. It is the aspect of gentrification that most deserves our attention, because it undermines social structures and causes real hardship. And people often land in worse places.

In times of growth, gentrification is inevitable. The only way to stop it is to stall growth, which no city wants, or to increase the supply of housing in already well-off neighborhoods. Usually, this can be accomplished only through up-zoning (increasing the allowed density), which well-off neighborhoods are quite effective at stopping. Daniel Hertz notes that housing supply in Chicago's wealthy Lincoln Park neighborhood actually dropped by 4.1% between 2000 and 2014, as larger houses took the place of smaller ones.[54] Well-off people gentrify poorer neighborhoods when they cannot find housing they can afford in well-off neighborhoods.[55] This, too, is not about to change.

While gentrification is inevitable, displacement is not. Surprisingly, more displacement actually takes place in our poorest neighborhoods than in neighborhoods that are gentrifying. This points to the fact that, as the economist Joe Cortright notes, "the persistence and spread of concentrated poverty—not gentrification—is our biggest urban challenge."[56] But this fact doesn't mean that the displacement of lower-income people from their improving neighborhoods is not a crisis deserving dedicated policy. While

Park Place is one of many apartment buildings that the Champlain Housing Trust uses to maintain affordability in downtown Burlington, VT.

most gentrification leads to some displacement, cities can take steps to limit the amount. The following measures have shown success in reducing displacement from gentrifying communities:

Create a Community Land Trust. Pioneered in Burlington, VT, the Community Land Trust has proliferated as a tool for creating perpetually affordable housing by maintaining land ownership while selling homes with capped appreciation potential.[57]

Turn renters into owners. When it was creating a Transit Oriented Development at the Wyandanch stop of the Long Island Railroad, the Town of Babylon, NY, preemptively reached out to all local renters with a down-payment assistance program, funded by developer fees, designed to move them into homeownership.

Offer property tax freezes. Boston, Philadelphia, and other cities have introduced programs that allow longtime owners to cap and/or freeze their tax assessments. Some such programs allow taxes to be deferred until the home is sold.

Support production of attainable housing. Thanks to the law of supply and demand, it is a simple fact that new supply—of *attainable* housing—helps to limit displacement. This housing can be located anywhere in the metro area and, as already discussed (Rule 6), deserves City support in walkable areas. Critics are correct, however, that large all-luxury projects, despite their contribution to supply, are likely to increase displacement. If these cannot be banned outright from gentrifying areas, they can at least be disqualified from any public financial support.

RULE 14: Fight displacement with community land trusts, rent-to-own programs, property tax freezes, and by subsidizing the production of attainable housing.

15 | Enact "Housing First"

Bring to your community the most effective technique for limiting homelessness.

Whether or not you believe that shelter is a basic human right that should be provided by society, you are probably aware that the costs of homelessness are profound, and not just for the homeless. Emergency room visits—the way most homeless receive health care—are expensive. Policing services are expensive. Jail time is expensive. So are homeless shelters. And, from a pure walkability perspective, street people are cited by many as the reason they avoid walking around downtown. In some cities where few people walk, the majority of pedestrians appear to be homeless, reinforcing that condition.

In Seattle, each person who moved from the street into the Housing First program saved the city more than $29,000 per year.

Historically, a moralistic approach to homelessness has mandated a slow progression in which the homeless are expected to work their way through public shelters into transitional housing and eventually into independent housing, with each transition earned in part through clean living. These programs are not effective, because having a stable place to live can be a key component of overcoming substance abuse. How can your case worker visit you if you can't be found?

Beginning in the 1990s with the premise that shelter is a right, the Housing First movement reversed the process, and began providing long-term housing to

Ignoring homelessness is one of many approaches that has not produced good results.

the homeless, (almost) no questions asked. This housing was provided at a cost of 30% of the resident's income, whatever the income, and supplemented with wraparound social services, including mental health and substance treatment. [58]

As Housing First programs began to spread and be studied, few were surprised at their success at getting people off the streets. What surprised many, however, were the savings.

In terms of success: the State of Utah, an early adopter, managed to reduce homelessness by an astounding 72% in less than a decade.[59] Nationwide studies report that between 75% and 91% of Housing First participants remain housed after a year in the program, and most of these participants take advantage of the optional social services they are offered. This makes them considerably more likely to seek work or stay in school, stay off drugs and alcohol, and stay out of the hospital and jail.[60]

In terms of savings: the outcomes have been remarkable. One study found an average annual spending reduction of over $15,000 per person in emergency services alone.[61] In Denver, emergency room costs were reduced by 34%, hospital inpatient costs by 66%, and incarceration costs by 76%.[62] In Seattle, each person who moved from the street into the Housing First program saved the city more than $29,000 per year.[63] Results in Canada have been similar.

Still, despite all this evidence, most cities do not have Housing First programs.[64] To those cities, one can only ask this: Are you really willing to spend twice as much on homelessness, and have twice as much of it, because you believe that people should be punished for addiction and mental illness? If not, what's keeping you?

RULE 15: Create a Housing First program or expand the one you have.

PART IV

GET THE PARKING RIGHT

PARKING COVERS MORE ACRES OF URBAN AMERICA than any other one thing,[65] and yet planners neglected it for years. City leaders, meanwhile, tended to ask the wrong question about parking, which is, "how can we have enough of it?" Nobody seemed to be asking the proper question: "how can parking be planned, provided, and managed to help cities thrive?"

Fortunately, due mostly to the work of one man, Professor Donald Shoup of UCLA, we now have answers to that question. Shoup's important book *The High Cost of Free Parking*[66] has changed America's understanding of how parking works, and it is an unsurpassed reference for replacing the failed parking policies of most of our cities with practices that work.

Taking some liberties with Donald Shoup's framework based upon recent experience, this section reorganizes his three-legged stool of eliminating parking minimums, pricing parking based on its market value, and creating Parking Benefits Districts to spend parking revenues locally, in order to highlight three other key concepts: treating parking lots as a public utility, located as anchors in downtown; decoupling parking from other uses that often pay for it, so that its cost is not hidden; and organizing development so that parking lots can serve different uses around the clock.

16 Eliminate On-Site Parking Requirements

Replace parking minimums with maximums.

IN 2000, my colleagues and I wrote the following:

[The on-site parking requirement] is probably the single greatest killer of urbanism in the United States today. It prevents the renovation of old buildings, since there is inadequate room on their sites for new parking; it encourages the construction of anti-pedestrian building types in which the building sits behind or hovers above a parking lot; it eliminates street life, since everyone parks immediately adjacent to their destination and has no reason to use the sidewalk; finally, it results in a low density of development that can keep a downtown from achieving critical mass. All told, there is nothing to be said in favor of the on-site parking requirement. Cities that wish to be pedestrian friendly and fully developed should eliminate this ordinance immediately and provide public parking in carefully located municipal garages and lots.[67]

Since that time, a lot has changed. Many cities have eliminated the on-site parking requirement in their downtown cores, and many others are reconsidering their parking rules citywide. But most are not. Why they need to is well described in *The High Cost of Free Parking.* And if your city has good transit, then parking maximums, such as those in New York or Europe, are probably in order.

Even in car-dependent places, one need not worry that eliminating the parking requirement will result in too

"Removing off-street parking requirements will not eliminate off-street parking, but will instead stimulate an active commercial market for it."

little parking. As Shoup notes, "removing off-street parking requirements will not eliminate off-street parking, but will instead stimulate an active commercial market for it."[68] Developers will always meet the market; their financing usually requires parking anyway. But different developers should be able to meet different markets, and cities shouldn't get in the way of that with one-size-fits-all auto-centric requirements.

The ramp to ample parking for the formerly homeless at Alma Place in Palo Alto, CA.

Nationally, the trend is slow but sure. Washington, DC, has eliminated parking requirements for retail near transit. Minneapolis just did the same for residential.[69] The greatest barrier to progress usually comes in the form of nearby residents worried about competition for on-street spaces.

Shoup tells the story of Alma Place, a 107-unit single-room-occupancy hotel that was proposed three blocks from the commuter train station in wealthy Palo Alto, CA. Given the high cost of providing parking, the need for affordability, the lower car ownership rates among its clientele, and the proximity to transit, the housing authority asked the city to waive its on-site parking requirement.

The city gave in—partway—reducing the requirement to 0.67 cars per unit. When it was built, this reduced parking still added a whopping 38% to the cost of construction.

Why did the city insist on making the cost of this "affordable" housing so high with unnecessary and unwanted parking? Because local residents were afraid of their new neighbors competing with them for a limited number of on-street parking spaces.

What if the City, instead of simply giving in, had come forward with a "Parking Preservation Plan:" a commitment to create and refine a resident-only permit system to protect existing abutters? Such a plan would have likely included a requirement that new renters sign leases proscribing car ownership. Such has been the proposal for several developments in Washington, DC.

A final counterintuitive note: in cities with good transit, eliminating the parking minimum results in less competition for on-street spaces, not more. Because when you allow a developer to put up a building without parking, the tenants show up without cars.

RULE 16: Eliminate on-site parking requirements; institute maximums where transit is ample. Where needed, create Parking Preservation Plans to protect current residents.

17 Make Downtown Parking a Public Utility

Provide parking in consolidated facilities.

ELIMINATING THE ON-SITE PARKING requirement is the clear best choice for every main street and downtown. Eliminating parking is not. Many American downtowns need to provide new parking as they grow, especially as ugly surface parking lots become building sites. The typical way to densify an unwalkable urban area into a walkable one is to turn surface parking lots into structured decks with a smaller footprint. How that parking is built and managed can be key to a place's success or failure.

Most of the parking for a new performing arts center, for example, should be located at least a block away.

In most places, the best and easiest way to transition away from on-site parking to something better is through *in-lieu fees.* Instead of being required to build parking, new developments are required to pay a similar amount into a fund that is then used to build large, collective parking facilities. This effort can be managed by the city, by a parking authority, or even by a master developer, but the outcome is the same: parking that serves an entire district, located and designed to help that district thrive.

How much in-lieu fees to pay should be based loosely on how much that parking costs to provide, minus anticipated net revenue from users. Fees per space across the United States range from $2,000 in Northampton, MA, (too low) to $27,520 in Carmel, CA, (too high?). As of 1999, Donald Shoup had identified thirty-one different North American cities with in-lieu fee programs, including Chapel Hill, NC ($7,200), Lake Forest, IL ($9,000), and Vancouver, BC ($9,708)[70] Keep in mind that, since municipal spaces are shared among many users, fees can typically be based on a parking requirement that has been adjusted well downward.

However you pay for it, municipal parking lots should be carefully located, with an understanding of the important role that they play in downtown. Effectively, they are anchors: receivers and disgorgers of large quantities of pedestrians. Like in a shopping mall, they should be located at some distance from the other anchors, to give

In Northampton, MA, a municipal lot anchors shopping and offices downtown.

business to the shops in between. In this way, downtowns need to be organized cunningly, with a strategic separation of origins and destinations.[71] Most of the parking for a new performing arts center, for example, should be located at least a block away.

This is the opposite of what usually happens in US cities. Frank Gehry's Walt Disney Concert Hall sits directly atop its six-level, $110-million parking garage, built at a cost of $50,000 per space[72]—about twice what it would have cost to build it on the empty lot one block east. This nonsense needs to stop.

The downtown parking discussion is given a new twist by car-sharing, ride-sharing and ride-hailing services, and the anticipation of driverless cars. Futurists tell us that it is folly to build any new parking facilities, since they will be obsolete in a decade or two. Whether or not these predictions are accurate, the fact remains that some downtowns need more parking now. In utterly car-dependent cities like Las Vegas and Tampa, getting new growth financed means a commitment to more parking.

Or does it? In a plan for the River District, an expansion of downtown Elkhart, IN, the City had determined that a 600-car parking structure was needed to serve a new aquatic center, and funded it at $10 million. With careful analysis and a healthy dose of skepticism, it was determined that—with shared parking, satellite parking, and high-tech demand management—all parking needs could be met using existing facilities. The $10 million has been rededicated to squares and parks within the District.

RULE 17: If on-site parking minimums cannot be eliminated entirely, replace them with in-lieu fees supporting shared parking lots. Regardless of how they are funded, locate large parking structures strategically as downtown anchors. And don't build them unless no other option exists.

18 Decouple and Share Parking

Bring the price of parking closer to its value, while rewarding efficient use.

LIKE DRIVING, low-priced parking is a "free good:" people use it much more than they would if its cost were closer to its value, which creates a powerful incentive to drive. For this reason, any serious attempt to make a city more walkable has to include a commitment to eliminate free parking at home and at work, the two places where it has the biggest impact on car ownership and use.

Doing so is relatively easy, if done fairly. What exists now in many places is a system in which people who don't own cars subsidize the lifestyles of those who do. When an apartment house or workplace provides free parking, the cost ultimately comes out of everyone's rent or salary, whether they drive or not.

In true mixed-use environments, one parking space can serve a morning café patron, a daytime office worker, an evening shopper, and an overnight resident.

In truly urban areas, most residential landlords have figured this out, and charge for parking separately. Not every apartment comes with parking, and those that do cost more. Ideally, parking spaces are rented (and sold) separately from residences, a practice called *decoupling*. But not every landlord does this, especially in more suburban areas; it should be required by law.

The workplace is a different matter. Few employers charge for parking at work. Donald Shoup calculates that, across the United States, this generosity

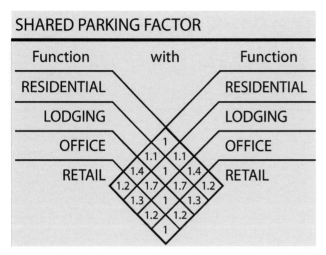

SHARED PARKING FACTOR

Function	with	Function
RESIDENTIAL		RESIDENTIAL
LODGING		LODGING
OFFICE	1 1.1 1.1	OFFICE
RETAIL	1.4 1 1.4 1.2 1.7 1.7 1.2 1.3 1 1.3 1.2 1.2 1	RETAIL

Sharing opportunities vary in different places, but the SmartCode offers these ratios as a rule of thumb for determining the increased efficiency of spaces shared among different uses.

amounts to an average subsidy of 22 cents per mile, which lowers the cost of commuting by a whopping 71%.[73] Employers feel compelled to offer free parking as they compete for talent, so what is to be done? The answer can be found in California, which mandates certain employers to offer something called *parking cash-out*. Following this all-carrot-no-stick program, these employers must allow workers to trade their parking space for its cash equivalent, which in turn reduces the parking requirement for the workplace. What the companies spend in incentives, they save in parking construction. Where used, this program has reduced driving commutes by more than 10%.[74]

As discussed in Rule 13, many downtown parking lots sit empty overnight, every night. The waste is staggering, as thousands of parking stalls costing $20,000 to $30,000 apiece go unused three quarters of the time. Similarly, parking lots at residential developments are mostly vacant every weekday from nine to five. These parking loads are utterly complementary; if they could somehow be combined, almost half of our parking spaces could be eliminated.

Of course, they can be combined, and often are. In true mixed-use environments, one parking space can serve a morning café patron, a daytime office worker, an evening shopper, and an overnight resident. All four of these users may even be the same person, who then might not choose to own a car at all.[75] Parking requirements in mixed-use communities, whether top-down or self-imposed, need to fully reflect two separate factors: the complementary schedules of different uses, and the lower car ownership rates among urban residents.

Aside from avoiding wasteful overbuilding, shared parking has been the key to financial viability in many recent mixed-use projects. For example, the City of Petaluma, CA, struggled for years to rebuild the south end of its downtown, but the City's conventional zoning code required too much parking for new developments to pencil out. A new form-based code, with shared parking ratios determined by Nelson\Nygaard, changed the math. With its parking requirement reduced from 1,200 spaces to only 530, the six-block, $95 million Petaluma Theatre District was built shortly thereafter.

RULE 18: Pass laws mandating the decoupling of residential parking and employee parking cash-out. Incentivize mixed-use development with reduced shared-parking requirements.

19 | Price Parking Based on Its Value
If the curbs are full, the parking is underpriced.

WHEN DRIVING is too cheap, roads get too crowded. When parking is too cheap, parking gets too crowded. And when people park too much, a bunch of bad things happen: people circle in search of spots; they double park; or they get frustrated and drive back home without shopping. Next time, they drive to the mall instead.

which constantly changes prices based on occupancy measured by in-road sensors. Or it can be achieved, with slightly less accuracy, by setting a price that changes once or twice a day based on a little bit of testing. Since most places currently price their parking so arbitrarily, a switch to an unsophisticated system that merely *tries* to respond

> *Since most places currently price their parking so arbitrarily, a switch to an unsophisticated system that merely tries to respond to demand can have a profound impact.*

For a downtown area to function rationally, its parking must be priced rationally. This means that price must reflect value, with the most desirable spots getting the highest price. In many places, this price should vary around the clock to reflect changing demand.

What's the right price? Donald Shoup suggests that parking be priced at the amount that results in 85% occupancy, which means that there is one empty spot on each curb face. This outcome can be achieved in high-tech ways, such as San Francisco's sophisticated *SFpark* system,

to demand can have a profound impact. And remember: the laws of supply and demand are not suspended at 6 p.m. or on Sunday, so properly priced parking shouldn't be either.

Shoup documents how, in city after city, a switch to properly-priced parking has changed merchants' fortunes for the better. He reminds us that the parking meter was introduced (in 1935) by store owners in order to improve revenue by creating more churn at the curb and encouraging workers to park elsewhere. Still, whenever someone

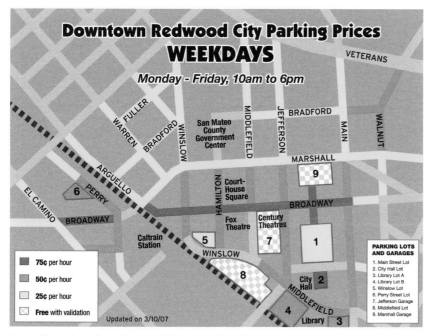

One of the earliest plans of its type, the 2007 Redwood City, CA, parking plan priced different spaces based upon their desirability, to allocate demand efficiently. Streets closest to the action cost the most, and underutilized parking structures were free.

suggests raising the price of parking in over-parked areas, it is almost always the local merchants who fight it the hardest.

In some cases, no amount of evidence or reason is adequate to change a merchant's mind. One restaurateur in Norwalk, CT, recently printed up a flyer. It says: "Donald Shoup's theories are right—just not here in Norwalk."[76]

For this reason, Shoup introduced one other great idea, the Parking Benefits District (PBD). A PBD makes a commitment to the merchants that the additional revenue collected from higher meter prices will be spent in the location where it is earned. Typically, it can be directed toward street and sidewalk improvements, street furniture like lighting and benches, new trees and landscaping, and even facade improvements to private businesses. Eventually, it can pay for new parking structures as well. PBDs are an excellent carrot for merchants, but they are potentially much more.

Probably the most effective PBD is the one that Shoup helped establish in Old Town Pasadena. Begun in 1993, it paid for all of the benefits mentioned above, as well as a team of public service officers, the burying of overhead wires, and the conversion of a rear alley network into a lovely pedestrian zone. There are no dumpsters in Old Town; each block has its own industrial trash compactor.

The experience in Pasadena has been truly transformative: a virtuous circle in which improvement has led to more visitors, which has led to more meter revenue and more improvement. Within five years of its inception, property tax revenue from the district tripled and sales tax revenues quadrupled.[77] Clearly, this is an effort worth copying.

RULE 19: Reprice parking with an eye to Shoup's 85% rule, and establish a Parking Benefits District to direct revenue toward local improvements.

PART V

LET TRANSIT WORK

IT IS DIFFICULT TO DISCUSS improved transit infrastructure when so many of America's existing transit systems are in scandalous disrepair, due principally to chronic underfunding. As the delays, derailments, fires, and (thankfully occasional) deaths mount, we must resist the urge to place our politicians on the first plane to Moscow—not in exile, but to experience the miracle of 90-second rush-hour headways on all lines. One need spend only an hour zipping around under Moscow—or Zurich, Paris, or even Vancouver—to realize how much better our transit systems could be. Meanwhile, most of them are getting worse. Do our leaders not realize how much more traffic their limos would face if everybody stopped taking transit?

Against this backdrop of neglect, it is comforting to know that good solutions exist—solutions that are already being deployed around the United States. Some of the most promising of these involve the redesign of bus networks. Lifestyle trends also suggest a resurgence in transit: about half as many sixteen-year-olds hold driver's licenses now as did in the 1980s.[78] While certainly not a response to improved transit service, this development suggests that a future of less driving could well be possible.

While driving one's own car used to be the definition of freedom, the mire of congestion enshrouding all of our major cities has changed the equation. More and more, it is frequent and convenient transit use that holds the real promise for mobility in our traffic-choked lives. Providing such service is possible, but it requires clearer thinking about mobility than we have seen in the recent past.[79] Such thinking mandates that transit and land use visions be developed in tandem, and evolve together. It reorganizes bus systems around a frequent network of direct paths with quick transfers. And it recognizes streetcars as more of a development catalyst than a mobility tool, while not forgetting about the role of transit vehicles as shared social spaces.

Several recent developments have complicated this picture in interesting ways. Bikeshare has given people an even healthier way not to drive, while ride-hailing services like Uber have turned both drivers and transit riders into backseat passengers. Eventually, autonomous vehicles are likely to transform urban mobility, but almost certainly not in the way that most people imagine.

Because density is at the heart of urbanism, and cars obliterate density, mass transit—in some form—is key to our urban future, and the topic of this section.

20 | Coordinate Transit and Land Use

Have a long-range plan that makes the two work together.

IT'S THE OLDEST LINE IN PLANNING. Why, then, do so few cities do it? Transportation systems beget land use patterns. Then land use patterns beget transportation systems. If they are not addressed together, with the same principles and goals—and the same map—mobility and quality of life suffer.

In his landmark book, *Human Transit,* transportation planner Jarrett Walker lays out some best practices for long-range land-use and transit planning.[80] These include the concepts below.

Twenty years out: For a long time, twenty years has been considered the proper window for long-range planning, and for good reason. It is soon enough to imagine, but so far in the future that most people and businesses are likely to have relocated.

A shared map: The centerpiece of any plan is a map, a drawing that should hang on the wall of every city office as a constant reminder of the community's shared vision for its future. This map should be clear and simple, and show principally two things: where the city intends to locate its transit-ready (higher-density) growth; and where the city

intends to locate its frequent-service transit network. Hint: they must be the same places.

A public process: The first step of this process should be a citywide comprehensive plan that is conducted—as required by planning ethics—fully in the public sphere, with as much participation and fanfare as can be mustered. Such a planning effort is needed both practically, to set a direction for growth, and politically, to create a foundation of public support for future planning and transportation actions in support of the plan.

An iterative process: Both in creating the comprehensive plan and in its subsequent refinement, the city's planning and transportation departments should establish a protocol of handing the document back and forth for continuous improvement. Typically, a proposed land use pattern will suggest a certain frequent-transit network that connects key destinations efficiently. That network will, in turn, suggest certain modifications to the land use pattern, to ensure that new areas of dense growth are located "on the way" while low-density areas are not. These modifications may in turn suggest tweaks to the

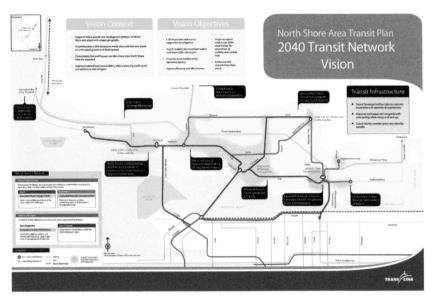

Vancouver's long-range transit plan links frequent service to high residential density, and vice versa.

love buying toys. But technology is unpredictable, and can't be trusted as the basis for twenty-year visions. What matters, when it comes to coordinating land use with transportation, is simply where the frequent-transit lines are located. When you are planning a transit line, the questions to answer are three: is service frequent or infrequent, is it rapid or local, and does it fit together with other lines to provide a network for going all over the city? A fixation on technology hijacks transit strategy away from making those choices that impact and respond to land use.

A basis for funding: The other purpose for a long-range transit vision is that it gives you something official to raise money around. More and more American cities, tired of waiting for uncertain state or federal funding, have created local referenda around sales taxes and other funding sources that allow them to plan their own transit destiny. Citizens have shown a surprising willingness to tax themselves in support of transit. A plan makes it possible.

transit plan. This process should never stop, so that the plan is always looking twenty years out.

Independent departments: Some cities consider merging their planning and transportation departments into a single entity, or forcing them to meet continually. That's a nice concept in theory, says Walker, but in practice it is "a great way to make the bureaucracy grind to a halt."[81] An iterative handoff process allows staff to spend more time planning and less time in meetings. The shared map (mentioned earlier) makes this possible.

Don't sweat technology: It is a common human trait—or at least an American one—to think more about transit technology than transit service. We all

---

RULE 20: Create a twenty-year land use and transportation plan, continually refined through an iterative interdepartmental process, which is used as a basis for funding transit.

21 Redesign Your Bus Network

Take advantage of current best practices to make the most of your transit investment.

IN MOST AMERICAN CITIES, your bus network is your real public transit workhorse. If it has not been comprehensively redesigned within the past two decades, chances are it should be, for three main reasons: First, we know a lot more about transit design then we used to. Current best practices may suggest an organization different from your current one. Second, most bus networks have received many tweaks over time, minor individual changes that may have made sense individually but that collectively have undermined the logic of the system, causing inefficiency, confusion, and potentially lost ridership. Finally, as discussed by Jarrett Walker, cities change. Each generation of growth is likely to alter working and living patterns in a way that impacts transit needs, and each generation of humans will have different values and priorities that govern its transit choices. Only a comprehensive redesign can address these changes rationally.

In approaching a bus network redesign, Walker encourages us to pay close attention to the following criteria.[82]

Ridership vs. coverage: Most transit systems must balance the two competing goals of serving the greatest number of people and serving those who may need transit most. A network that only serves people who live and work in densely settled areas will achieve high ridership, but at the expense of serving those who are more isolated—and vice versa. Before embarking on a network redesign, a transit agency must explicitly decide how much of its resources it wants to dedicate to each goal. In Houston, the transit agency board decided to direct 80% of its budget toward pursuing ridership.

The Frequent Service Network: Only when transit service is frequent does it provide true usefulness and freedom for its riders. Transit agencies pursuing ridership should determine their Frequent Service Network and distinguish it from the remainder of their service, with its own route map. Worth noting is that *high frequency* implies all-day service and extended hours; people need to get back home from wherever they are going.

Connections not complexity: A system that requires few transfers between buses will necessarily be more complex, requiring more independent routes. For any given number of buses, more routes means reduced frequency on each route. Since frequency is key to ridership, the most effective bus networks are based on connections, not complexity.

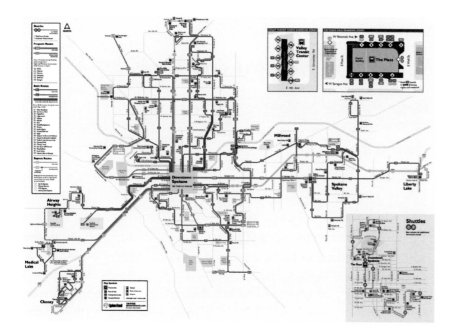

Spokane's redesigned bus network, shown here in part, highlights (in red) the frequent-service network that connects concentrations of housing and jobs.

Asterisk, spiderweb, or grid? Historically, most bus networks were like asterisks, making all connections through downtown. This pattern still makes sense in traditionally organized cities in which most jobs and activities remain at the center, but it may no longer be valid in the typical sprawling city, where paths through the downtown can add tremendous distance to trips at the periphery. In these circumstances, adding circles or squares to the asterisk—to make a sort of spiderweb—creates a network that allows for the most efficient deployment of transfers. Finally, in multicentered cites like Houston, the best solution may well be a simple grid, allowing quick L-shaped single-transfer trips from any one point to any other. Presuming a good street network and a modicum of walkability, covering a sprawling city in a grid of frequent bus routes one mile apart may be the most effective approach to providing mobility.

Dedicated lanes: In congested cities, the key to efficient bus service is to allow the bus to run in a dedicated lane, unimpeded by traffic. Everybody know this, so the challenge is more political than practical, and the best arguments come from politicians, like Bogota Mayor Enrique Penalosa. He wisely notes that, if all people are equal under the law, than "a bus with 100 people has a right to 100 times as much road as a car."[83]

RULE 21: Redesign your bus system with the goal of creating a frequent service network of simple routes—ideally in dedicated lanes—with efficient connections between them.

22 Build Streetcars, but as a Development Tool

Trolleys should be funded by the property owners they enrich.

STREETCARS—TRAINS THAT RUN IN STREETS, mixing with traffic—are far from the most efficient way to move people around. They are essentially buses that can't change lanes. Unless they have a dedicated travel way, as bona fide light rail, they are subject to the whims of traffic,

But the RideKC Streetcar is free, which points to the fact that these systems need an outside funding source to operate in the black. Unlike many places, Kansas City is doing it right: they established a Transportation Development District drawn tightly around the trolley line, within which a 1% sales

At the turn of the twentieth century, every city with a population greater than 10,000 had at least one trolley system, almost all of them built by real estate speculators in order to bring value to developable land.

which can mean all sorts of delays. And unless they are well integrated into a larger transit network, they are unlikely to expand freedom for many people.

Despite their limitations, new streetcar systems continue to be built across North America. Atlanta, Charlotte, Cincinnati, Salt Lake City, and Washington, DC, are but a few of the cities with shiny new trains running through their streets. Some are exceeding ridership projections, while many fall short. The biggest recent story may be Kansas City, MO, where the new trolley has doubled its first year projections of 2,700 rides per day.

tax and roughly 0.5% annual assessment on all property (even tax exempt) goes straight into RideKC operations.

Many streetcars are funded with sales tax, but Kansas City's extremely local focus on both sales tax and property value reminds us that the principal beneficiaries of streetcar development are the owners of the properties that the streetcar serves. This has always been the case. At the turn of the twentieth century, every city with a population greater than 10,000 had at least one trolley system,[84] almost all of them built by real estate speculators in order to bring value to developable land.[85]

In Portland, the streetcar is funded largely by the development it helped create.

No surprise then, that America's most successful recent line, the starter leg of the Portland Streetcar, was first imagined as a tool for creating real estate value. The goal was not just to "get a streetcar," but to bring downtown property values and activity north into the abandoned Hoyt Rail Yards. The streetcar plan was completed—as it always should be—as part of a comprehensive neighborhood plan, one that included an eight-fold density boost in exchange for affordable housing, parks, and other urban amenities.[86]

In this scheme, what did the streetcar do? Two main things: it created a permanent infrastructure commitment (unlike a more flexible bus line) integrating the new neighborhood into the downtown—and into Portland's sixty-mile TriMet rail network—and it took a distance that was a bit too far to walk and made it reachable. As Mayor Charlie Hales noted, streetcars are less transit systems than they are "pedestrian accelerators:"[87] tools for making walking more useful.

Together, these changes had the desired effect. In short order, more than $3.5 billion in new investment sprung up around the trolley line—sixty-four times the cost of the system—and local property values rose between 44% and 400%, well above baseline appreciation in Portland.[88] It was in anticipation of that appreciation that local landowners had happily paid the lion's share of the initial construction costs. Operating funds now come in part through property tax assessments from a Local Improvement District along the line.

A similar strategy was recently employed in Seattle around the new South Lake Union Trolley (yes, the S.L.U.T), where landowners including Microsoft contributed half the cost in anticipation of growth. Meanwhile, Detroit's new streetcar is being credited with over $7 billion in new investment along the line,[89] yet none of the profiting landowners seem to have been pressed to fund it. One suspects that this condition may not last.

Streetcars are development tools more than transit. Their planning and long-term funding should reflect this fact.

RULE 22: Plan streetcars where they can be funded by the landowners they will benefit, as part of comprehensive neighborhood planning around growth.

23 Consider the Transit Experience

Provide transit-by-choice that entices drivers out of their cars.

IN THE BIGGEST, most urban American cities, transit plays a large and indispensable role providing mobility to a large segment of the population. But most American cities are not big, and even fewer are truly urban. In these cities, few people take transit if they have the option to drive, since driving is so much more efficient. When your commute takes two transfers and ninety minutes, you find a way to get a car if you can.

Only with maximum wait times of ten minutes or less do schedules become dispensable.

In such places, transit for those without choice must remain as an essential social service. But there is justification for another type of transit, transit by choice, conceptualized as an urban amenity for those who might otherwise drive. Happily, transit by choice is also of great use to those who don't own cars, but its principal role is to make walkable areas more successful by allowing people to get around them and between them without driving.

These services, like downtown circulators, offer workers the opportunity to leave the car at the office while they attend a baseball game. They offer college students a convenient campus–downtown connection. And they offer downtown residents an incentive to go carless, by making walking more useful.

Because they tend to benefit downtowns, these services are often sponsored by the city itself or a downtown development authority, rather than by a transit authority. This is probably for the best, because they require a different skill set, one more focused on hospitality than efficiency. Still, many of these services seem to forget what features makes a transit experience appealing. These characteristics can be summarized as urbanity, clarity, frequency, and pleasure.

Urbanity: Urban transit should offer the benefits of urban life. Stops should be located alongside coffee shops, pocket parks, and other places where people want to be anyway. Why have a shelter when you can place a bench under the awning of a shop with great windows? Where needed, shelters should have (non-obtuse) artwork, and also whimsy, like Montreal's musical swings. Never should

Santa Barbara's open-air downtown shuttle was designed to attract riders with a choice.

a transit stop be located across a parking lot from a main street, the "problem of the last 100 yards" that haunts too many bus hubs and train stations.[90]

Clarity: Riders are more comfortable with routes they can easily conceptualize—simple straight lines. Any diversion represents an added discomfort, and also annoyance. Great wayfinding is a big help here; route maps should present appealing graphics, use simple place names, and indicate frequency. Smartphone apps should be equally transparent. Clarity of payment is also essential; many people who avoid transit do so because they are afraid of being befuddled by the fare mechanism. Most downtown circulators should be free, both to entice riders and because

it is difficult to communicate the fare on the outside of the vehicle. Collecting fares on circulators is pound foolish, anyway; they quash ridership and never come close to covering cost.

Frequency: Beyond being key to the larger network, frequency is also essential for transit by choice, since its riders are loathe to look at schedules. Only with maximum wait times of ten minutes or less do schedules become dispensable. Shorter headways may suggest using a smaller vehicle; better to have people standing than a ton of empty seats. And even with short headways, time-to-arrival clocks are also key to attracting customers, as the removal of uncertainty makes the wait more bearable.

Pleasure: In *My Kind of Transit,* Darrin Nordahl reminds us that public transit is "a mobile form of public space,"[91] and the design of that space can have a profound impact on its success. Benches should face inward, not forward. Windows should be big and not darkened by ads. In mild climates, open-air is a plus. Cuteness sells, but vehicles should be Apple cute, not Disney cute; a black-suited attorney should not feel silly climbing in.

While these four characteristics—urbanity, clarity, frequency, and pleasure—are called out as essential to downtown circulators and other similar services, they should be considered when providing any type of transit. Just because a bus serves many commuters does not mean that it won't do better if reconsidered through the lens of hospitality.

RULE 23: All transit should endeavor to satisfy the objectives of urbanity, clarity (of route and fare), frequency, and pleasure. Downtown circulators should be free and as small as practical.

24 Create Bikeshare that Works

Bring the latest bikeshare technology to your city.

AS OF THIS WRITING, there are only 119 docking bikeshare systems in the United States. We say "only 119" because every city of significant size should have one, and most still don't.

Still, the uptake has been impressive. Modern bike-dock technology has been deployed in the United States for less than a decade, and already the country's ten largest systems boast more than 2,500 docks among them.[92] Spartanburg, SC, population less than 40,000, has a successful 5-dock system. But there are 880 US cities larger than Spartanburg.

In many places, an investment in bikeshare is unwise without similar investment in improved cycling facilities.

After more than 100 million bikeshare trips, there is a lot to be known about best practices.

Promote bikeshare as transit. In a Denver study, 41% of bikeshare trips were found to have replaced driving trips.[93] Bikeshare makes transit systems more effective by providing last-mile service. Cities should support bikeshare for the same reasons they support transit.

Build a coalition. Successful bikeshare systems can be city owned or privately owned, but most are privately run. Whatever the structure, leadership

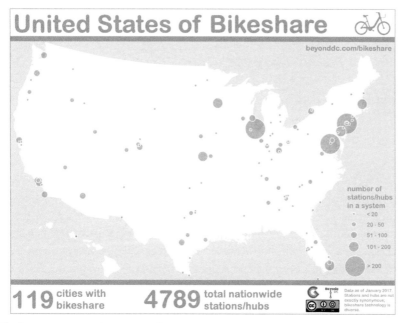

Bikeshare programs continue to spread.

Don't require helmets. While there were other factors involved, it is telling that the only large bikeshare system in the United States to fail (Seattle) had to attract ridership in the face of a helmet law. When Mexico City rolled out its Ecobici bikeshare program, it abolished its helmet law.[95] Because bicyclists are safer in larger numbers, helmets don't make riding safer if they depress ridership. (See Rule 54.)

Use Smart Bike technology. Portland's BikeTown system offers financial incentives for customers to redistribute bikes, rather than relying on vans. Meanwhile, despite some initial hiccups, GPS-enabled dock-less bike share threatens to make conventional systems obsolete.

Consider ebikes. It appears that Raleigh, NC, is pioneering electric bikeshare in the United States, following the lead of Madrid. More hilly cities should be even more interested.

Locate stations with care. Do not rely solely on conjecture or polling. (The most likely cyclists are often underrepresented in on-line outreach.) Be sure to review the valuable NACTO *Bike Share Station Siting Guide.*[96]

should include a steering committee representing all those institutions that see bikeshare as something that supports their mission. Foremost among these is the city itself, which has every reason to provide major support.

Subsidize lower-income riders. About a quarter of all US bikeshare programs offer lower-cost ridership to those who qualify. When such a feature was added in Philadelphia, the percentage of new riders earning less than $35,000 jumped from 27% to 44%.[94]

Don't stop with bikes. Bikeshare is not well used in places where it is unsafe to bike; it's also potentially negligent. In many places, an investment in bikeshare is unwise without similar investment in improved cycling facilities.

RULE 24: If your city is somewhat bikeable, introduce the most advanced bikeshare system possible, subsidized for those who need it, in conjunction with bike lane investment.

25 Don't Mistake Uber for Transit

Support public transportation in the face of ride-hailing.

MOST OF US use Uber, Lyft, or a similar ride-hailing app. The ubiquity of ride hailing is inevitable. Even as some progressive cities like Austin have tried to create trade barriers, it represents too good a value proposition for users to be held at bay for long.

Does a small surcharge on each ride in support of transit not seem prudent?

Ride hailing is amazing for mobility, especially in the suburbs, where few alternatives exist. But there is some question whether ride hailing is good for cities. On the plus side, there is likely a lot less drunk driving. A recent study found that New York City's four most urban boroughs experienced a 25% to 35% reduction in alcohol-related collisions after the rise of Uber.[97] It is hard to find another cause for this decline, and there is no temptation to do so. Most of us know people who used to drink and drive but now take Uber instead.

On the minus side, Uber is bad for transit, and for traffic. As many of New York's drivers were switching to Uber, so were transit riders. After years of increases, bus ridership has been declining since 2013, subway ridership has been declining since 2016, and street traffic is measurably worse.[98] According to one study, ride-hailing services are responsible for a 3% to 4% jump in traffic citywide, about six hundred million miles per year.[99]

The argument that the transit decline might be mere coincidence was largely dismissed by a recent study that polled Denver Uber and Lyft riders on what travel mode they would have taken had the ride not been available. A full 22% had switched from public transportation—and 12% would have otherwise biked or walked. Those data suggest that fully one third of all ride-hailing trips in Denver are new traffic caused by ride hailing.[100] And Denver has a fraction of the transit riders of New York.

But it gets worse, because the ride has to get to you first. The same Denver study, conducted by Alejandro Henao—who worked as an Uber and Lyft driver while earning his PhD, as well as a 5-star rating—found that for every 100 miles of moving customers, his car had to move 169 miles.[101] (And Alejandro parked his car immediately after every ride.) Uber's own data are similar, and that fig-

DOWNTOWN ENFORCEMENT EFFORTS APRIL 1, 2017–JUNE 30, 2017

VIOLATION	# OF VIOLATIONS	# IDENTIFIED AS TNC
7.2.72 TC (Drive in Transit Lane)	1,715	1,144
21209 CVC (Drive in Bike Lane)	18	15
21211 CVC (Obstruct Bike Lane)	10	7
7.2.70 TC (Obstruct Bike Lane or Lane of Traffic)	239	183
21950 CVC (Failure to Yield to Ped.)	50	26
21202 CVC (U-Turn in Business District)	57	42
Other Transit Violations	567	306
TOTAL	**2,656**	**1,723**

The San Francisco Police Department recently reported that Uber and Lyft drivers were responsible for fully 64% of traffic violations downtown.[106]

ure does not take into account commuting to and from the first and last customer.[102]

So if Uber generates more travel, what is the transportation payoff? Theoretically, it is a reduction in car ownership, which over time would be expected to lower road use, since ride hailing raises the variable cost of each ride. (Car owners more readily travel by car, because their principal costs are fixed.)

Evidence of a reduction in ownership is starting to trickle in.[103] According to a Reuters poll, approximately 2% of Americans recently ditched their cars thanks to ride hailing.[104] But think about it: if 2%—or even 20%—of Americans drive a bit less, is that enough to make up for the fact that each ride travels 69% farther? Environmentalists who support ride hailing are not doing this math.

Conversations with Uber and Lyft drivers would seem to teach a different lesson: to the typical moderate-income car owner, Uber and Lyft are less likely to be seen as an opportunity to lose the car than an opportunity to work for Uber and Lyft. Indeed, in South America, ride hailing is catching on as a platform for car ownership, allowing drivers to buy personal vehicles that they would otherwise not be able to afford.[105] These increases in ownership are likely to outweigh any eventual reductions in the United States.

Given these circumstances, cities may want to reconsider their policies regarding ride-hailing services. Since talented professionals want ride hailing, and cities want talented professionals, it does not seem wise to keep them out of town. But concerns about congestion and the viability of existing transit systems would suggest that a more defensive stance is warranted. Does a small surcharge on each ride in support of transit not seem prudent? At the very least, all but the most suburban cities need to stop wondering if ride hailing is a smart alternative to transit. If you have congestion, it's not.

RULE 25: City policy should reflect the fact that ride-hailing services increase congestion, undermine transit, and offer little social benefit beyond reduced drunk driving.

26 Anticipate Autonomous Vehicles

Unless we make rules now, they are likely to do more harm than good.

IT SOMETIMES SEEMS THAT ALL ANYONE WANTS TO TALK about these days in cities is Autonomous Vehicles (AVs). How soon will they arrive? Will they swarm? How are they likely to change our cities, and our lives?

Proponents of AVs are quick to tout all the potential benefits. These include a dramatic drop in driving deaths, reduced car ownership, less congestion, more personalized transit service, and the elimination of much on-street parking, allowing a ton of street space to be rededicated to walking, biking, and greenery. Unfortunately, a more careful thought experiment, informed by a fuller understanding of American cities and their governance, leads to some less optimistic conclusions.[107]

When it comes to transit, even AVs must follow the laws of physics, and there is no getting around the fact that one New York City L Train carries as many commuters per hour as 2,000 cars.

History would suggest that the widely held vision of swarming public fleets, uninterrupted by private and non-autonomous cars, is unlikely to happen in the United States, where no city has ever shown the willingness to limit private car use in any meaningful way, despite crippling traffic. Unlike in less libertarian coun-

As travel becomes cheaper and time wasted in traffic becomes more pleasant, AVs threaten to make congestion worse.

tries, American cities must plan for incomplete, uncoordinated AV adoption.

And while car ownership may decline with AVs, car use will not. Zipcar founder Robin Chase, former NYC mayor Michael Bloomberg, and many other thoughtful people predict a massive increase in car trips as a result of autonomy, due to the likelihood of lower driving costs.[108] But that's not all. Since time wasted in traffic is currently the principal constraint to driving, any boost in roadway efficiency (through tighter vehicle spacing) will increase car use, as will the fact that time in traffic will become productive for work or play. Bloomberg and others suggest regulation through laws,[109] but there is a simpler way: regulation

through lanes. In an AV future, each city street would ideally be allocated a limited number of driving lanes, no more than currently present. Only in this way will our downtowns remain welcoming to more than just cars.

Moreover, cheap automobiles were the principal enabler of suburban sprawl. As autonomy makes it even cheaper to access far-flung locations, there is danger of a second wave of exurban dislocation. Cities that wish to avoid the long-term balance-sheet burden represented by low-density suburbia must double-down on efforts to promote "smart growth," which mostly means eliminating all hidden subsidies for sprawl.

When it comes to transit, even AVs must follow the laws of physics, and there is no getting around the fact that one New York City L Train carries as many commuters per hour as 2,000 cars. Each city bus replaces about 50 cars.[110] Even swarming AVs will never come close to providing the services of a well-used transit vehicle. Replacing transit with small AVs in congested city centers would cripple mobility. They must be understood as a supplement, not a solution.

For that reason, only cities with no congestion and insignificant transit ridership should plan to convert transit to autonomous cars. Unfortunately, the prospect of such service is already threatening transit investment in certain congested American cities, like Mountain View, CA, where dedicated bus lanes were recently defeated in part due to the promise of autonomy.[111] Cities must show informed leadership on this challenging issue.

RULE 26: Do not allow the arrival of AVs to result in a net increase in driving lanes; do not allow AVs to undermine large-vehicle transit in places with significant traffic congestion.

PART VI

ESCAPE AUTOMOBILISM

AS FRED KENT, the founder of Project for Public Spaces, likes to say, "If you plan for cars and traffic, you get cars and traffic. If you plan for people and places, you get people and places."[112] But it is actually more of a struggle. Never in the history of cities has a car not taken all the space that it was given and asked for more.

There are many things that can be measured in cities, each of which has its own impact on success. Density, diversity, walkability, property value, resource conservation, life expectancy, educational attainment, the production of patents, GDP, carbon footprint, free-flowing traffic: all of these relate to a city's well-being, attractiveness, and future prospects. Yet only one of them, the last one, is routinely used to direct decision making around a city's growth, and ironically, it is the one that works to the detriment of all the others.

Let that sink in. The one aspect of urban life that has the most impact on city planning, traffic flow, exists in almost perfect opposition to all the other good things a city can have. Time and time again, studies find a clear inverse correlation between easy driving and every other measure of success. The more dense, diverse, walkable, and desirable a city is, the more it is likely to be congested. The less fuel it burns and the lower the obesity rate, the worse the traffic. Ditto that on educational attainment, patents per capita, and GDP.[113] (Every 10% increase in traffic delay correlates to a 3.4% increase in per-capita GDP.[114])

In the United States at least, greatness brings congestion. Why, then, is design controlled by congestion, and not by greatness?

For putting fears of congestion in their proper place, the first step is to understand the phenomenon of induced demand, and how more roads mean more traffic and fewer roads mean less. Once this understanding becomes more widespread, a city may be ready to stop widening roads and building new highways. It may even be willing to remove a redundant highway, a bold measure that has paid off wherever it has been tried.

Meanwhile, congestion pricing—the one tool that actually limits congestion—may finally be ready for its North American debut. And pedestrian streets and zones, discredited in the United States for good reason, seem to merit a second look.

27 Understand Induced Demand

Acknowledge that more lanes means more traffic.

TRAFFIC ENGINEERING THEORY is straightforward: a street is congested because the number of drivers exceeds its capacity. If you enlarge the street, you will eliminate congestion. Unfortunately, seventy-five years of evidence tells us that this almost never happens. Instead, what happens is that the number of drivers quickly increases to match the increased capacity, and congestion returns in full force. It's called induced demand. These new drivers are the people who were taking transit, carpooling, commuting off-peak, or simply not driving because they didn't want to be stuck in traffic. When the traffic went away, they changed their habits. Maybe they even moved farther away from work, as the time-cost of their commute went down. Unfortunately, thanks to them and others like them, this honeymoon couldn't last long.

This makes sense once you realize that, in congested systems, the principal constraint to driving is congestion. The question is not whether roads will be congested at rush hour, but how many lanes of congestion you want.

This phenomenon has been well documented over many years. The data tell us that every new mile of roadway that you build will typically be 40% filled up with new trips immediately, and 100% full within four years.[115]

Sometimes it happens faster. When California's 405 freeway was recently expanded, a $1.6 billion nightmare that included two complete shutdowns, it actually opened to congestion that was worse—and stayed worse—than it had been before construction.[116]

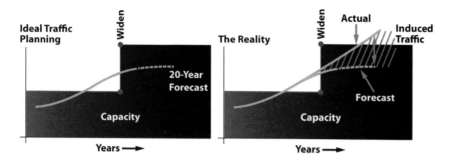

Walter Kulash's classic illustration of traffic theory: Congestion occurs when traffic (in yellow) outpaces capacity. Widening the road absorbs the extra trips.

Walter Kulash's traffic reality: Eliminating congestion induces people to drive more, and congestion returns quickly.

Likewise, Texas, with federal help, paid $2.8 billion to turn the Katy Freeway into "the world's widest highway," in order to reduce congestion. Within four years of completion, the morning commute was taking 30% longer, and the afternoon commute was taking 55% longer than before construction.[117]

Induced demand is one lesson that engineers—and politicians—never seem to learn. The graphs on these pages are older than many of the people reading this book, yet, almost no traffic studies even consider induced demand. At the time of this writing, more than a dozen states have major highway expansions ready to happen, and almost all of these are being justified first and foremost by traffic congestion. Rest assured, these thirteen projects, which total over $31 billion, will not do a thing to reduce congestion for more than a few years.

There may be some progress: Not too long ago, Caltrans placed a link on its website to a policy brief entitled "Increasing Highway Capacity Unlikely to Reduce Congestion."[118] Finally, a State DOT admitting induced demand! Shortly thereafter, the link was gone.[119] One hopes the staffer responsible landed on their feet.

There may be legitimate reasons in certain cases to widen roads or highways. Congestion just isn't one of them.

RULE 27: Do not widen roads or build new ones to fight congestion.

28 Tear Down a Highway

Replace downtown highways with walkable boulevards.

IF YOU UNDERSTAND the Law of Induced Demand, you will not be surprised to learn that it works in reverse: *Build It and They Will Come* becomes *Remove It and They Will Go.* Quietly.

Happily, this counterintuitive claim is backed by evidence. When structural damage caused Manhattan's West Side Highway to shut down in 1973, a NYDOT

Boulevards create real estate value, while highways—especially elevated highways—sunder real estate value.

study showed that 93% of its traffic did not shift to other streets; it just went away.[120] Similarly, when San Francisco's Embarcadero and Central Freeways had to come down after the 1989 Loma Prieta earthquake, the anticipated "carmaggedon" never arrived. People simply adjusted their travel patterns: they took different routes, took different modes (like the F-Line streetcar) or just shifted their travel a bit off-peak. For the first time in years, overall travel times in San Francisco dropped.[121]

More recently, and in the face of a huge outcry, Seoul, South Korea, tore down its fabled and congested Cheong-gyecheon Freeway, which boasted a daily traffic count of 168,000 vehicles. In its place, they built a gentle boulevard lining the lovely river that the highway had been squatting on. Sixteen lanes were replaced by four, and traffic congestion dropped.

In all fairness, these teardowns were not done in isolation: they were accompanied by investments in transit and walkability. The F-Line along the Embarcadero now moves more people per day than the highway it replaced.

How were these projects paid for? First, it should be noted that, when an elevated viaduct needs to be rebuilt, replacing it with a surface boulevard is almost always the cheapest alternative. Roads in the air cost more than roads on the ground. Second, and more important, replacing a highway with a boulevard generates a tremendous amount of wealth. Boulevards create real estate value, while highways—especially elevated highways—sunder real estate value. In both Seoul and San Francisco, properties surrounding the removed viaducts quickly escalated 300% in value, and continue to appreciate.[122] Empty lots have filled up with

San Francisco's Embarcadero Boulevard sits on land once occupied by an elevated highway.

buildings. The resulting increased tax revenues make a massive transit investment look small in comparison.

Some highways are easier to tear down than others. The best candidates are spurs and ring roads—routes that provide mostly redundant access to city centers. But, under the right circumstances, major interstates deserve replacement as well, such as I-81 in downtown Syracuse.

A good dozen "Freeways without Futures" are now under serious consideration across the United States, with several removals underway. [123] Rochester, NY, is slowly dismantling its sunken Inner Loop, hoping to undo some of the damage that it wrought when, in 1965, they built a depressed highway and got a depressed city. (Or, as described by city engineer James MacIntosh: "We built an evacuation route. It worked: everybody evacuated."[124])

Recent experience in Oklahoma City suggests an important detail: when turning a State highway into a City boulevard, it is essential to transfer ownership to the City before, not after, design and construction. When you're a hammer, everything looks like a nail, and when state highway engineers design local streets, they end up looking like highways.

Finally, as with any intervention that is expected to dramatically increase property values, any highway removal must be accompanied with a program to ensure that existing residents are not displaced by raising rents or property taxes.

RULE 28: Replace urban highways with City-designed urban boulevards in locations where doing so will create a great increase in land value, simultaneously investing in transit along the corridor.

29 Congestion-Price City Centers

Fight traffic with the only tool that works.

WHY DOES INDUCED DEMAND HAPPEN? The short answer is that, for most of us, time wasted in traffic is the principal cost of driving. When that time is shortened, driving effectively becomes cheaper, and people do more of it.

But why is time the principal cost? What about. . . cost? The fact is that we pay only a small fraction of the true cost of driving. Through one mechanism or another—mostly hidden subsidies—drivers are not footing the bill for a long list of direct and indirect costs including roads, parking, policing, fire services, fuel security, pollution (a.k.a. climate change), and so on. According to one study, subsidies to roads and parking alone add up to between 8% and 10% of our Gross National Product.[125] As illustrated in Rule 1, it is estimated that we are paying less than one tenth of the true cost of our driving.

No surprise, then, that the only real remedy to congestion is to bring the cost of driving back in line with its value.

This makes driving what economists call a "free good." When something is a free good, you use it as much as possible, and the market for it goes haywire. Our streets are too congested for the same reason that the Soviets couldn't keep bread on the shelves: artificially low pricing spikes demand.

No surprise, then, that the only real remedy to congestion is to bring the cost of driving back in line with its value. Such is the goal of Congestion Pricing, in which the cost of driving on a busy road or in a crowded downtown is raised in an attempt to reflect demand, often varying over time as demand changes.

The United States already has a few congestion-priced roads in the form of High-Occupancy Toll (HOT) Lanes, mostly in California. But, despite some attempts, it has yet to see any congestion-priced city centers of the type spreading around Europe and elsewhere. America's HOT Lanes, also called "Lexus Lanes," have raised questions of equity. These questions are valid, mostly because congestion-priced roads offer few of the social benefits of congestion-priced downtowns.

To understand the benefits, one need only look at what happened in London on February 17, 2003, when Mayor Ken Livingstone introduced one of the world's largest congestion pricing schemes. Suddenly, it cost roughly $15 to bring a car into central London on weekdays between 7 a.m. and 6 p.m.

Fairly quickly, congestion dropped 30%, trip times dropped 14%, bus delays dropped 60%, and air pollution dropped 12%. More than a billion dollars in net revenue was collected, much of which was put into alternative transportation. Eventually, bus reliability rose by 30%, and cycling went up 20%.[126]

Central London is still congested—the toll may need to be better calibrated to demand—but the impact is clear, and the principal beneficiaries are those who take buses, ride bikes, and live along busy roadways. These people are, on average, poorer than those who arrive by car. Unlike with Lexus Lanes, the equity benefits of downtown congestion pricing clearly outweigh the burdens placed upon those who still make the choice to drive.

Congestion pricing in city centers is now a fact of life in Singapore, Stockholm, and a few other places—far fewer than would benefit from it. Michael Bloomberg's 2007 attempt to introduce Congestion Pricing to New York City was killed by the State legislature, favoring suburban voters as states usually do. Cities less dependent on state-level approval should not be deterred from pursuing this powerful tool.

Stockholm's congestion tax is carefully calibrated to demand around the clock.

RULE 29: If your downtown is congested, introduce a variable congestion-based toll for entry, and invest the proceeds in alternative transportation.

30 | Close a Street to Cars—Maybe

In the right circumstances, pedestrian streets can thrive.

AN IDEA THAT IS POPPING UP in many American cities right now is to turn the downtown's best street into a pedestrian mall. In many of these cities, this idea is being raised by someone who has no idea of the sobering history of that concept.

More than two hundred North American main streets were turned into pedestrian malls in the 1960s and 1970s, most at great expense. All but about ten of them went straight downhill, and all but about thirty have been expensively retrofitted back to welcome cars again.

Stay light and flexible, and see what arrangement works best.

The successes are remarkable, and make you want to build more. Church Street in Burlington, Main Street in Charlottesville, Lincoln Road in Miami Beach, State Street in Madison, Pearl Street in Boulder, 3rd Street in Santa Monica. . . which is your favorite? Most of them are in either college towns or resort cities. But there are exceptions, like 16th Street in Denver, Downtown Crossing in Boston, and just about any street that anyone closes in Manhattan. These exceptions teach us about what it takes for a main street to survive without cars. You'll never guess what it is: *stores that don't need cars.*

This sounds obvious enough, but nobody stopped to consider it the first time around. When main streets were closed to cars in Buffalo, Des Moines,

Grand Rapids, Memphis, and two hundred other places, not even the merchants raised much of a stink about the fact that most of their customers had always arrived in vehicles and parked nearby. It worked well in Europe, and it was going to work well here, too.

It still works well in Europe. Most sizeable European cities have one or several main streets that are pedestrian-only. Copenhagen, famously, has a central pedestrian zone of more than 25 acres.[127] In the United States, it can sometimes be hard to tell how car-dependent a shop or restaurant may be; merchants often overestimate it. The debates can go on for years, but the good news is that you don't have to guess: you can close the street for a few days and find out.

Many main streets have tried this already. They start with a holiday, then try a regular weekend day, then maybe a whole weekend. Each success allows another test. Key to this strategy, even if it succeeds, is to not spend a lot of money on landscape that makes the change permanent—at least, not at first. Stay light and flexible, and see what arrangement works best.

When you have the confidence to make the car ban permanent, lay down epoxy gravel like in New York. If it keeps working for years, we can talk about adding beautiful pavement and permanent plants and trees. But these things may not be needed; the success of a pedestrian zone depends more on location and access than on materials and beauty.

New York City's new car-free spaces started out temporary and cheap.

RULE 30: If your city has a main street that might thrive without cars, test it temporarily. Once it demonstrates continued success, make it permanent and test another.

PART VII

START WITH SAFETY

THERE ARE A HUNDRED REASONS to make cities more walkable, but perhaps the easiest one to explain is safety. It is also the one that is hardest for opponents to fight; nobody likes seeing people get hurt. In any effort to improve walkability, safety has to be front and center.

Fortunately, safety is the aspect of walkability that cities are most able to influence in the short term. The General Theory of Walkability, discussed in *Walkable City*, explains how, for a place to be walkable, the walk must be simultaneously useful, safe, comfortable, and interesting. Of those four, the categories of usefulness, comfort, and interest are principally the result of the buildings that line the street. Do they serve diverse uses, shape public space well, and have lively edges? These are qualities that a city can control only over the long run, through its plans and codes.

But the safe walk can be provided in the short run, because most cities own their streets, and most city streets are currently not as safe as they could be, principally because their design

encourages drivers to travel at speeds well above the posted limit. This fact, more than any other, needs to lead public conversation around those efforts.

Also important to discuss is the fact that some safety improvements will lead to slightly longer commutes. Rather than being swept out of sight, these tradeoffs should be communicated honestly. When they are properly understood, most enlightened politicians will choose safety over speed.

A few tools exist to help cities along this path. The first is the rapidly propagating Vision Zero movement, which provides a powerful framework as well as a toolkit for making city streets safer. Next, downtown speed limits, while less impactful than street design, are nonetheless effective in reducing crashes and injuries, especially if properly publicized and enforced. Finally, the controversial red-light camera (and speed camera) is an undervalued tool that is overdue for mass adoption.

31 Focus on Speeding

Street improvements should be linked to keeping speeding in check.

IT'S THE SPEED, STUPID.

Roughly the next fifty points—half of this book—address different aspects of the street, and how they are designed and managed. Many of these points may serve multiple objectives and audiences, but they all aim back, in one way or another, at a single issue: vehicle speed.

Streets must be designed to encourage the speeds that we have set for them, or the result will be illegal, deadly speeding.

While many different factors influence the safety of humans in cities, none matters nearly so much as the speed at which vehicles are traveling. The relationship between vehicle speed and danger is, to put it mildly, exponential.

The diagram at right is one of many that can be found to communicate this relationship. Others show people falling out of buildings, with 20 mph equaling the second floor and 40 mph equaling the seventh. The basic message to remember is that you are about five times as likely to be killed by a car going 30 as a car going 20, and five times again as likely to be killed by a car going 40.

This threshold zone of 20 to 40 mph, is basically where it all happens—the difference between bruises, broken bones, and death. And 20 to 40 is roughly the range of speeds that we find cars traveling on the best downtown

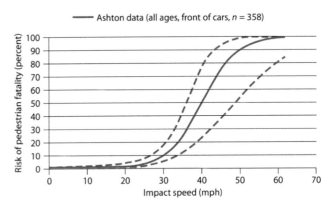

The risk to pedestrians from vehicles takes a dramatic upturn at 25 mph.

streets. Keeping cars on the lower end of that range, therefore, must be the central objective of urban street design.

The speed of the impact itself is not the only factor. As cars move faster, the likelihood of a crash also rises. Drivers and pedestrians alike have less time to respond to conflicts, stopping distances lengthen, and the driver's cone of vision narrows. These factors multiply the impact of speed beyond those indicated in the above graph. It is safe to say that a car traveling 30 mph is probably at least three times as dangerous as one going 25.

Many cities have a downtown speed limit of 25. All should—or lower, as discussed in Rule 34. These limits simplify the conversation, because it is no longer necessary to talk about "slowing drivers down." Who wants to be slowed down? That sounds like congestion.

Instead, we can simply talk about "reducing illegal speeding." Streets need to be redesigned so that fewer people will speed on them. This cannot be accomplished with speed limits alone, because people do not drive the posted speed; they drive the speed that is implied by the street design. Streets must be designed to encourage the speeds that we have set for them, or the result will be illegal, deadly speeding. That is the central message, and the street designer's mandate.

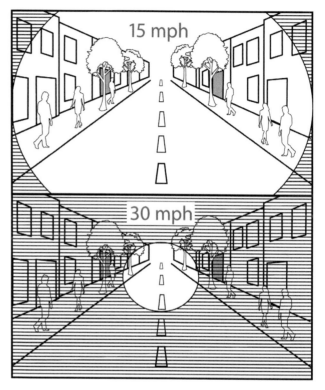

As drivers move more quickly, their cone of vision narrows, making crashes more likely

---

RULE 31: Street design and design discourse should focus on reducing illegal speeding.

32 | Discuss the Time Cost of Safety

Be forthright about tradeoffs.

MANY REDUCTIONS TO SPEEDING can be accomplished without lengthening commute times. When drivers are gunning it from red light to red light, introducing a slower design speed can make life better for everyone.

This was the case on Brooklyn's Prospect Park West, when Janette Sadik-Khan's team at NYCDOT introduced a new protected bike lane, narrowing the roadway from three lanes to two. Speeding remarkably dropped from (an impressive) 71% of all vehicles to only 17%, yet travel times were no longer than before, because drivers had just been speeding from red to red.

Would you rather have a downtown that is quick to drive through, or one worth arriving at?

But this is not always the case. Improvements to a downtown's safety—essential for its vitality—can sometimes lengthen travel times. This is probably most evident when one-way streets are reverted back to two-way, and commuters are no longer able to "surf the green wave"

of synchronized lights in and out of town (see Rule 39). Commutes take a bit more time.

The same is true of reducing a downtown speed limit, or intentionally changing—notice we did not say "lowering"—a street's Level Of Service from, say, B to E. The increased commute times are not hard to model, and usually add up to just a minute or two. These delays, while small, are real, and matter to people.

These concerns should not be dismissed out of hand. There are many people who commute in and out of downtown each day who have no other use for downtown—at least, not in its current state. They brown-bag their lunches and don't linger after work for cocktails. Most are constrained in both money and time.

Some of these people will never have interest in a safer, more vital downtown. Even if it becomes remarkably more appealing, with new public spaces and activities springing up, they will not make use of it. But these people are the exception. Almost everybody, at the very least, wants a downtown they can be proud of. And most suburbanites, when a downtown becomes a destination, will want to visit it on occasion.

This graphic by the transportation planning firm Nelson\Nygaard shows how slower downtown speeds have only a minimal impact on typical commute times.

Moreover, these people's desires need to be weighed against the desires of all downtown stakeholders. In most places, the majority of downtown workers care a lot about its safety and quality. All downtown residents certainly care. The same goes for merchants, property owners, and other investors. It is in this context that the trade-offs between commute time and safety need to be made clear, and the key question asked: would you rather have a downtown that is quick to drive through, or one worth arriving at?

In most cases, getting a struggling downtown to reach its potential depends on bringing speeding drivers in check. People avoid sidewalks they don't feel safe on, and without people on sidewalks, cities don't thrive.

The arguments in favor of slightly slower commutes are especially powerful when lives are being lost. Between 1990 and 2014, 186 people were killed in car crashes along New York City's Queens Boulevard. That's one death roughly every seven weeks for a quarter-century, most of them people walking. Finally, the city invested a mere $4 million in improved pedestrian and cycling facilities, and not a single person has died since. Speeds have dropped by about 4 mph along the corridor.[128] Few would argue that this slight inconvenience is worth even a single life.

So, citizens and city leaders should be presented with a clear and honest choice. Where commutes will take a little longer, it's important to say so. But, given the whole story, most people have shown themselves willing to spare a minute or two for the good of their city and fellow citizens.

RULE 32: Discuss tradeoffs between speed and safety honestly, with an eye to downtown vitality, civic pride, and lives saved.

33

Adopt Vision Zero

Make a political movement around traffic safety.

IN EVERY MAJOR AMERICAN CITY, pedestrian deaths are a part of life. Often, the victim is a child. The news cycle is predictable: first comes the victim blaming, then the driver blaming—sober drivers are almost never punished—then perhaps a discussion about speed limits and enforcement. Through it all, the crash is called an "accident," as if it was not preventable. Rarely is the design of the roadway itself considered. And never—*never*—is there any reconsideration of the professional engineering standards that created the hazard in the first place.

Vision Zero does not focus exclusively on roadway design, but it is one of the first programs of its type to stress its importance.

The Swedes, those geniuses of driving safety, know better. For some time, the leadership of the Swedish traffic safety profession has acknowledged that street design is at the heart of street safety, and modified its engineering standards with an eye to lowering speeds in urban areas. The results are astounding. Their traffic fatality rate as a nation is about one quarter of the United States',[129] but the biggest difference is in the cities. In 2013, Stockholm, with a similar population to Phoenix, lost six people to car crashes. Phoenix lost 167.[130]

Remarkably, Stockholm made it through 2016 without a single pedestrian or cyclist dying.

When children die in a crosswalk, it is natural and appropriate to investigate the driver. Rarely do we investigate the crosswalk.

Welcome to *Vision Zero,* the Swedish path to eliminating traffic deaths. Now a decade old, Vision Zero has become an international movement, and joining it in earnest means making a commitment to its goals. As of this writing, there are more than thirty "Vision Zero Cities" in the United States, including Austin, Boston, Denver, Fort Lauderdale, Los Angeles, New York, Seattle, and Washington, DC.

Each of these cities has approached the commitment in its own way, but joining the Vision Zero network can be a key first step to identifying the elimination of traffic fatalities as an important goal and reorienting policy and investment around that goal. In New York City, for example, the Vision Zero program has organized the insertion (at last count) of 18.5 miles of protected bike lanes, 776 Leading Pedestrian Interval traffic signals (see Rule 74), and 107 left-turn calming treatments, and also overseen a dramatic crackdown on speeding and failure-to-yield violations.[131] The result? After holding fairly steady for three years, pedestrian fatalities dropped by a whopping 32 percent between 2016 and 2017, from 148 to 101.[132]

In Seattle, too—where city engineer Dongho Chang tweets daily about bike lanes, curb extensions, and other safety improvements his department is installing—the impact of Vision Zero is clear. Vision Zero does not focus exclusively on roadway design, but it is one of the first programs of its type to stress its importance. While not stated outright, both its goals and its execution fly in the face of a half-century of negligent engineering practice.

Vision Zero presents cities with a tremendously useful framework for both raising the profile of pedestrian safety and making real change to support it. Advocates should rally publicly around the tragedy of road deaths to overcome hurdles to its adoption.

RULE 33: Get your city to join the Vision Zero Network.

34 | Adopt a Downtown Speed Limit
To make speed limits stick, make them district-wide.

SPEED LIMITS DON'T MATTER, MUCH. But they matter. Speed limits in cities have limited impact because of the way that drivers set their speed in cities. It is the opposite of what occurs on highways. Think about your own experience, and how you set your speed on a highway.

In New York City, guerilla speed police have posted their own neighborhood signs.

If you are like most people, you wait for a speed limit sign, and then set your cruise control for a speed a little bit above it.

Now think about how you set your speed downtown. Chances are you don't look for speed limit signs, but you drive the speed at which you feel comfortable. That comfort is an outcome, mostly, of the street design. In this context, it is shocking to learn that, for years, traffic engineers have insisted that city streets be designed to support speeds well in excess of posted limits. This mistaking of city streets for highways has probably killed more Americans than any other form of professional negligence.

But speed limits do have an impact, especially if they are so prominent and memorable that they work their way into a community's collective unconscious. One way to do that is with constant, vigilant ticketing. In Sun Valley, ID, locals drive 25 mph on downtown streets that look like interstates, because the police there are utterly rabid—they even ticketed Jimmy Kimmel.[133]

The other way to make a speed limit stick in people's minds is to create a public campaign around a limit that applies to an entire area, especially a well-defined area like downtown. Having a catchy name doesn't hurt either. That's why the *20's Plenty for Us* movement has had such an impact. More than 15 million people, most of them Britons, live in jurisdictions that have adopted or will soon adopt neighborhood-wide 20-mph speed limits.[134] About one third of London is now so posted.[135]

The data from *20's Plenty* programs are slowly coming in. One study found an average speed reduction of only 1 mph throughout the posted area.[136] Another, though, found a 20% reduction in serious casualties.[137] It would be interesting to compare the two cases; outreach and enforcement were probably important factors. But, since even a speed reduction of only 1 mph is correlated with a 6% reduction in collisions,[138] it seems clear that district-wide speed limits do help.

More than 15 million people, most of them Britons, live in jurisdictions that have adopted or will soon adopt neighborhood-wide 20-mph speed limits.

Aside from a number of citizen-led rogue movements, *20's Plenty* has yet to catch on in the United States, probably because we have so few cities in which driving 20 mph doesn't feel just ridiculous, thanks to the street design. In these places, though, district-wide speed limits still make sense, and 25 mph does not seem too much to ask. Combined with eye-catching signs, public outreach, and some concerted ticketing, one can imagine a 25-mph campaign making a big difference. How does *25 Keeps Us Alive* sound?

But be more ambitious if you can. Portland recently enacted a 20-mph rule on 70 percent of the city's total street miles.[139]

Speed limits are more likely to be remembered if they apply to an entire district and the signs say so.

RULE 34: Post a district-wide 25-mph speed limit in downtown areas (or 20 mph if you can get away with it) in conjunction with a bold public campaign, special signage, and strong enforcement.

35 Install Red-Light Cameras and Speed Cameras

It's time to embrace these effective tools.

RED-LIGHT CAMERAS AND SPEED CAMERAS are automated devices that issue citations to drivers who run red lights or drive above the speed limit. These citations have a limited cost—often $50—and have no impact on a driver's license "points" or insurance rates. While there have been conflicting reports through the years, the evidence is now conclusive that these cameras save lives, and do so in a way that is revenue-positive for the cities that use

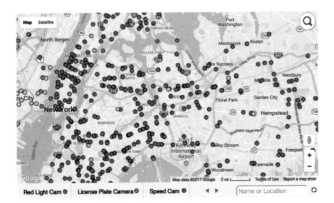

New York City is one place where automated ticketing is well established and saving lives.

them. As a supplement to in-person enforcement with the teeth to get repeat offenders off the street, they are simply too effective to ignore.

As of this writing, 421 communities have red light cameras and 142 have speed cameras.[140] While many more municipalities would like to use them, state government has often stood in the way. Sixteen states, including Michigan, South Carolina, and Utah, outlaw them completely, while others have placed constraints upon their use. The justification for these restrictions are usually that they do not improve safety (now disproved) or they violate the privacy of drivers (ruled as false by the Seventh US Circuit Court of Appeals). With these concerns put to bed, these devices are poised to become more ubiquitous. Recent data from New York City provide a strong incentive.

The City was severely restricted by the NY State Assembly, which in 2013 grudgingly allowed speed cameras to be installed only in school zones, and switched on only during school hours—even though a DOT study found that fewer than one in ten speeding deaths occur in these hours.[141] Nonetheless, by 2016, these cameras were issuing more than 1.3 million citations per year.[142] Compared to beforehand, injury crashes have declined by 15%, and pedestrian injuries are down 23%.[143] Speeding in the school zones dropped by 63%. Apparently impressed with these results, the State Assembly recently voted to more than double the number of speed cameras in the city, to 290.[144]

In Montgomery County, MD, researchers concluded that speed cameras resulted in a 39% reduction in the likelihood that a crash involved an incapacitating or fatal injury.

Even stronger data have been collected elsewhere. In Seattle, a red-light camera program led to a 23% decline in collisions, while crashes involving pedestrians fell by almost a third. The cameras even reduced rear-end crashes by 15%, which is meaningful, given past speculation that cameras would cause an increase in rear-enders.[145] In Montgomery County, MD, researchers concluded that speed cameras resulted in a 39% reduction in the likeli-

hood that a crash involved an incapacitating or fatal injury. Beyond that, they estimate that the County's decade-old camera program has averted more than 500 incapacitating injuries or deaths during that period. [146]

What would you spend to avert 500 life-changing collisions? The answer is immaterial, since these programs make money. Over three years, New York City's speed camera program collected $123 million in fines, of which $70 million went to costs and $53 million was surplus. The high ratio of cost to net revenue is the final item that upsets the critics of these programs, who see them as industry boondoggles and opportunities for graft. No doubt the speedcam companies are raking it in. One would hope that, as camera and data-processing technology becomes increasingly cheap, and the field more competitive, cities can negotiate better deals with their providers. For these programs to remain popular, a focus on transparent and widely advertised competitive bids will be essential.

In the meantime, however, it is important to fight Tea-Party small-government pressures with the most impactful rhetoric. Try this: Speed cameras are only popular in those places where parents value the lives of their children.

RULE 35: Put red-light and speed cameras wherever you can, prioritizing places where injurious crashes have occurred. Shame state lawmakers into removing their restrictions.

VIII. OPTIMIZE YOUR DRIVING NETWORK

PART VIII

OPTIMIZE YOUR DRIVING NETWORK

SPEED LIMITS, PUBLIC EDUCATION, AND SPEED CAMERAS all make a difference in limiting speeding. Ultimately, though, however you post it, promote it, or enforce it, a safe speed limit has little effect when the road itself tells drivers to speed. And most do.

This is not by accident. Traffic engineers are still taught that the way to make a road safe is to design it for speeds higher than the posted speed limit. This approach makes sense in theory, until one realizes that there are humans involved. When humans see a street designed for a higher speed, they drive a higher speed, and the road becomes more dangerous.

About a dozen different factors contribute to driving speeds. The first two of these are the size of the blocks—smaller is better—and whether traffic on multilane streets is two-way (safer) or one-way (not). Most of this section addresses the national trend to revert dangerous one-way street networks back to two-way. But first, it is necessary to review the street network as a whole.

36 | Understand Network Function

Choose porous networks over dendritic sprawl,

and take advantage of their virtues.

FOR ROUGHLY FIFTY YEARS, the dominant ideology of roadway planning was to eschew street networks in favor of *dendritic* (branching) systems. In such systems, which characterize suburban sprawl, parking lots and cul-de-sacs lead to collectors, which lead to arterials, which lead to

In dendritic sprawl, most streets are cul-de-sacs and loops, so connectivity falls to a small number of collector streets that are designed as highways.

highways, and there is typically only one direct path from any one location to any other.

As early as the 1930s, development manuals advocated for dendritic systems over networks because they reduce the number of intersections, and each intersection is theoretically an accident waiting to happen. Developers were quick to take the bait, as buyers jumped at houses on cul-de-sacs.

As often happens, reality intervened. The data now show that areas developed with a large percentage of cul-de-sac streets are considerably more dangerous than traditional networks, with 270% more fatalities.[147] They are also the areas with the least walking, the least transit use, the least social capital, and the greatest obesity. Why this has happened becomes evident as one exits the cul-de-sac into the larger street system beyond: because most streets don't go anywhere, those few that do are burdened with tremendous amounts of traffic. As a result, these streets are designed exclusively around the task of moving as many vehicles as possible as quickly as possible; they are effectively traffic sewers.[148] Their noxious quality causes housing subdivisions to turn their backs to them and put up walls.

As can be seen in the image at left, it is not uncommon for a collector road to hold not a single address.

What results from this strategy are individually safe local streets isolated within a gantlet of life-threatening roads, and a system in which the paths to most destinations involve a confounding number of reversals and switchbacks, enough to make cycling frustrating, transit ineffective, and walking out of the question.

The data now show that areas developed with a large percentage of cul-de-sac streets are considerably more dangerous than traditional networks, with 270% more fatalities.

But let's face it, walking never was the question. Without the presumption of universal car ownership, dendritic street systems don't make any sense. How ironic then, that this approach, designed entirely around cars, actually works worse for cars. Because there is only one path from each origin to each destination, one engine fire on the collector road is enough to shut the whole system down.[149] Contrast that with a porous urban grid, in which there are a handful of ways to get anywhere from anywhere else. The ramifications for emergency response are also painfully clear.

Even without an emergency, dendritic systems have proved themselves to be unduly prone to crippling congestion. Due to their inherent inflexibility, most cannot be easily modified to accommodate new intensifications of land use. Unlike in traditional urban grids, where buildings often molt into taller structures, dendritic suburbs choke on very small increments of growth. They can never really grow up into something more urban.

In addition to putting an end to the cul-de-sac, we need to correct the ways that decades of dendritic planning have infected thinking about proper street networks, which are generally considered to be less flexible than they truly are. Often, when considering such things as the insertion of a bike lane, we regard each street individually, paying little attention to the fact that, within a grid, traffic can easily switch from street to street in response to congestion. If we remember that each car within a grid is an "intelligent atomic actor" maximizing its utility at every corner, we realize that we can manipulate networked street systems with much greater freedom than we would have in sprawl. Gridded streets can and do absorb each other's traffic every day; we see this clearly when one street is narrowed or closed for repairs.

RULE 36: In all new development, build a porous network of streets and blocks rather than branching (dendritic) systems. When considering changes to individual streets, understand that traffic within a network can shift to parallel routes.

37 | Keep Blocks Small
Intersection density is what makes cities safe and walkable.

ON THE LEFT BELOW IS PORTLAND, OR— famously walkable, and famous (to planners) for its tiny 200-foot blocks. On the right is Salt Lake City—famously less walkable, with its huge 600-foot blocks. So different are these street networks that it is hard to imagine that they were laid out in the same era (mid-1800s). While each has

its benefits, the advantages of Salt Lake City do not include the safety and comfort of its pedestrians.

The problem is that, while a 200-foot-block city can be principally a two-lane city, a 600-foot-block city is often a six-lane city. Given a similar density of development, it takes many more lanes of traffic to move the requisite number of vehicles around such large blocks.

And it's probably not the same number of vehicles: wider streets make walking less comfortable, so more people are likely to give up walking for driving. Portland's streets can be smaller because each street serves less land area, but also because the delightful result gets people out of their cars.

The alternative is not pretty. Salt Lake City has done a lot of great things in recent years, especially around light rail and cycling, but it inherited "bad bones." It's one of those places where they give you orange flags to wave as you cross the street, so that nobody mows you down.

Where things really get grisly, though, is not in America's big-block downtowns, but in our many postwar auto-centric "cities," in which dendritic street networks result in some truly elephantine blocks. Los Angeles may have only

You can fit almost nine Portland blocks into a single Salt Lake City block.

150 intersections per square mile compared to 1,500 in Venice, Italy. But Irvine, CA has a mere fifteen.[150]

According to a thorough study conducted by Reid Ewing and Robert Cervero, no other measure is more predictive of walkability than block size; not land-use mix,

A study of twenty-four California cites found that as block size doubled, the number of fatal crashes on local roads roughly quadrupled.

not population, not jobs per acre, and not even transit coverage.[151] Block size is certainly predictive of safety. A study of twenty-four California cites found that as block size doubled, the number of fatal crashes on local roads roughly quadrupled.[152]

Smaller blocks are also better for retail. A walk in downtown Portland exposes you to about 50% more storefronts than the same walk in downtown Salt Lake City, thanks to all the corners. It also gives you a lot more choices, and many more opportunities to vary your path between destinations.

The only thing small blocks don't do well is hide parking, which can be embedded in the centers of bigger blocks. This fact can lead to some clear tradeoffs. When building new suburbs, the best solution can be blocks as large as 300 x 600 feet, in which buildings surround midblock parking lots (see Rule 92). But as places become more urban and less auto-dependent, the mandate for small blocks is clear.

This mandate is particularly apparent when it comes to the act of superblocking. Most American cities have a place where the demands of a hospital, a stadium, or a convention center have led to the consolidation of multiple historic blocks into a single huge property. These are often the places in downtown where walkability ends. Wherever connections are snipped, places become less vital.

For that reason, superblocking should be avoided where not essential, and then directed to the edges of neighborhoods, where walking is already in short supply. The stadium belongs where the neighborhood ends.

RULE 37: Build new places with small blocks; aim for a 1,000-foot maximum perimeter in cities and 2,000 feet in suburbs. In existing downtowns, resist street closures that create superblocks, and locate them at neighborhood edges only.

38 Revert Multilane One-ways to Two-way for Business

In many cities, one-way networks are holding business back.

IF YOUR CITY DOES NOT HAVE any multilane one-way streets, you can skip this section and the three that follow. But most sizeable American cities do, and many small cities as well. How this happened, mostly between 1950 and 1980, is well covered in *Walkable City* in a section titled "The One–Way Epidemic," which attempts to

Whether in Durham, NC, Davenport, IA, or Cornelius, OR, there is always an old-timer who can tell you how the one-ways came to town and the shops left, pronto.

convey the extent of the damage wrought by this nation-wide error. Since that book was written, more data and stories have been collected, and it is hard to find a city planner who is not aware of the national movement to revert one-way streets back to two-way travel. Still, many American cities remain unwilling to reconsider their downtown one-ways, and some are even—double take!—introducing

new one-ways as we speak. Las Vegas just decided to turn its Main Street one-way. At least it's got a bike lane.

Because Las Vegas refuses to follow even the laws of physics, this would be a good time to point out that there are exceptions to every rule. One-way main streets thrive in New York City, Boston, Philadelphia, Palm Beach, and a few other places. But, as with pedestrian malls, the successes are relatively rare. Much more common, in fact typical, is what happened in Savannah, GA, when East Broad Street was made one-way in 1969, and two thirds of its businesses disappeared. (Happily, it was reverted back to two-way in 1990, and promptly saw the number of business addresses rise by 50%.)

Anecdotes are not data, but it is remarkable how similar the stories are that one hears echoed in city after city when working as a planner over a few decades. Whether in Durham, NC, Davenport, IA, or Cornelius, OR, there is always an old-timer who can tell you how the one-ways came to town and the shops left, pronto. It is also surprising how many times one meets suburbanites who say that they don't come downtown because they are "afraid of getting lost in the one-way streets."

Vine Street in Cincinnati's Over-the-Rhine neighborhood began its revitalization with a two-way reversion.

Another benefit of decades of practice is to witness firsthand the main street revivals that have followed many two-way reversions. Again, from West Palm Beach, FL, to Vancouver, WA, stories abound about how the change from speedy one-way to calm two-way boosted revenues to retailers. Vancouver's comeback was hailed in *Governing Magazine* as "The Return of the Two-Way Street," in that important 2009 article.[153]

Yet, despite all the evidence, most cities exhibit tremendous inertia on this topic. Case in point: Cincinnati. The story that everyone hears about Cincy these days is the remarkable revival of OTR, the Over-the-Rhine neighborhood north of downtown. The city is riding a wave of success spurred in large part by the transformation of this community from Cincinnati's most dangerous neighborhood into a hipster haven. This revival was centered on Vine Street, and began after the City reverted that street to two-way traffic in 1999. Most city officials know this.

Meanwhile, for more than a decade, the City has been pondering reverting nearby Main Street to two-way traffic, for a mere quarter mile. Every two years or so, an article appears about how this may happen. It hasn't. More studies are recommended. Similar stories of two-way success followed by the inability to reach for more of it could be told in a dozen other American downtowns.

Why are multilane one-way streets so bad for business? First, there is the speed and the jockeying of the cars. Second is the visibility problem: stores on cross streets whose facades face the direction of flow are never seen by passing drivers (think about it). Finally, one-ways create a feast-or-famine scenario depending on whether a street is on the morning or evening commute. Restaurants and bars will not thrive on a one-way that is inbound; few people dine or drink (we hope) on the way to work.

For these reasons, two-way reversions are sweeping the nation. . . just not fast enough. The only good reason not to revert a moribund one-way back to two-way travel is fear of the displacement that can come with revitalization (see Rule 14). This fear is justified, and should lead to planning for the retention of existing businesses whenever such an improvement is made.

RULE 38: Retail one-way streets should be reverted to two-way travel in places where improvement is desired.

39 | Revert Multilane One-ways to Two-way for Safety

In many cities, one-way networks create unnecessary danger.

TRAFFIC SAFETY is often counterintuitive. Many people assume that multilane one-way streets are safer than two-way, because you have to look in only one direction to cross, and there are fewer chances for head-on collisions. The problem with this thinking was summed up in a Traverse City, MI, editorial of 1967, asserting that "one way traffic made for a faster, safer flow of vehicles in the downtown area."[154]

We now know this phrase to be self-contradictory. Judging from the collision data already discussed (Rule 31), there is no such thing as faster and safer. Higher speed causes more collisions and more death.

A choice of lanes provides the opportunity to jockey.

Why do people speed on multilane one-ways? First, due to that lowered risk of head-on collisions. Second, because a street with many lanes in the same direction just feels like a highway. Third, because a choice of lanes provides the opportunity to jockey. This may be the most decisive factor; on a normal street without a passing lane, the slowest driver sets the speed, for better or for worse. In places where people walk, it's for better.

For this reason, where data has been collected, two-way reversions have been shown to save lives. Probably the best study so far was conducted in Louisville, where William Riggs and John Gilderbloom looked at four adjacent one-way streets, two of which were reverted to two-way traffic in 2011. The reverted

PROPOSED TWO-WAY REVERSIONS

Burdened by speeding, New Albany, IN, recently reverted almost all of its one-way streets for a total cost of $4 million. This plan went from proposed to complete in less than three years.

then speed to the front of the wave. For this reason, speeds on signal-timed one-way streets often far outpace the signal progression.

And that's not all. These drivers, as they turn onto the one-way, focus their attention over their shoulder in the direction of oncoming traffic. They tend not to look straight ahead, where there may be a pedestrian in the crosswalk. In Lancaster, PA, where PennDOT one-ways lace the downtown, crashes and near-misses of this nature are a regular occurrence.

Interestingly, one-way streets also appear to invite crime. In the same Louisville study, total reported crimes dropped by about 23% on the reverted streets, while going up 3% on the streets that remained one-way.[156] The causes of this relationship are many, but it is interesting to notice that one-ways provide "shadow zones" between buildings in which people can hide. In the same way that one-ways hurt businesses whose facades face the direction of traffic and are therefore never seen by drivers, they also create many areas where people can loiter unobserved.

With the reduction of speeding and crime on the two-way streets, property values increased dramatically. Home sales on Louisville's Brook and 1st streets reflected an annual appreciation of 21.6%, as citywide housing values—and prices on the one-ways—declined slightly.

Increased property values result in higher tax revenue. Decreased crashes and crime reduce the cost of policing. Most significantly, saving lives is good. These outcomes should motivate more cities to revert more of their one-way streets back to two-way travel.

streets, Brook and 1st, experienced a collective drop in total collisions of about 49%, despite attracting more vehicles daily than before the change. At the same time, crashes on the two one-way streets went up by about 10%.[155]

It is sometimes suggested that the danger of multilane one-ways can be mitigated by timing the signal progression at a moderate speed. Most cities that have such streets have coordinated the signals to create a slow "green wave" of flow to keep speeding in check. But signals are not always present and, even where they are, another problem arises: drivers turning onto the one-ways from side streets learn that, if they gun it around the corner, they can catch the end of the wave, beating a red light. If traffic is thin, they

---

RULE 39: One-way streets with significant crash occurrence should be reverted to two-way travel to improve safety.

40 | Revert Multilane One-ways to Two-way for Convenience

The choice is not as simple as vitality and safety vs. smooth traffic.

THERE IS LITTLE DOUBT that a wave of green lights allows drivers to zip through a downtown area more quickly than they could in a typical two-way network in which signals are not timed. However, it is not necessarily correct to assume that having a green wave in and out of town is the most efficient way to organize a street network, or that a switch back to two-way traffic is likely to increase congestion, for a number of reasons.

Circuitous trips: In one-way systems, many trips begin and/or end with a doubling-back that would not take place

The protracted loop from Hyatt parking to Hyatt pickup in Tulsa.

in a two-way network. The traffic engineer Vikash Gayah at Penn State University has demonstrated how, for short trips, such looping causes one-ways to actually perform worse than two-ways when many trips are short.[157]

Extra trips: In some places, one-way systems even create trips that would not otherwise take place. In Tulsa, valets at the Hyatt hotel, in order to bring a guest her car, must embark on a half-mile odyssey from garage to front door involving four turns and five traffic signals. It should also be noted that, to the degree that one-way systems encourage speeds that discourage walking, they scare would-be pedestrians into their cars, putting more drivers on the street.

Green waves: A cascading series of green lights is possible not only on one-way streets. It can also be introduced to two-way systems where there is a dominant path of rush-hour travel in and out of downtown.

Left-turn lanes: Introducing dedicated left-turn lanes allows a two-way network to perform almost as efficiently as a one-way system. However, it should be noted that left-turn lanes should be avoided if their presence requires the removal of a significant amount of parallel parking, which can be essential to the success and safety of a downtown.

Emergency response and resiliency: Police, fire departments, and other emergency responders are often delayed and frustrated by one-way systems that lengthen their path to a crisis. Additionally, when a crash or other incident closes a street, one-way systems require more distant detours than two-way networks, in which a shift of a single block will suffice.

> *Police, fire departments, and other emergency responders are often delayed and frustrated by one-way systems that lengthen their path to a crisis.*

Fewer signals: Often, when a one-way network is reverted to two-way, it is possible to eliminate some traffic signals in favor of all-way stop signs. This opportunity arises because signals are typically required where two multilane one-ways meet, but may not be warranted when two 2-lane two-ways meet. In addition to saving lives (see Rule 76), all-way stop signs can make paths through a downtown more efficient by eliminating the need to sit idling at red lights. They are also considerably less expensive to install and maintain than traffic signals.

This rule and the two prior ones lay out a comprehensive series of arguments in favor of reverting multilane one-way streets back to two-way traffic. Further evidence should

not be needed. Still, it is difficult to spend public dollars changing the direction of traffic on a street on which, not that long ago, you spent public dollars changing the direction of traffic. Motivation can perhaps be found in those places where successful two-way reversions have already been completed, including Albuquerque, Arlington (VA), Ann Arbor, Atlanta, Austin, Baltimore, Boise, Buffalo, Cedar Rapids, Charleston, Charlottesville, Chicago, Cincinnati, Colorado Springs, Columbus, Dallas, Davenport (IA), Dayton, Denver, Detroit, Durham, Edmonton (AB), El Paso, Evansville (IN), Fort Collins (CO), Fort Wayne (IN), Hamilton (ON), Holland (MI), Huntington (WV), Indianapolis, Iowa City, Jackson, Kalispell (MT), Kansas City (MO), Kichener (ON), Kokomo (IN), Lancaster (PA), Lawrence (MA), Louisville, Los Angeles, Lowell (MA), Lubbock (TX), Mankato (MN), Melbourne (FL), Mexico City, Michigan City (IN), Milwaukee, Minneapolis, Mt. Pleasant (SC), Nashville, New Albany (IN), Oklahoma City, Omaha, Ottumwa (IA), Pittsburgh, Roanoke, Rochester (NY), Raleigh, Redmond (WA), Richmond, Sacramento, San Francisco, San Jose, San Marcos (TX), Savannah, Seattle, Somerville (MA), South Bend, Sturgeon Bay (WI), Tampa, Toledo, Tulsa, Tucson, Vancouver (WA), West Lafayette (IN), West Palm Beach (FL), and Winchester (VA).

The above list is incomplete and will soon be out of date, as more and more communities work to correct the mistakes of the last century.

RULE 40: Question assumptions and studies that suggest that reverting a one-way system to two-way traffic will increase congestion.

41

Revert Multilane One-ways Properly
Many years of such projects suggest some best practices.

REVERTING MULTILANE ONE-WAY STREETS back to two-way traffic is a tricky business, but it is not as difficult as its detractors may lead you to believe. To revert a one-way network properly, you must give consideration to the following issues.

Two-way to one-way splits: Often, when such reversions are proposed, people point to the fork where the two one-ways diverge from their two-way source as an impediment to a two-way reversion. "How will we resolve traffic motions at the fork?" they ask. The answer is that such

Removing half the parking from a retail main street in order to make it two-way is probably a mistake.

motions are almost always easily resolved one or two blocks back from the divergence. The two diagrams at right show the current and proposed reconfiguration of one such fork, in Lancaster, PA.

Highway interfaces: Similar but simpler challenges exist when pairs of one-way streets lead to and from

highway on- and off-ramps. This is a common occurrence: one-way systems were often introduced to cities when interstates were constructed through their centers. In this case, the switch to two-way traffic must be held back a block or two from the end of the highway ramp. In this location, new traffic approaching the highway off-ramp must be made to shift right or left to a parallel street.

Preserving parking: As noted in the previous point, the desire for smooth traffic can cause two-way reversions to include left-turn lanes at intersections. If a three-lane street is being reverted, this is no problem, as the full center lane can be devoted to left turns. But in a two-lane street, the introduction of a center turn lane means that something else has to go. In most cases, that something is parallel parking, which is often vital to the safety and success of a downtown street. The best solution here is probably to introduce very short left-turn lanes, such that only two or three parking spaces at each corner are cut. Beyond that, one must carefully consider the tradeoffs present; removing half the parking from a retail main street in order to make it two-way is probably a mistake.

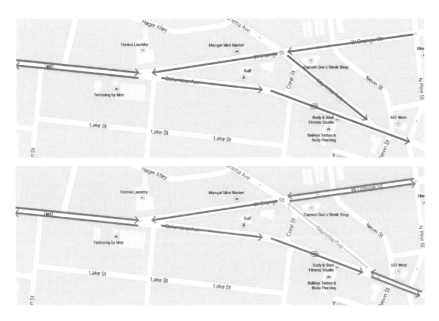

Before two-way reversion in Lancaster, Pennsylvania.

After reversion. In this case, traffic motions are resolved by reversing flow on Marietta Avenue.

Adding bike lanes: Similarly, there are instances when maintaining one-way flow is the best way to find room in a street for high-quality cycle facilities. It is much easier to put a two-way cycle track on a one-way street than on a two-way street, especially when turn lanes are also competing for asphalt. When one-way networks are considered comprehensively for two-way reversion, it sometimes makes sense to preserve one or two one-way pairs in order to optimize the cycling network.

Phasing of work: The principal cost in reverting one-way networks back to two-way is the reconfiguration of traffic signals. While a large price tag may suggest completing this work in phases, doing so may add significantly to the ultimate expenditure. If a north-south pair is reverted in a first phase, and an east-west pair is reverted in a second phase, then the four intersections where they meet will need to be re-signalized twice. Additionally, if an intersection is designated as a good location for a four-way stop sign instead of a signal, this conversion cannot occur until both streets entering the intersection are reverted to two-way. For these reasons, it may be worth biting the bullet and avoiding a phased approach.

RULE 41: When reverting one-way streets back to two-way, use tested methods to address forks and highway interfaces; weigh the benefits of two-way travel against any tradeoffs associated with parking and biking; and understand that gradual implementation adds considerably to cost.

PART IX

RIGHT-SIZE THE NUMBER OF LANES

THE MORE DRIVING LANES A STREET HAS, the more dangerous it is. But, since the most common complaint that one hears in most cities is about traffic, there is always pressure to add more lanes (see Rule 27). Moreover, many cities' public works departments, fearing future congestion, have already built lanes that may not be necessary. A key approach to keeping a place walkable is to resist pressures to add more lanes, and a key technique for making a place walkable is to remove any lanes that can be cut without unduly impacting the experience of drivers.

The first step to keeping the number of driving lanes within reason is to challenge the assumptions and practices that currently misdirect the practice of street network design in most cities. Of these, three stand out: *Traffic Studies,* which are typically overdemanded, overvalued,

and based on faulty assumptions; *Level of Service,* the A–F rating systems that steer planners toward creating unwalkable streets; and *Functional Classification,* the organization of streets according to the branching hierarchy of sprawl, which has been spuriously expanded to apply to most urban networks as well. A critical approach to all three of these items is often needed if we are to avoid an oversized road system.

Once a proper intellectual foundation is laid for considering a city's supply of lanes, three main opportunities exist: cutting the extra lanes that can be demonstrated as redundant; road-dieting any inefficient four-lane roads down to three; and eliminating unwanted turn lanes while shortening those that are too long. Together, these changes can have a profound impact on a community's safety and walkability.

42 Challenge Traffic Studies

They are probably inevitable but can be managed.

IN ANY CITY OF SIGNIFICANT SIZE, and many much smaller, it is impossible to make meaningful changes to any but the smallest roadway without first conducting a traffic study. This policy reflects a popular opinion that congestion is fixable and that avoiding congestion must be the dominant inviolable rule in the design and management of our streets.

Never mind that, in America, the cities with the most traffic congestion are the ones with the greatest productivity, the highest per-capita income, the healthiest citizens, and the least carbon emissions from traffic (it's true).[158] Never mind that, as explained in Rule 27, fixing congestion is a fool's errand, since congestion is the principal constraint to driving. You can preach priorities and provide evidence all day long, but, in all but a handful of American cities, the goals of health, wealth, sustainability, and happiness will all be set aside whenever they run up against the demand for free-flowing traffic. Which is all the time.

We can fight these battles and win, on occasion, in Boston, New York, Seattle, and San Francisco. But the reality almost everywhere else is that traffic studies delimit the redesign of the public realm, and any proposal for changing

the number of driving lanes on a street must be demonstrated to not threaten the flow of vehicles currently or into the foreseeable future.

Fortunately, in most places, this fact is not an impediment to making real change, because not all streets are congested (see Rule 45), and because engineers conducting

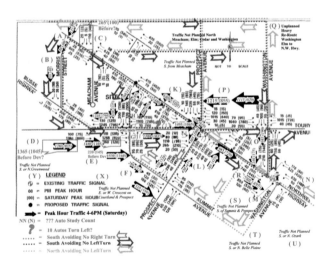

The traffic study has become the most inevitable act of urban planning.

traffic studies are allowed to exercise judgment—and even creativity. How an engineer approaches a traffic study, and with what attitudes and prejudices, remains the most significant factor in how that study turns out.

For this reason, the key step in transforming a street or a street network is usually hiring the right engineer. Most often, this means bringing in a consultant who is prepared

How an engineer approaches a traffic study, and with what attitudes and prejudices, remains the most significant factor in how that study turns out.

to counter the often incorrect assumptions of local public works officials. These assumptions influence the traffic study's inputs, especially the key items of *vehicles per lane per hour* and *background growth.*

Vehicles per lane per hour: There is no general consensus on how many vehicles a lane should process each hour, with estimates running from below 500 to above 800. The saturation rate on a highway is about 2,000, but we are talking here about local streets, which offer more flexibil-

ity. The State of Iowa uses a figure of 750, which many engineers would consider too aggressive, but it's a good place to start, because: Iowa.

Background growth: Background growth is a prediction about the rate at which the amount of driving in your city will increase over time. Since many traffic studies look forward twenty years, this figure can easily torpedo a proposed road modification. Some traffic engineers unthinkingly apply a figure of 2% (compounding), which means that, in twenty years, traffic will increase close to 50%. The simple fact about background growth is that nobody knows. Moreover, cities have to ask themselves how much traffic they want to have into the future. An understanding of both induced demand and the profound downsides of increased car-dependence would suggest that background growth is a dark self-fulfilling prophecy that should not be allowed to control the design of our cities. Since background growth is unknowable and unwanted, the more reasonable approach to a traffic study is to set it at zero.

Optimizing a traffic study's assumptions is half the job of a good traffic engineer. The other half is to apply the proper priorities in reviewing the outputs from the traffic model in order to propose a solution. Key in this regard is a critical stance toward *Level of Service,* discussed next.

RULE 42: Challenge the value of traffic studies, but, when they are unavoidable, involve a progressive traffic engineer who is experienced at challenging their assumptions and critically assessing their outcomes.

43 | Challenge *Level of Service*

LOS is the wrong measure for urban places.

LEVEL OF SERVICE is the system that traffic planners use, often exclusively, to determine the success of a street network. Level of Service (LOS) rankings run from A to F, with A representing unimpeded flow and F representing bad delays. Clearly, gridlock must be avoided, but beyond that, we must ask ourselves: what is the target LOS for a healthy downtown?

Many engineers aim for an LOS of A or B, because. . . A's and B's are best, right? To an engineer's mind, the less congestion the better. But this belief ignores the fact that an LOS of A or B corresponds to cars moving at higher speeds than are safe for an urban center. Moreover, experience teaches us that there hardly exists a single successful, vital, main street that would earn an A or B rating. When it comes to retail performance and street life, LOS could aptly be said to stand for Lack of Success.

Wise municipalities understand that an LOS of E is perfectly appropriate for an urban center.

Thankfully, more sophisticated engineers understand that a certain amount of congestion is inevitable and desirable in city centers, and aim to provide an LOS of C or D downtown.

But wait! Picture a lively city center. In your imagination, how fast are the cars moving, and how far apart are they? Readers will be surprised to learn that an LOS of D means that cars are roughly eight car-lengths apart.[159]

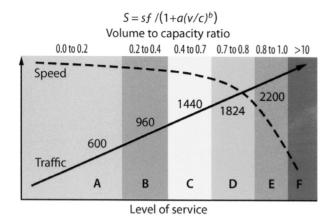

$$S = sf /(1+a(v/c)^b)$$

Everyone wants to get an A and not an F, but the goal of safety would turn the LOS rating system on its head.

That's one or two cars moving *per block.* It is clear that the LOS system, which was created to assess highways, is the wrong measure for determining the success of a city. Or, perhaps it is useful, but only if we consistently aim for an LOS of E.

The chart above, from the car-centric Transportation Research Board, helps to clarify the discussion. Only as a LOS of D merges into E do we see a significant drop in driving speeds. Even a high F would seem to provide a slow but steady flow of traffic, ideal for a main street.

Wise municipalities understand that an LOS of E is perfectly appropriate for an urban center. In a recent project to restripe all the streets in its entire downtown, the

City of Des Moines has been willing to accept E as its rush-hour condition, and even a few F's in challenging locations.

Better than intentionally aiming for a certain level of congestion—low or high—some municipalities have decided just to ignore LOS entirely. Such is the case in Yolo County, CA, just west of Sacramento. You only live once, so why let a little traffic bring you down?

Few cities are willing to go that far, so redirecting traffic studies at a target LOS of E is probably an easier move. There is, however, one place from which LOS needs to be permanently expunged, and that is our environmental regulations. Because congestion is spuriously associated with pollution, it once seemed wise to impose upon new development a burden of maintaining a high LOS. This approach ignored the fact that the most free-flowing traffic is found in those places where people drive the most miles—that smooth traffic is indeed an inducement to driving—and thus our most congested cities make the lowest per-capita contribution to greenhouse gases. In light of this new understanding, the State of California recently eliminated LOS from its environmental review process, and replaced it with a focus on reducing VMT: Vehicle Miles Traveled.

Under the old rules, ironically, environmental regulations would stop you from adding a bike lane to a street if a traffic study showed a negative impact on the flow of cars.[160] This still happens in many places. But California has regained its sanity and is once again leading the way in limiting the environmental impacts of driving.

RULE 43: If Level of Service cannot be removed from the process entirely, streets in potentially walkable urban areas should be designed with a target LOS of E.

44 Challenge *Functional Classification*
This system created for sprawl does not apply to urbanism.

WHEN TRADITIONAL NETWORKS OF BLOCKS were replaced by dendritic sprawl as the dominant technique for organizing streets in the latter half of the twentieth century (see Rule 36), a new concept was born: *functional classification*. Functional classification derives from the dendritic (branching) street design system, in which the hierarchy up from *local* through *collector* to *arterial* to *highway* is organized to correspond with the spectrum of trips from closest and slowest to farthest and fastest. Traffic volume also plays a role, with arterials generally expected to hold more traffic than collectors, which are expected to hold more traffic than locals. It makes sense to organize streets this way when the street pattern is dendritic, since it is easy to know which types of trips will make use of which class of street.

However, not long after it was created to organize the design of rural and suburban streets, the functional classification system was also assigned to urban streets as well. Like the zoning codes imported from the suburbs that caused new buildings in cities to be incompatible with their historic fabric, this application created a mismatch. Designed for a branching system, functional classification was not meant to be applied to the urban grid, which operates in an entirely different way.

The essence of the dendritic system is *concentration*: trips of any significant distance are kept off of local streets and forced onto roads that are further up the hierarchy. In contrast, the essence of traditional urbanism is *dispersion*: trips are distributed among a large number of parallel streets so that no one street is overwhelmed with traffic, yet every street receives the beneficial supervision of people passing through. Some thoroughfares, like avenues and boulevards, carry more trips than others, but all are designed to support street life as well.

In a traditional street network, trips from origin to destination can take many different paths—and often do—based on a variety of factors. The typical street in a downtown grid handles trips of all types—local, midrange, and distant—in defiance of its functional classification assignment. This wouldn't necessarily be a problem if each functional classification didn't bring with it a set of required standards. Key among these is *design speed,* the speed that a street has been designed to support. On highways, design speed appropriately keeps lanes wide and curves loose, so that speeding drivers don't crash. But it doesn't just support higher speeds; it invites them—it is set well above the

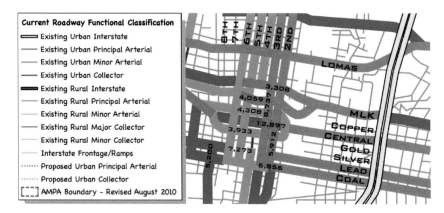

Current Roadway Functional Classification
- ▭▭ Existing Urban Interstate
- —— Existing Urban Principal Arterial
- —— Existing Urban Minor Arterial
- —— Existing Urban Collector
- ▬▬ Existing Rural Interstate
- —— Existing Rural Principal Arterial
- —— Existing Rural Minor Arterial
- —— Existing Rural Major Collector
- —— Existing Rural Minor Collector
- —— Interstate Frontage/Ramps
- ······ Proposed Urban Principal Arterial
- ······ Proposed Urban Collector
- [ ] AMPA Boundary - Revised August 2010

Within Albuquerque's downtown grid, there is no observable relationship between functional classification and traffic volume.

speed limit—and this fact becomes particularly impactful in downtowns.

People wonder why drivers speed in downtown Albuquerque. For an explanation, they need look no further than functional classification. The image above shows the downtown's principal arterials in red, its minor arterials in green, and its urban collectors in blue, as well as the daily car trips on each. The first thing to notice is that, contrary to the system's intention, there is absolutely no correlation between street hierarchy and traffic volume. The principal arterials average roughly 5,800 trips per day, the minor arterials average roughly 5,100, and the lowly collectors handle roughly 9,000.

Next, we need to turn to Albuquerque's old Development Process Manual, which sets the standards for each class of street, including its design speed. Brace yourself: urban collectors must be built at a design speed of 35 mph, minor arterials at 45 mph, and principal arterials at a whopping 50 mph.

In case this isn't clear: even though we know that speeding increases fatalities, and higher design speeds increase speeding, Albuquerque's downtown segments of 2nd, 3rd, Lomas, MLK, Central, Lead, and Coal Streets have all been designed to a 50 mph standard. These are all streets in a pedestrian-oriented part of the city in which moderate driving speeds should be encouraged, universally; there is no reason why cars should be driving at higher speeds on some streets than others, since pedestrians and cyclists are present everywhere.

Since completing a walkability study in 2014, the City of Albuquerque has been working to modify these standards. Many other cities are still beholden to similar regulations, with dangerous results.

RULE 44: If possible, remove the functional classification designation from would-be walkable streets in traditional urban areas. At the least, do not allow these areas' streets to be designed according to standards set by such a system.

45 Cut the Extra Lanes

When lanes are not needed for traffic,

all they do is cause speeding.

STREETS THAT HAVE MORE LANES than they need cause more injury and death than they otherwise would. The more lanes a street has, the more it feels like a highway, and the more drivers are induced to speed. The more lanes it has, the more opportunities arise for dangerous jockeying from lane to lane. The more lanes it has, the farther pedestrians have to cross. These factors add up to a clear mandate to remove all lanes that are not deemed necessary.

The first step of any good neighborhood plan is to complete a quick lane audit that compares the supply of lanes to the demand for lanes on each potentially walkable street.

The definition of *necessary* varies, but we as a society have shown a tremendous propensity to sacrifice lives for smooth traffic. We lose more people per capita per year to car crashes than almost any other developed nation,

Before redesign, Oklahoma City's Hudson Avenue carried 8,400 cars per day, few enough to be served by two lanes.

but that has never stopped us from adding lanes. A clear minority of American cities have made the decision to stop increasing their street capacity, and only a small handful are willing to remove lanes from streets that are already congested; the driving public, unaware of the dynamic of induced demand, simply won't allow it.

The good news is that almost all American cities, even the congested ones, contain at least a few important streets that have more lanes than they need to handle the traffic

On Oklahoma City's Sheridan Street, extra lanes became parking spaces, bike lanes, and landscaped medians.

that they receive. These lanes are doing nothing but wasting asphalt and causing mayhem. When this fact is properly communicated, they can be removed.

Such was the case in Oklahoma City in 2009. After *Prevention* magazine named it the "least walkable city in the entire country,"[161] Mayor Cornett commissioned what may have been the first-ever *walkability study.* That study quickly found a tremendous mismatch between the supply of lanes and the demand for lanes. Fully seven streets running though the downtown were four- to six-lane arterials, even though they averaged fewer than 7,000 car trips per day.

By right-sizing these streets to meet their anticipated future demand—yes, there was a traffic study—the City was able to double its supply of on-street parking in the downtown, a real boon to businesses. It was also able to create a cycling network where there had been none before, all while reducing speeding and improving safety. According to the mayor, these changes have sparked a downtown renaissance.

The first step of any good neighborhood plan is to complete a quick lane audit that compares the supply of lanes to the demand for lanes on each potentially walkable street. Wherever a mismatch is found, the extra lanes can be put to better use. A good rule of thumb, allowing for growth, is that streets with fewer than 1,000 trips at peak hour need only two lanes. (This generally equates to about 10,000 trips per day.) Adding a center turn lane allows the street to handle as much as twice that amount. Only as a street approaches 2,000 peak-hour trips are more than three lanes needed.

RULE 45: Find those streets in your city where the supply of lanes exceeds the demand for them, and convert the extra lanes to other uses.

46 | Road-Diet Your Four-Laners
The Classic American Road Diet saves lives without adding congestion.

WE NOW KNOW THAT THERE IS NO REASON for any urban street in America to have four lanes. It cannot be justified.

It took a while to figure it out, but the data are clear. When a four-lane street is converted to a three-lane street, in which the center lane is reserved for left turns, the capacity of the street does not drop.

When Edgewater Drive in Orlando was dieted, injuries to road users dropped by 68%.

How this happens requires some explanation. First, it must be acknowledged that four-lane roads are dangerous. Because the turning lane is also the passing lane, drivers speed in the same lane in which drivers stop. Drivers that jockey right to avoid rear-ending a stopped vehicle are often rear-ended themselves. Additionally, cars turning left can be T-boned by approaching drivers whose views are blocked by parallel traffic.

But, conversely, because the passing lane is also the turning lane, drivers that wish to continue straight often find their paths blocked, and cars jockeying from lane-to-lane create wave-pulse congestion impacts that slow traffic.

It comes as no surprise that four-lane to three-lane road diets save lives. When Edgewater Drive in Orlando was dieted, injuries to road users dropped by 68%. What many do find surprising, however—and are unwilling to believe—is that a road diet does not reduce a street's capacity. A study of twenty-three different four-to-three-lane road diets across North America demonstrated, overall, a very slight average *rise* in the number of vehicles using the streets each day.

And then there's the other win, the 10 to 12 feet of recovered asphalt that can be put to better use. This can become two bike lanes, a lane of parking, additional sidewalk, or landscape. Bike lanes are the simplest solution, as the change can be made with little more than paint, requiring minimal investment. To the degree that more budget is available, it is probably best spent on inserting a median with trees in those places where no left turns occur. In the best road diets, the center turn lane is not continuous.

Like one-way to two-way conversions, road diets are sweeping the country. Seattle has done thirty-four of them.

On average, these 23 road diets compiled by the consulting firm Nelson\Nygaard did nothing to reduce the overall vehicular through-put of their streets.

Most road diets convert four-laners into three-laners, but some cities have also converted roads from six lanes to five, with similar outcomes. Because most congestion occurs at intersections and can be resolved with center turn lanes, municipalities should modify their standards to not allow four- or six-lane roads in urban areas.

Since the data are so powerful, public education is an important and effective component of the road-diet process. The greatest resistance often comes from merchants who worry that the diet will dramatically lower the number of potential shoppers passing their businesses. Again, the data suggest otherwise. When Oakland's Telegraph Avenue was dieted, retail sales went up 9%, most likely due to the fact that the amount of pedestrian activity doubled.

AREAS OF ROAD DIET IMPLEMENTATION—VOLUME CHANGES

LOCATION	STREET	ADT BEFORE	ADT AFTER
Oakland, CA	High Street	22,000	24,000
San Francisco, CA	Valencia Street	22,200	20,000
San Leandro, CA	East 14th Street	17,700	16,700
Santa Monica, CA	Main Street	20,000	18,000
Orlando, FL	Edgewater Drive	20,500	21,000
Charlotte, NC	East Boulevard	21,400	18,400
Reno, NV	South Wells Avenue	18,000	17,500
East Lansing, MI	Abbott Road	15,000	21,000
East Lansing, MI	Grand River Boulevard	23,000	23,000
Duluth, MN	21st Avenue East	17,000	17,000
Ramsey, MN	Rice Street	18,700	16,400
Helena, MT	U.S. 12	18,000	18,000
Toronto, ON	Danforth	22,000	22,000
Toronto, ON	St. George Street	15,000	15,000
Lewistown, PA	Electric Avenue	13,000	14,500
Bellevue, WA	Montana Street	18,500	18,500
Bellevue, WA	120th Avenue, NE	16,900	16,900
Covington, WA	State Road 516	29,900	32,800
Kirkland, WA	Lake Washington Boulevard	23,000	25,900
Seattle, WA	Dexter Avenue, N,	13,606	14,949
Seattle, WA	North 45th Street	19,421	20,274
Seattle, WA	Madison Street	17,000	18,000
Seattle, WA	W. Gov't Way / Gilmen Ave.	17,000	18,000

RULE 46: Do not build four-lane roads in urban areas, and convert all four-lane roads to three lanes, putting the recovered asphalt to other use. Insert treed medians where budget allows.

47 | Limit the Turn Lanes
Road diets aside, turn lanes are not a panacea.

REPLACING TWO LANES with a center turn lane is a clear win, but that win should not be misinterpreted as advocacy for putting center turn lanes in every street, a common habit in many American cities. Among public works officials, it has become considered a best practice to insert such lanes wherever they will fit, since they make intersections more efficient.

> *When unnecessary left-turn lanes are provided, the extra pavement width encourages speeding, lengthens crossing distances, and takes up roadway that could otherwise be used for on-street parking or bike lanes.*

But left-turn lanes should by no means be the universal approach to intersection design. They should be used only at intersections where undo congestion is caused by cars turning left; otherwise, they make the street more dangerous for drivers, pedestrians, and cyclists alike.

When unnecessary left-turn lanes are provided, the extra pavement width encourages speeding, lengthens crossing distances, and takes up roadway that could otherwise be used for on-street parking or bike lanes. In contrast, when no turn lane is inserted, the occasional pauses that drivers must make for other vehicles turning contributes properly to the everyday friction that keeps speeding in check.

Eliminating unnecessary left-turn lanes was an important part of the effort to improve walkability in Oklahoma City. Laura Story, the City's lead engineer on the project, insisted that no street handling fewer than 10,000 cars per day would qualify for left-turn lanes. Despite much resistance from consulting traffic planners, this mandate prevailed. The result is a safer street network that does not suffer from the congestion that these consultants predicted.

A similar story hails from Bethlehem, PA, where Wyandotte Street on the south side of downtown was unfortunately also PA Route 378. As state highway planners are wont to do, the street was restriped with a new left-turn

In Bethlehem, PA, an unnecessary and overlong turn lane eliminated a block of curb parking to the detriment of storefront businesses.

lane. Longer than a football field, the lane served a cross street three blocks long and holding only twelve houses. This utterly unnecessary facility was created by eliminating an entire flank of parallel parking, a move that essentially wiped out the half-dozen businesses lining the sidewalk. Subsequent to a 2009 walkability study, the state allowed the parking to return. . . just not at rush hour, when the businesses would most likely make use of it.

The length of turn lanes is a key issue. When justified, they should be just long enough to hold the number of cars that stack in them in standard rush-hour conditions, and no longer, for the same reason: extra roadway causes speeding.

Unlike left-turn lanes, exclusive right-turn lanes are rarely justified in urban locations where people are likely to be walking, and only make occasional sense where heavy pedestrian activity causes queuing right-hand turners to dramatically impede through-traffic. This condition rarely occurs in most American cities. Because right turns are never opposed by oncoming traffic, adding an exclusive lane for them provides only a limited increase to a street's vehicular capacity, while dramatically undermining pedestrian comfort. This tradeoff rarely makes sense in streets meant to encourage walking and biking.

When properly implemented, turn lanes have a lot going for them. Since most congestion occurs at intersections and not at midblock, allowing turn lanes at intersections can be the trick to keeping the rest of the street narrow. A two-lane street with left-turn lanes at intersections can usually handle just as much traffic, more safely, than a four-lane street. The key is to limit turn lanes to where they are truly needed, and to keep them as short as possible.

RULE 47: Place left-turn lanes only at intersections where undue congestion is caused by cars turning left, and make them no longer than the typical rush-hour queue. Generally avoid the use of right-turn lanes.

PART X

RIGHT-SIZE THE LANES

LIMITING THE NUMBER OF LANES is only half the battle; limiting their size is the other. Over the past half century, the design of roads in the United States has experienced a dangerous mission creep, such that a typical residential street that used to be as narrow as 25 feet (with two sides of parking) is now required by many cities to be 40 feet wide. The mindless application of high-speed highway standards to would-be walkable streets has contributed mightily to the dangers of walking and our subsequent reliance upon automobiles.

Perhaps the key step to making our communities walkable again is to get our driving lanes back to their historical proportions. This means busy urban lanes that are only 10 feet wide—not 11 or 12—and the reintroduction of slow-flow and yield-flow streets with lanes that are even narrower. Any lane that is wider than necessary should be understood as a health risk and addressed with appropriate alarm. Responding to that risk should be made an explicit mandate of fire departments and other emergency services.

Any campaign to right-size a city's driving lanes produces a valuable by-product: free asphalt. This leftover roadway can be repurposed into bike lanes, on-street parking, and other uses that make places more vital.

48

Adopt a 10-Foot Standard for Free-Flow Lanes

Any wider is an invitation to speeding.

SIMPLY PUT, different-width driving lanes correspond to different driving speeds. A typical American urban lane has historically been 10 feet wide, which comfortably supports speeds of 45 mph. A typical American highway lane is 12 feet wide, which comfortably supports speeds of 70 mph. Drivers instinctively understand the connection between lane width and driving speed, and speed up when presented with wider lanes, even in urban locations. For this reason, any urban lane more than 10 feet wide encourages speeds that increase risk to people walking.

These lanes are everywhere. In the second half of the twentieth century, city engineers began importing highway standards into their downtown cores, such that many American cities now have a lane-width requirement of 11 feet, 12 feet, or more. Omaha, NE, is one of many cities that has 12-foot lanes, and drivers can be observed approaching highway speeds when using them. It is surprising to learn, then, that the correlation between lane width and driving speed, accident frequency, and accident severity is a very recent discovery of the traffic engineering profession and contradicts decades of conventional wisdom within that profession. Even today, many traffic engi-

To quote Andres Duany, "the typical street to the typical American subdivision is now wide enough to allow you to experience the curvature of the earth."

neers will still claim that wider lanes are safer. Fortunately, a number of recent studies provide ample evidence of the dangers posed by lanes 12 feet wide and wider.

These studies, published by the National Cooperative Highway Research Program and others, demonstrate that

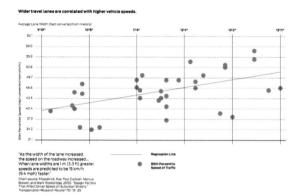

Wider travel lanes are correlated with higher vehicle speeds.

This study shows that wider travel lanes are correlated with higher vehicle speeds.

urban and suburban 12-foot lanes are clearly associated with higher speeds and higher crash frequencies than 10-foot lanes.[162] Additionally, a June 2015 report by the Canadian Institute of Transportation Engineers found that lanes wider than 10 feet generate risk for higher crash severity.[163]

Given that 10-foot lanes handle no less traffic than 12-foot lanes—also documented[164]—there is clearly no justification for 12-foot lanes in urban locations. In acknowledgement of this body of research, numerous organizations and agencies, like the National Association of City Transportation Officials, have recently begun to endorse 10-foot lanes for use in urban contexts. NACTO's *Urban Street Design Guide* lists 10 feet as the standard, saying, "Lane widths of 10 feet are appropriate in urban areas and have a positive impact on a street's safety without impacting traffic operations." They add: "Narrower streets help promote slower driving speeds which, in turn reduce the severity of crashes."[165]

This same conclusion was reached by ITE, the Institute of Transportation Engineers. According to the *ITE Traffic Engineering Handbook, 7th Edition,* "Ten feet should be the default width for general purpose lanes at speeds of 45 mph or less." That statement is very telling, as it implies, accurately, that lanes wider than 10 feet encourage speeds greater than 45 mph. And 45 mph is a full 20 mph over the posted speed limit in most downtowns.

RULE 48: Replace all urban lane standards greater than 10 feet with a 10-foot standard.

49 Restripe to a 10-Foot Standard

Put dangerously wasted pavement to better use.

NOW THAT WE'VE GOT A 10-FOOT STANDARD, what do we do with it? The answer to this question is wondrous indeed.

Every urban lane in your city that is more than 10 feet wide represents both an obligation and an opportunity. The obligation is clear: the extra width is only doing one thing, and that's causing drivers to speed, creating a completely unnecessary risk to themselves and others. The opportunity is manifold, and depends on the total number of extra feet available.

If the extra space is less than 5 feet, there are few options. But don't give up too soon. . . if the parking stalls are more than 7 feet wide, they can be narrowed too. Harvard Street in Boston has 5-foot bike lanes sandwiched between 10-foot driving lanes and 7 feet of parking— hardly ideal, but much better than the wide-lane alternative. But if 4 feet or less is all you have to play with, the safest solution is to add it to the width of the parking lanes. This will slow drivers slightly.

Five feet and above, the best approach is usually to add a bike lane. Beyond 7 feet, you could instead add a flank of parallel parking, if one is missing. The choice

between biking and parking is a tricky one, and must be considered with an eye to the larger bike network. (More on that in Rule 55.)

As yet more space becomes available, more options present themselves, including cycle tracks, angle parking, and—if there's a good budget—wider sidewalks. Most often, economy dictates a solution in which curbs are not moved (see Rule 97).

What about buses?

When all other hurdles to 10-feet lanes seem to have been cleared, that's when the transit agency shows up and demands 11 feet for its buses.

Most buses are 8'6" wide, plus mirrors. When a bus in a 10-foot lane passes a car in a 10-foot lane, there is no friction. When a bus passes another bus under similar circumstances, the resulting squeeze requires the bus to slow down slightly for a moment that is too short to impact bus schedules but has a positive impact on the safety of the street for all users.

A few rare transit agencies appreciate the traffic-calming value of 10-foot lanes. The administrators of DART, in

Before and after: Many streets that should have been built 35 feet wide are 40 feet wide. Inserting a bike lane, whether it is needed or not, will make these streets safer.

Des Moines, advocate for 10-foot lanes, reminding us that "every transit ride begins and ends with walking, and without walkable streets we are undermining the opportunities for public transit in the community."[166] But DART is the exception, so most transit agencies need to be reminded that streets that kill pedestrians threaten their customer base.

What about snow?

It is useful to discover that some of the communities with the skinniest streets have a ton of snowfall. Somehow they manage, even under many feet of snow, to maintain higher property values than nearby places that have been designed around the needs of the snowplow. Allowing snow-emergency inconvenience to override neighborhood livability is to confuse the end with the means.

But try telling that to a local public works department. More useful arguments include the fact that, in a snow emergency, a parking lane is typically a snow storage lane, and that, in a true crisis, bike lanes can serve the same purpose—at least in America. In Copenhagen, they plow the bike lanes first.

Cities should be admonished to remember that, the wider a street is, the more there is to plow.

RULE 49: Restripe streets with wide lanes to a 10-foot standard, allowing parking lanes to become as narrow as 7 feet in order to gain space for other uses. Then, with that extra space:
    —Less than 5 feet, widen the parking spaces.
    —5 to 7 feet, insert a bike lane.
    —Above 7 feet, insert bike lane(s) or curb parking, as appropriate.

50

Build Slow-Flow and Yield-Flow Streets

In most streets, a 10-foot lane is still too wide.

TEN FEET IS THE PROPER WIDTH FOR A LANE in a street that handles a lot of traffic. But experience demonstrates something that many cities' codes completely ignore: there are other types of streets. The majority of any community's thoroughfares do not carry more than a thousand trips per day. So why do so many of them have lanes that are 10 to 12 feet wide?

If you had the privilege of growing up in one of America's older single-family neighborhoods, you probably spent much of your outdoor time playing in skinny streets.

The great dumbing-down of development codes that happened across the US in the second half of the twentieth century erased the fact that there are actually four different types of traffic flow: *speed flow* for highways, *free flow* for busy streets, *slow flow* for less busy streets, and *yield flow* for quiet residential streets. As noted, speed-flow lanes are about 12 feet wide, while free-flow lanes are about 10 feet wide. The other two are yet narrower.[167]

Slow Flow

As you drive around older cities, you occasionally find yourself on streets where you feel you have to slow down as another car approaches. You experience some anxiety while passing, but your mirrors do not hit. This is called a slow-flow street, and its lanes are about 8 feet wide. The discomfort aroused by passing without braking is what makes it considerably safer than a free-flow street. It is a small price to pay for saving lives.

There is no official rule of thumb, but it's fair to say that most streets experiencing fewer than 300 trips during peak hour can be designed for slow flow. That adds up to about five cars every minute. Stop reading for twelve seconds and you will see that this is a longer time between cars than you might imagine.

Slow-flow streets need not have centerlines, and probably shouldn't (see Rule 71). They also do not need bike lanes, as the speed of cars should approach that of bikes. Slow-flow lanes are not appropriate on shopping streets, on bus routes, or in places with heavy truck traffic. A slow-flow street should be about 24 feet wide if it is parked on one side, and about 31 feet wide if parked on both sides.

Yield Flow

If you had the privilege of growing up in one of America's older single-family neighborhoods, you probably spent much of your outdoor time playing in skinny streets. It truly was a privilege to live in an environment where your parents could let you roam free without fearing what has become the leading cause of death for children. One reason that car crashes kill more children than they used to is the eradication from the development codes of the "yield street." Yield streets are thoroughfares in which a single driving lane about 12 feet wide handles travel in both directions. This sounds preposterous, which is one reason why they were eradicated by people who clearly did not have eyes to see, since they exist almost everywhere and are inevitably the most desirable streets in any city.

But why trust experience when logic is so obvious: how can two cars possibly pass each other in a mere 12 feet? The answer is found in the parking lane, where gaps between cars offer the opportunity to pull over slightly when another car approaches. This maneuver happens every day in thousands of yield-flow streets around the United States, and the fact

Many of us grew up on "yield-flow" streets, but they are now illegal in most places.

that it is necessary is what makes yield-flow streets the safest streets of all.

Again, there is no hard rule, but a street serving only single-family homes—freestanding or rowhouses—experiencing fewer than 150 trips at peak hour is a good candidate for yield flow. A yield-flow street should be about 20 feet wide if it is parked on one side, and about 26 feet wide if parked on both sides.

In most communities, the greatest impediment to creating slow- and yield-flow streets is the fire chief. This challenge is addressed in Rule 51.

RULE 50: Build streets with light traffic with slow-flow dimensions, and build local single-family residential streets with yield-flow dimensions.

51 Expand the Fire Chief's Mandate

Shift the focus from response time to public safety.

PERHAPS THE MOST IRONIC DAY IN THE LIFE of every city planner is the one on which she discovers that her greatest opponent in making her city's streets safer is the fire chief. How this bizarre circumstance has come to occur in city after city across the United States is a veritable morality play on the topics of siloed thinking, the confusion of ends and means, and Murphy's Law. It goes something like this:

A faster response time is good, but not at the expense of life safety.

The fire chief's job performance is typically judged on response time. The fire department's budget is often based on the number of calls that fire trucks respond to. These two facts conspire to replace a fire chief's natural mandate, optimizing the life safety of the community, with a much narrower focus: sending out lots of trucks, and getting them to their destinations quickly.

Into this mix, we can throw two additional ingredients: union make-work and the fire-equipment upsell. Over the years, firefighters' unions have introduced contractual language stipulating the minimum number of firefighters on a call. Simultaneously, firefighting equipment suppliers have infiltrated the ranks of the organizations drafting official guidelines for firefighting equipment. The unsurprising outcome: ever larger fire trucks.

As a result, most cities have found themselves under the protection of fire chiefs who, when introduced to the planning conversation, advocate for three things that make their cities more dangerous: wider streets, broader intersections, and the introduction of unwarranted traffic signals.

Wider streets: Rule 50 discussed 8-foot lanes and two-way 12-foot lanes, two things that increase safety in most older, walkable cities, and which are impermissible according to something called the "20-foot clear." The 20-foot clear appears in the Universal Fire Code—not a law, but a standard that many cities adopt—and requires that all streets maintain 20 feet of clear space between any obstructions such as parked cars. Many fire chiefs apply this law indiscriminately, not realizing that it hails from cul-de-sac suburbia, where there is only one path to each fire. When a street can be entered from both ends, there is no longer a need to do what the 20-foot clear allows, which is to park

Acknowledging that only 1.1% if its emergency calls were fire related, the City of Beaufort, SC, saved $500,000 by replacing two pumpers with these smaller all-purpose vehicles.[168]

allow drivers to speed around corners without applying the brake, while lengthening the amount of time that pedestrians are exposed to oncoming traffic. In most cities, these standards have been applied as a short cut to someone doing the (not very) hard work of designing each intersection independently with a fire-truck-turning template to make sure that the trucks can fit. When this is done properly, the curb radii become much smaller, especially when it is understood that fire trucks are allowed to cross into the opposing lane when making a turn. (They have sirens.)

Unwarranted traffic signals: As demonstrated ahead in Rule 76, replacing unwarranted signals with four-way stop signs results in great reductions in injuries. But fire chiefs prefer signals, because only with signals can you have signal preemption, which allows you to clear an intersection of cars as the fire truck approaches, speeding response time.

And a faster response time is good. But, as with the other two examples, not at the expense of life safety. If wider streets, broader intersections, and unwarranted signals all improve response time, while killing and maiming untold numbers of citizens in the process, it is clear that the cart is leading the horse. It will continue to do so until mayors and city managers provide their fire chiefs with different performance metrics, and a different job mandate.

a big truck, put down its stabilizers, and drive another big truck past it. Some fire chiefs, but not all, are willing to reject the 20-foot clear once they learn that it was written for cul-de-sacs.

Broader intersections: Many cities have minimum curb return radii for their corners, put in place to serve large fire trucks. The curb return radius measures how much swoop there is at the corner. Larger swoops allow big trucks to turn the corner without going into the opposing lane; they also

RULE 51: Rewrite the fire chief's mandate to optimize public safety, not response times. Replace the 20-foot clear and minimum curb radii with more precise measures. Do not add or keep unwarranted signals in the name of preemption. Size new fire trucks to the community and not vice versa.

PART XI

SELL CYCLING

THERE ARE TWO MAIN THINGS to understand and promote about cycling in cities: The first is that it is an unmitigated good. The larger your city's biking population, the better off your city will be. The second is that biking population is primarily a function of biking investment. Those cities who prioritize biking—and whose finances reflect that priority—will be the ones that become biking cities.

Convincing a city's leadership to invest in cycling facilities often means getting non-cyclists to make the case in non-cycling terms. The best allies are those who care about public health, social equity, and economic competitiveness, all of whom can be armed with powerful arguments in support of cycling investment. Such an effort can lead to big change in cities with any climate.

52 | Justify Biking Investment
Studies show that bike lanes pay for themselves many times over.

WHILE IT IS FAR FROM EASY, designing an effective cycling network is the easy part of bringing more biking to cities. The hard part is convincing governments to accept that network and then to invest in it. In representative democracy, such a task typically requires a great deal of public education and outreach around biking's many benefits. To be effective, this outreach should focus on the following key issues.

Public Health

The most powerful arguments in favor of developing a larger cycling population center on public health. The studies are piling up, and they are astounding. The most recent one followed 263,450 people over five years and found that those who biked to work had a 41% lower risk of dying prematurely. This included a 46% lower risk of developing heart disease and a 45% lower risk of developing cancer.[169]

Any study of health benefits must also consider the risks of injury and death that cyclists face, especially in the United States, where cycling is roughly twice as likely to kill you as it is in Europe. The best study on this subject was British and found that the health benefits of biking outweigh the risks by twenty to one.[170] Cut that in half, and it's still impressive, but the better news is that, in city after city, a strength-in-numbers relationship would seem to prevail. In New York, Washington, Chicago, Minneapolis, Portland, and Seattle, increases in cycling over the past fifteen years have lowered the rate of serious injury by an average of more than 64%.[171]

> *A study found that a $10 million biking investment in 2005 provided New Yorkers with approximately $230 million in net societal benefit.*

In terms of public health investment, it is hard to imagine a more efficient wonder drug than bike lanes. The average person will lose thirteen pounds during their first year of biking to work.[172] A University of Northern Iowa study found that cycling saves the state's riders about $87 million in health care costs.[173] Another study found that a $10 million biking investment in 2005 provided New Yorkers with approximately $230 million in net societal benefit. This figure included the improved health of nonbikers as well, from cleaner air.[174]

Equity

Most people, when they think of cyclists, imagine middle-age men in Lycra—MAMILs—and assume them to be relatively well off. This impression is statistically false; poor people are almost twice as likely to bike to work. The lowest-earning quartile of Americans make up almost 40% of the bike commuting population.[175] Investments in bike facilities disproportionately improve the safety of your community's construction laborers and restaurant workers, and help to free them from the huge financial burden of car ownership.

Economics

Whether it comes to talent attraction and retention, job creation, household expenditures, home value, retail performance, or limiting costly externalities, bike lanes mean business. Young creative and tech workers often cite bike infrastructure as a high priority in deciding where to live and work.[176] A study shows that public dollars spent on bike infrastructure generate roughly twice the jobs as money spent on driving infrastructure.[177] In Indianapolis, proximity to bike paths was demonstrated to add an average of 11% to the value of a house;[178] in Brooklyn, the number was 16%.[179] Retail sales to businesses along new bike lanes in Manhattan were seen to increase as much as 49%.[180] Finally, unlike cars, bikes do not exacerbate the costly impacts of climate change,

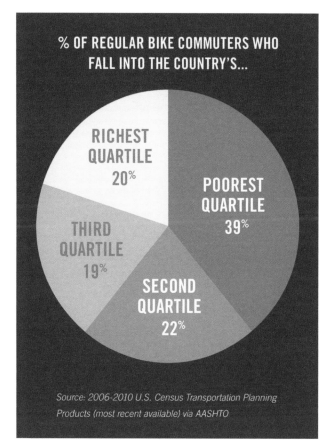

Most US bike commuters are not well off.

oil addiction, and 40,000 driving deaths per year. The data make it clear: it would be difficult for a city to find an investment that pays off better than bike lanes.

RULE 52: When advocating for bike network investment, cite data surrounding public health, equity, and economics.

53 Understand That Cycling Follows Investment

Topography, climate, and culture can't compare.

IN THE 1970s, people in Portland, OR, biked not much more than people in the rest of the United States. Over the ensuing forty years, the city invested about $60 million in cycling infrastructure—enough money to pay for about one mile of urban freeway. Now, people in Oregon bike to work at a rate that is more than fourteen times the national average.[181]

Observing that few people bike in a place without a good bike network is like saying that you don't need a bridge because nobody is swimming the river.

The same story can be told of many European cities, except with more dramatic outcomes. By the 1960s, cars had begun to dominate the landscape of Amsterdam and Copenhagen, just like in the typical American city. But then, national and local policies directed investment away from highways and toward comprehensive urban cycling networks, with an emphasis on safe bike lanes largely protected from automobile traffic. Now, in the Netherlands,

A high-quality bike network enabled this bike-based maid service in Washington, DC.

36% of people list cycling as their most common way of getting around, and the percentage in urban centers is even higher.[182] Meanwhile, in Copenhagen, after $150 million was invested in the past decade alone, a whopping 62% of residents commute to work or school by bicycle—almost seven times as many as go by car.[183]

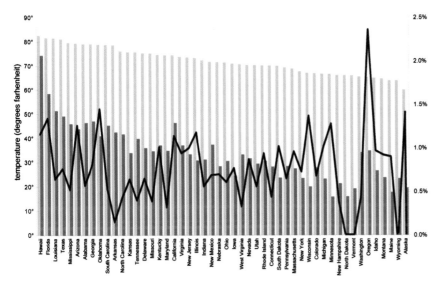

State by state, the bouncing line that bears no relationship to weather represents commuting trips by bike.

It snows a bit in Copenhagen—the City famously plows the bike lanes before the car lanes—and of course it rains a ton in Portland, about 150 days per year. It snows there too. There's a saying in Portland: "There's no such thing as bad weather, just bad gear." This brings up another point, which is that weather, once thought so important to bike ridership, seems to not have much of an impact on outcomes, and neither does topography. Twice as many people commute by bike in Canada's northern Yukon Territory than in California[184], and hilly San Francisco has double the cycling rate of relatively flat Denver.[185]

Clearly, hot weather can be a problem, which is why development regulations encouraging showers at work—as the LEED green-building certification does—are a key part of the picture. But climate, hills, and other local factors cannot legitimately be cited as insurmountable hurdles to growing a cycling population, when the evidence clearly suggests otherwise.

The most befuddling red herring of all is "culture." Often is it claimed that "nobody will bike here because nobody bikes here." Observing that few people bike in a place without a good bike network is like saying that you don't need a bridge because nobody is swimming the river.

In sweaty Macon, GA, past city officials installed three noncontiguous blocks of bike lanes and then pointed out that nobody used them. Last year, they striped eight miles of pop-up bike lanes and witnessed cycling increase by more than 800%.[186]

RULE 53: Refute all claims that any factor other than biking investment will have a significant impact on biking population.

54 | Avoid Common Cycling Pitfalls

There are plenty of mistakes to learn from.

WITH MORE OR LESS AMBITION AND LUCK, American cities have been trying to install bike lanes for many decades. Even a limited exposure to these efforts teaches lessons about some common pitfalls that can be better avoided if properly anticipated.

In New York City, injuries have dropped an average of 22% on streets with new bike lanes.

Us vs. them thinking: One thing you are ideally taught as a planner is to avoid using the words *driver, cyclist,* or *pedestrian* in public documents. Instead, you should use the terms *people driving, people biking,* and *people walking,* and for good reason. We are not so different from each other. We all belong to the same species, and, in fact, many of us are one and the same: depending on the day, the time, and the weather, we may choose to drive, bike, or walk. The language we choose can reinforce or undermine that fact. Additionally, there is the "One Less Car" phenomenon, the exasperatingly ungrammatical but all-too-necessary

T-shirt campaign that deserves greater attention. Most *people driving* could use a reminder that each *person cycling* is potentially a *person driving* in their lane, gumming up their commute.

Zero sum thinking: Many people assume that gaining a bike lane means losing a driving lane or a parking lane. Sometimes it does, but sometimes it doesn't. More often, a good bike network will take road space away from cars where it simply isn't needed, and where it is contributing mostly to speeding and danger. As discussed under road diets (Rules 45 and 46) and just ahead, adding bike lanes can improve safety for *all* road users without reducing car capacity at all.

Cyclists vs. pedestrians: Here's a favorite—about once a day, somewhere, someone stands up at a planning hearing and tries to stop a bike lane because they once heard a grisly news story about an old lady plowed down by a bike messenger. The proper response to this comment is to explain calmly how good bike lanes actually improve pedestrian safety; the data are clear: in New York City, injuries have dropped an average of 22% on streets with new bike lanes.[187] The improper, but sometimes necessary, response is as follows: "Each year, more people are

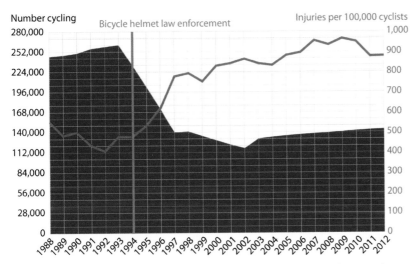

Number cycling — Bicycle helmet law enforcement — Injuries per 100,000 cyclists

When New Zealand began enforcing helmet laws, cycling dropped by 51% and injury risk roughly doubled.[190]

crushed to death by vending machines than the number of pedestrians killed by cyclists."[188] Next question.

Helmet laws: You should wear a bike helmet, because biking in America is dangerous, much more dangerous than it is in places like Europe where people don't wear helmets. But, if you are concerned for your safety, you should never require anyone else to wear a helmet, because doing so makes cycling more dangerous for everyone. Helmet laws suppress cycling, and fewer cyclists means greater risk. It also means worse public health outcomes, and more people driving. It is no coincidence that those few places (Seattle, Australia) where public bikeshare has failed are places with helmet laws.[189]

Bad "polling:" In 2017, the City of Des Moines began to aggressively pursue a multi-modal street-design strategy, after many years of tentative measures. As recently as three years prior, the situation there was similar to what one still finds in many American communities: the City leadership, City staff, and a robust cycling community all wanted better bike infrastructure, but felt unable to pursue it because "public opinion" was against it. How was public opinion measured? By online polling, which asked such questions as, "do you want to see new bike lanes on Ingersoll Avenue?" People self-selected to participate in the polls and, as with most online forums, the grumpiest naysayers showed up in droves, voting early, often, and against. "Polling" does not count as polling unless it is random, cross-sectional, and not limited to those who seek it out. Trusting conventional online polls is a great way to stop any good change from coming to your city, including cycling facilities.

RULE 54: Use language that reflects the commonalities among drivers, cyclists, and pedestrians; demonstrate how what is good for cycling can also be good for driving; deflate worries about bike/pedestrian collisions; eliminate helmet laws; only conduct public opinion polls if you can do so scientifically.

PART XII

BUILD YOUR BIKE NETWORK

IN NORTH AMERICA, a proper urban cycle network is made up of a variety of facilities that all work together. In decreasing order of comfort, these are bike paths, bicycle boulevards, cycle tracks, and conventional bike lanes. There is a lot to be known about how to design and distribute these facilities well. Sharrows (shared-lane markings), while they have a role to play, are not effective cycling facilities. A proper cycling network will likely contain a variety of facilities as well as a large number of local roads in which bikes simply mix with low-speed traffic.

55 | Understand Bike Network Function

The goal is to make cycling useful and safe.

A CONTROVERSIAL SENTENCE from *Walkable City* bears repeating: "The dream is to get bicyclists where they need to go, not to apportion them a slice of every road, tied up with a bow."[191] Even under the best political circumstances, placing bike lanes in every street is simply not possible, nor is it the best outcome. As implied by the concept of *strength in numbers,* it is safer to concentrate cyclists on fewer routes, where drivers expect to see them, rather than to disperse them like a mist throughout an entire city.

Just as the goal with improving transit networks is to focus on frequent routes, the goal with improving cycling networks is to focus on low-stress routes.

This approach ideally results in a bike network in which most cyclists can spend most of their trips in a low-stress environment, largely separated from cars and trucks. Then, as they approach their destination, they might briefly need to use an unprotected bike lane, claim a slow driving lane,

or just walk their bike on the sidewalk. Few cyclists find such a network wanting, but few American cities have even that much. Where to begin?

When one looks at any urban street network, opportunities arise. Most are made possible by the "extra pavement" salvaged by right-sizing the driving lanes (see Rules 45–50). These opportunities should be collected and plotted against the larger regional picture, so that trails and other large-scale facilities are all tied together. If all goes well, it will then be possible to lay in a cycle network that allows mostly low-stress travel between most destinations.

This network will be made up of a wide range of facility types, to be covered ahead, organized from least to most stressful.[192]

Bike paths: These are cycling trajectories that are located apart from city streets, which they may cross on occasion, with such crossings carefully designed for safety. In the United States, most of these have been built in disused rail beds.

Bicycle boulevards: Less common, these are low-volume, low-speed streets—typically residential—that are specifically modified to encourage bike travel and discourage nonlocal driving.

Cycle tracks: A more recent arrival that is now proliferating, the cycle track, also known as a protected bike lane, is located within a street right-of-way but physically protected from it, often by a row of parked cars.

Conventional lanes: The most common facility, these are striped lanes located adjacent to driving lanes, and often sandwiched between them and parked cars, creating a door hazard.

Slow-flow and yield-flow streets: Where low-volume streets are properly designed for low speed, they can be shared among cars, trucks, and bikes, without markings. These are good for local travel, but rarely comprise regional networks on their own.

Sharrows: Sharrows are conventional driving lanes that have been marked with cycling symbols and/or lined by "Share the Road" signs. It is becoming evident that a sharrow is actually not a cycling facility, as discussed ahead (Rule 62).

Most American cities have vastly inadequate cycling networks, especially downtown, where cycling is most productive. Just as the goal with improving transit networks is to focus on frequent routes, the goal with improving cycling networks is to focus on low-stress routes. In most cases, this means finding opportunities for bicycle boulevards and cycle tracks, such that cyclists need only shift a few blocks laterally to access one. In busy streets where a cycle track can't fit, Integrated Lanes can still play an important role, especially when it comes to eliminating the extra asphalt that causes speeding.

In the small downtown of Lancaster, PA, a limited amount of street space led to a proposed downtown cycle network made up of a range of facilities.

RULE 55: Create cycling networks that concentrate cycling onto low-stress routes within easy reach.

56

Turn Existing Corridors into Bike Paths

Nothing beats dedicated bike/run/walk facilities.

BIKE PATHS, ALSO CALLED BIKE TRAILS, are cycling trajectories that are located apart from city streets and are therefore the safest and most attractive places for biking. They tend to be located in disused rail beds or along coasts, rivers, and canal lines. They can also be found in highway rights-of-way or, occasionally, along electrical transmission lines.

In Boulder, CO, properties adjacent to paths sell for fully 32% more than similar properties 1,000 yards away.

Key to the safety and success of a bike path is limiting and properly treating its interruptions. Depending on the circumstances, street crossings will require stop signs, flashing signals, or even full signalization. In places where car travel is not heavy, it is the crossing street that should receive the stop sign, not the bike path. Too often, it is the bikes who are made to stop, even where requiring cars to do so would not cause congestion; this outcome suggests unhealthy priorities.

Sometimes a bike path will disappear temporarily and merge with city streets as it passes through a downtown. How this condition is treated can have a large impact on the success of the path, especially as a recreational facility, where inexperienced users may well turn around if they lose scent of the trail. In-street lanes and bold signage are key to letting users know that the path continues beyond the interruption.

As with most transportation facilities that have become the realm of specialists, there exists a tendency to oversize bike paths to best serve their users, which can lead to excess cost and threaten viability. Some planners, optimizing biking and walking, ask for cyclists and pedestrians to each receive five feet of pavement for each direction of travel, resulting in a preposterous twenty feet of asphalt. While there are urban, high-intensity uses in which more pavement is warranted, there is no reason for a typical two-way path to be more than ten feet wide. Recreational and commuting cycling is not the Tour de France, and riders should be expected to use their brakes on occasion.

The Rails-to-Trails movement has been a great success, and there are many resulting regional bike paths that deserve to be celebrated. Some of the best dovetail with transit, like Massachusetts' Minuteman Bikeway, in which a ten-mile bike path ends at the western terminus of the MBTA Red Line, a quick ride from downtown Boston. Ample bike storage is provided at the station.

Bike paths contribute tremendously to the cachet and the quality of life of their communities. Yet, like clockwork, most attempts at creating new facilities are met with significant local opposition, often from neighbors who are convinced that hoodlums will use the paths to "come in from the city and steal my television." Such fears remain a common refrain at local meetings, despite the fact that bike paths have never been linked to increases in crime.

To the contrary, the data show that a nearby bike path is likely to have a significant positive impact on a home's property value—about $8,800 per home, according to one University of Delaware study.[193] In Boulder, CO, where biking has become more established, properties adjacent to paths sell for fully 32% more than similar properties 1,000 yards away. In Massachusetts, houses located along bike paths take three weeks less time to sell than houses elsewhere.[194]

And once a path becomes large enough, it can be an economic engine in its own right. The 35-mile Virginia Creeper Trail is documented as contributing about $1.6 million in annual revenue to its region, and is singlehand-

In Detroit, the Dequindre Cut uses an old rail corridor to provide cyclists a quick and safe trajectory through downtown.

edly credited with the revival of the City of Damascus, VA, where more than thirty new businesses have sprung up to serve the trail's 130,000 annual visitors.

There may be one good reason not to create a bike path—specifically a Rails-to-Trails bike path—and that is the potential of those rails, which once held trains and could again. Ripping them out could possibly end up crippling a future attempt at commuter rail service in certain locations. For this reason, new Rails-to-Trails proposals must be carefully considered in light of realistic opportunities for future transit.

RULE 56: Identify corridors with potential for bike paths and use economic analysis and recent experience to justify investment in them.

57 | Build Bicycle Boulevards

This underutilized tool is ready for prime time.

THE BICYCLE BOULEVARD is a concept that has begun to proliferate on the West Coast, and shows great potential for increasing the safety and population of cyclists across the United States. It is also a catchy term, like *Bus Rapid Transit* and *New Urbanism,* which is easily co-opted and risks losing its meaning through half-hearted imitation. What, exactly, is a bicycle boulevard? A proper one has five characteristics.

When a bicycle boulevard crosses a major street, the signal should be designed to improve the efficiency of the bike facility.

Long and calm: Bicycle boulevards gain their value by being regional facilities, so the good ones are measured in miles, not blocks. To function properly, they should serve very little car traffic, typically only those cars that "live" on the block. They do not make sense in high-density or commercial areas that attract traffic. When a bicycle boulevard enters a downtown, it typically must transform into a more urban facility, ideally a cycle track.

Low speed: Bicycle boulevards should be signed for low speeds—typically 20 to 25 mph—but also designed for low speeds, which ideally means not too wide. If a street attracts speeding, it should receive *speed cushions, pinch points, chicanes,* or other features that slow down cars without affecting the speed of bicycles, which can dodge them easily. Parallel parking is not out of keeping with a bicycle boulevard, as it helps keep speeds low.

Marked and branded: From block to block, a Bicycle Boulevard looks a lot like a normal street but with emphatic pavement markings. Beyond just the bike logo, it makes sense to write "BLVD" in the street, to call out the facility as special. A vertical sign at each corner, giving each Boulevard a unique name, helps with branding and marketing, and reminds drivers that bicycles are intended to be the dominant user. Centerlines should also be eliminated.

Hobbled to through-traffic: Because bicycle boulevards are efficient and direct routes through a city, they will quickly be inundated by cars and trucks if vehicular through-traffic is not discouraged. This end can be achieved, painfully, through signs and enforcement, but is more easily accomplished by installing impediments at intersections. The most effective such tool is a short raised median in the cross street, with a small central gap, so that only cyclists can zoom from block to block without turning at each cross street.

Signed and signalized for bikes: When a bicycle boulevard crosses a minor street, that street should receive stop signs. When it crosses a major street, the signal should be designed to improve the efficiency of the bike facility,

Berkeley, CA, has a network of seven bicycle boulevards that girds the entire city.

with a green wave timed to bicycle speed or quick-response sensors (or pushbuttons) for cyclists.

In both cases—but especially where conflicts are likely to occur—highlighting the visibility of the Bicycle Boulevard with signage, pavement markings, flashing beacons, and/or a raised crossing can be instrumental in improving the safety of the facility.

As with most bike facilities, the best guidance on the design of bicycle boulevards can be found in the *Urban Bikeway Design Guide* published by NACTO, the National Association of City Transportation Officials.

RULE 57: Introduce regional bicycle boulevards located on calm streets that have low speed limits, no centerline, prominent markings, branded signage, and intersections designed and signed/signalized to prioritize bikes over cars and trucks.

58 | Build Cycle Tracks

Protected lanes are the quick, affordable path to promoting urban cycling.

STUDIES SUGGEST that if a city wishes to significantly enlarge its cycling population, it must provide a useful network of low-stress cycling facilities. In addition to proper bike paths and bicycle boulevards, such a network usually contains *cycle tracks,* also known as *protected lanes.* Cycle tracks are bike lanes that are located within vehicular rights-of-way but designed in a manner that limits potential conflict between drivers and cyclists, usually by placing some sort of barrier between driving and cycling.

In Europe, the typical cycle track occupies the outer edge of the sidewalk zone, where it sits above the street at sidewalk elevation. This configuration has only begun to infiltrate North American cities, but it is the ideal outcome to pursue when streets are being designed from scratch or fully rebuilt. One popular layout places the street trees between the cycle track and the sidewalk, to better define the distinct zones.

In the United States, most opportunities to create cycle tracks occur in already-existing streets, in which the more economical approach is to keep construction to a minimum. Under these circumstances, the best technique is to eliminate one lane of traffic and shift the parallel parking away from the curb to create a bike lane that is protected by a row of parked cars and buffer for swinging doors.

Bike lanes of this type are proliferating around the United States, with tremendous outcomes. When Janette Sadik-Khan inserted a cycle track into Brooklyn's Prospect Park West, that street's cycling use tripled, as speeding dropped from 75% to 17% of all drivers and the number of injury crashes plummeted by 63%.[195] This being New York City, there was an immediate lawsuit, but eventually, to quote the *Village Voice,* the "bike hating NIMBY trolls grudgingly surrender[ed] to reality."[196]

Depending on the amount of roadway available and the opportunity for additional parallel routes, cycle tracks can be one-way or two-way. Let there be no doubt: one-way cycle tracks are safer and more pleasant to use; Denmark has eliminated the two-way track as a *best practice.*[197] But if there is nowhere else to provide the opposing direction of travel, two-way tracks like the one along Prospect Park can be a blessing. Because they can cause confusion at corners, such tracks must be designed very carefully as they approach intersections—especially on two-way streets, where the opportunities for conflicts double. Indeed, while

Despite removing a lane of traffic, this cycle track did not negatively impact car volumes or travel times on Brooklyn's Prospect Park West.[198]

multilane one-way streets are generally best avoided (see Rule 39) it sometimes makes sense to preserve one or several of a city's existing one-ways in order to have a good place to put the cycle tracks.

Cycle tracks are best located where there are fewer cross streets or curb cuts, since the parallel parking must receive a gap for each one. For that reason, they are most effectively placed against parks, rail beds, and other linear features that result in long block faces. In these locations, where one side of a street has many curb cuts and the other has few, two-way cycle tracks on one flank make particular sense.

Often, the biggest question surrounding a cycle track is whether or not it makes sense to lose a flank of parallel parking in order to make room for one. The short answer is no,

because it is far better to remove extra driving lanes than parking lanes, which slow traffic and protect the sidewalk.

The longer answer is a bit more nuanced. On streets without retail, removing parking can be a good thing when it is politically possible—in other words, almost never. On streets that serve retail, this parking may or may not be needed for the merchants to thrive. If it can be determined that the parking is not essential for shopping, and also that no driving lanes may be eliminated without causing gridlock—an assertion always worth challenging—then a trade of parking for biking might make sense. In such a case, when parked cars are absent, a physical barrier such as curbs or planters is needed to make the bike lane into a true cycle track.

RULE 58: Build a network of cycle tracks, ideally by removing unnecessary driving lanes.

59 Build Cycle Tracks Properly

Get the details right.

DESIGN STANDARDS FOR CYCLING facilities in the United States are advancing at a pace unmatched by any other aspect of urban planning. We can hope that they will eventually achieve the quality of those found in Europe, and receive a similar share of street space and public works budget. In the meantime, certain configurations and measurements have begun to proliferate, and they constitute a best practice of sorts when it comes to serving cyclists. These are well documented in the NACTO *Urban Bikeway Design Guide*, and are further elaborated in the paragraphs that follow.

It is better to stripe 100 blocks of cycle tracks than to build 10 for the same cost.

A good size for a cycle track is 5 feet of pavement for each direction of travel, plus a 3-foot buffer against parked cars. In some cases, though, eliminating a lane of traffic only yields about 10 feet of pavement, theoretically not enough for a two-way track. Such was the case with Washington, DC's popular 15th Street cycle track, a two-way facility on the left flank of a one-way street. (Barring exceptional condi-

tions, the left flank is always the proper flank for a two-way track on a one-way street; think about the direction of flow to understand why.) The city settled on a solution in which two 3.5-foot bike lanes sit against a 3-foot buffer. While not ideal, this outcome was superior to losing one direction of travel, and it handles high volumes of cyclists. Also worth noting is how, while typical curb parking lanes are 8 feet wide, the parallel parking on this facility is only 7 feet wide. Because a buffer is easier to park against than a curb, 7 feet is an ample width for parallel parking against a cycle track.

How to design the buffer depends on budget and climate. In heavy snow areas, raised buffer zones can provide plowing challenges, but cities that are committed to high-quality facilities will build next to each crosswalk a small island that occupies the parking and buffer areas together. This is the technique that New York City has used on many of its facilities. In its ideal version, shown at right, this island is matched by another one that projects into the intersection in order to neck it down, tightening the curb radius so that vehicles don't speed around the corner. When two cycle tracks intersect, these details, which separate cyclists from both cars and pedestrians, are especially useful.

The ideal multi-modal intersection provides dedicated paths for people walking, biking, and driving. Note the islands that initiate the parking lanes as well as the neckdowns at the corners.

Away from intersections, it is a nice touch to raise the buffer zone with curbs—even to provide it with ground-cover—but this should be considered a luxury. It is better to stripe 100 blocks of cycle tracks than to build 10 for the same cost.

When inserting bike lanes into existing streets, bulb-outs (curb extensions) in the parking lane can appear to be an impediment to creating proper cycle tracks. The solution is to angle the bike lane away from the curb as it approaches the corner, essentially angling it through what was previously the parking spot closest to the intersection. This move should result in the loss of only one parking space on each intersection approach.

Cycle tracks and protected lanes should not be confused with what are called "buffered lanes." These provide some distance, but no substantial physical barrier, between the bike lane and the traffic that flanks it. The buffer is typically striped at an angle to indicate that it is a no-go zone for cars and bikes. In streets with parallel parking and room for a buffer, it is of course safer to provide protected lanes than mere buffered lanes, but the fire department often insists on the latter in order to maintain twenty feet of clear space in the roadway. As discussed in Rule 51, this requirement deserves questioning.

Most design guides recommend, in the absence of curbs, filling cycle track buffer zones with flexible vertical posts as well as angled stripes. While effective, the problem with these is that they are ugly, and result in a visually busy and discordant streetscape. While beauty should not trump safety, it seems reasonable to assume that, over time, as Americans become more accustomed to using this infrastructure, the posts can be removed and the stripes replaced with a simple contrasting pavement color.

RULE 59: Build cycle tracks using best practices as outlined in the NACTO *Urban Bikeway Design Guide.*

60 | Use Conventional Bike Lanes Where They Belong

For now, in-street lanes are still a useful tool.

CONVENTIONAL BIKE LANES, adjacent to moving traffic and sometimes parked cars, used to be good enough. Now, with the acceptance of cycle tracks, it is harder to advocate for them, but they still have a significant role to play in most American cities.

> *A six-lane road with unprotected bike lanes is not a "complete street," as many DOTs would claim; rather, it's a deathtrap.*

The disadvantages of conventional bike lanes are clear. They place the cyclist directly adjacent to moving traffic, often sandwiched between this traffic and parked cars whose doors may open without warning. As Amazon and other services make home deliveries more and more common, these lanes are often occupied by delivery trucks, forcing cyclists into traffic. Similarly, bike lanes are a favorite pickup zone for Uber and Lyft drivers. And then there is the New York City Police Department, whose officers love to store their cruisers in bike lanes while ticketing cyclists for not coming to a complete stop at intersections.

For all these reasons, bike lanes are inferior to cycle tracks, but they are still needed. In a typical urban grid, a rider should be able to find a bike lane by shifting one or

Nobody wants their daughter in the door zone, but bike lanes are a great way to slow cars on a street that is five feet too wide.

Unlike cycle tracks, conventional bike lanes invite delivery trucks and other obstacles.

two streets left or right at most. This means that one out of every three or four parallel streets should contain some sort of cycling facility, and there is often not room for cycle tracks on all these streets. Better a conventional bike lane than no bike lane.

The other good reason for a bike lane, discussed in Rule 48, is that some streets just have four to six feet too much pavement in them. For example, while a typical main street is 36 feet wide, with 8-foot parking on both sides, some have been built 40 feet wide. One way to make this street safer would be to narrow all the lanes slightly, placing a single 6-foot bike lane next to 10-foot driving lanes and 7-foot parking lanes. Now, if a street has seven feet too

much pavement, it would be better to insert a cycle track (a 4-foot lane with a 3-foot buffer), but with less extra width, only a conventional lane will fit.

There are some streets where conventional bike lanes do not make any sense. They do not belong on highways more than two lanes wide, given the driving speeds these streets invite. For the same reason, conventional lanes should not be part of any street with more than two lanes in any one direction. A six-lane road with unprotected bike lanes is not a "complete street," as many DOTs would claim; rather, it's a deathtrap. Wider, faster streets are where a choice must be made between protected lanes or no lanes at all.

RULE 60: To build a useful cycling network and to use up excess pavement, place conventional bike lanes where cycle tracks won't fit.

61 | Build Conventional Bike Lanes Properly

Get the details right.

Width: For many years, the standard width for conventional bike lanes was 5 feet. This number is now 6 feet, because wider is safer. However, you should stop there; if a bike lane is 7 feet wide or more, people will try to drive or park in it. Five feet is still a reasonable measure if wider is not possible, especially when a bike lane does not abut parallel parking. In an extreme pinch, it is acceptable to place a 4-foot bike lane between a driving lane and the curb, but that is not an acceptable width for a lane that sits in the door zone.

That bright stripe is effectively a horizontal billboard proclaiming that a city is progressive, healthy, and welcoming to young talent.

Buffers: When more than 6 feet are available for a bike lane, and creating a true cycle track is not possible, the excess width beyond 5 feet should become a diagonally striped buffer or buffers. There seems to be no consensus on whether the buffer should protect the bike lane from traffic or from the doors of parked cars; it probably makes most sense to split the excess width into buffers against both dangers equally.

Paint: Bright green paint has become the gold standard in marking bike lanes, either in key locations or for their entire length. There may be marketing reasons for painting your bike lanes entirely green; that bright stripe is effectively a horizontal billboard proclaiming that a city is progressive, healthy, and welcoming to young talent. Absent this motivation, it is probably wisest to allocate the paint budget to those places where bikes are most likely to come into contact with cars and pedestrians: at intersections, merges, and other locations where paths cross.

The technology for green surfacing keeps improving, so communities should investigate recent applications in places with similar climates to select an up-to-date material and brand that has shown its durability over several years. Do not be a guinea pig for untested products. And of course, green is not required; a unique color can be a source of local identity and pride.

Intersections: Bike lanes alone are not enough. An effective bike network must also include special facilities at intersections that allow cyclists to negotiate them safely. Chief among these are bike boxes and bike crossings. Bike boxes allow cyclists to stage in front of stopped vehicles when there is likely to be a conflict between bikes turning left across traffic or cars turning right across the bike lane. Bike crossings are like pedestrian crosswalks but for bikes and are warranted when an intersection poses a particular risk for cyclists. In these facilities, bike arrows or green paint is brought through the intersection in a dashed form, alerting motorists to the presence of bikes and helping cyclists stay on course. Details of both of these facilities, and others, can be found in the NACTO *Urban Bikeway Design Guide*.

Extent: As pertains to conventional bike lanes, but also the entirety of a city's bike infrastructure, it is important

Bike boxes are one of many important features for serving cyclists at intersections.

to remember that a cycling network only becomes popular when it is useful, and it only becomes useful when it allows people to meet most of their daily needs on bicycle. Unfortunately, the typical city's trajectory from having almost no bike infrastructure to having an effective network is long and potentially frustrating. Each new bike lane, alone, will not be enough to fundamentally change a place's experience and culture around cycling. For that reason, establishing such a network requires commitment, patience, and an ongoing political effort over many years. Throughout the process, it will remain necessary to remind the community that a significant cycling population will only arise once all the individual investments add up to an effective network.

RULE 61: Build conventional bike lanes using best practices as outlined in the NACTO *Urban Bikeway Design Guide*. Remind constituents of the need for a comprehensive network.

62 | Do Not Use Sharrows as Cycling Facilities

Speedy driving lanes with sharrow markings are not safe.

SHARROWS, OR SHARE-THE-ROAD MARKINGS, are biking symbols that are placed in a driving lane in order to inform cyclists and drivers alike that the lane is meant to serve both parties equally. They generally come in two forms, either placed in the center of a normal-width lane,

This would all be well and good if sharrows improved safety. The problem is that they don't.

or placed right-of center in a wide lane. In the former configuration, cyclists are meant to "claim the lane," with drivers patiently cruising behind them. In the latter, cyclists are supposed to stay to the right, with drivers exercising caution in passing them. The potential for conflict in each of these scenarios is not hard to spot.

For many years, sharrows have been a favorite of state DOTs and conventional public works departments, allowing them to check the box for providing cycling infrastructure while not in any way impacting the amount of roadway dedicated to vehicles. The typical traffic study

investigating the potential for bike lanes shows how inserting dedicated bike facilities will bring the traffic to a Level of Service of D or E, and then suggests turning two lanes into sharrows instead. Problem solved!

Remarkably, sharrows have also experienced a fair amount of support in the cycling community, particularly among those confident cyclists who would likely ride a bike even in more adverse conditions. In *The Cyclist's Manifesto*, an important book of 2009, Robert Hurst's called sharrows "art that conjures awareness, and that, as we've seen, is what traffic safety is all about."[199]

This would all be well and good if sharrows improved safety. The problem is that they don't. Since 2009, we have had ample opportunity to study them, and it turns out that streets with sharrows are not only more dangerous than streets with actual bike lanes, they may be more dangerous than streets *without* sharrows.

A recent University of Colorado study by Nick Ferenchak and Wesley Marshall compared cycling population and crash rates in areas of Chicago with sharrows, dedicated bike lanes, or no street markings at all. They found that, while all areas saw increased cycling and fewer injuries,

Highway 431 in Nashville, winner of planner Dan Kostelec's 2017 "Sharrows of Death" award.

The more accurate symbol suggested by Queen Anne Greenways.

those with dedicated lanes saw the most improvement, while those with sharrows saw the least, attracting fewer cyclists and experiencing more injuries (per cyclist) than even those areas where no street markings were added.[200]

Based on these data, and in response to a Twitter call for a more accurate version of the sharrow symbol, Queen Anne Greenways responded with the image shown above.

In this context, sharrows still do have a role to play. There are times where, due to the insertion of a turn lane or a pinch point in a road, a dedicated bike lane must disappear along its trajectory, and cyclists must merge with drivers. In these locations—hopefully rare—sharrow-type road markings are indeed necessary to alert drivers and cyclists to the merge. It can also be useful to add sharrows to a narrow, slow street, to let everyone know that cyclists are expected. But on larger roads, sharrows are an apology, not a cycling facility.

RULE 62: Use sharrow symbols to indicate bike lane merges and as wayfinding, but not as a replacement for real bike facilities.

PART XIII

PARK ON STREET

ASIDE FROM STREET TREES, no aspect of thoroughfare design is as undervalued as curb parking. Whether parallel or angled, on-street parking is a feature of almost every great North American street, where it plays an essential role in calming traffic and supporting mixed use.

In City Planning 2.0, currently being practiced in Europe and elsewhere, cars are removed from the streetscape almost entirely. This dream persists in the United States, and is achieved in a few remarkable places. But until cars become irrelevant to urban vitality, the proper place for parking them is between where people are driving and where people are walking.

63 | Put Curb Parking Almost Everywhere

Often undervalued, curb parking can be key to walkability.

CURB PARKING is an essential barrier of steel that protects the sidewalk from moving vehicles. Without it, sidewalks in urban areas do not feel safe. For proof, one need look no further than Fort Lauderdale, where a rush-hour parking ban on one side of Himmarshee Boulevard created a perfect experiment. Restaurants serving essentially the same bar food set up tables on both flanks of the street. Repeated happy-hour visits yielded the same results: groups of diners on the side with parking, and a ghost town on the side without. The restaurant on that side folded shortly thereafter.

This outcome makes perfect sense because nobody who values their safety wants to sit, or walk, in close proximity to cars moving at 30 mph. The protective presence of curb parking is so powerful that it is almost certainly better to have an 8-foot-wide sidewalk with parking than a 16-foot sidewalk without it.

Curb parking doesn't just protect sidewalks. It slows down drivers, who are wary of clipping a mirror, and who might also be looking for an empty spot. It replaces off-street parking, decreasing the need for large lots and expensive structures. It contributes to sidewalk life as drivers walk from cars to destinations.[201] And, according to

Prior to a walkability study, Fort Lauderdale banned curb parking on one side of Himmarchee Boulevard, a key spot for sidewalk dining.

the National Trust's Main Street program, each on-street parking space contributes about $10,000 in retail sales to nearby businesses.[202]

After a walkability study, Fort Lauderdale removed its rush-hour parking ban. So did Des Moines, recognizing

On the left, happy hour on the parked side of the street. At right, happy hour on the side without parking.

that rush hour is the best time to invite workers to linger and spend money in their downtown. Many cities are still unwilling to make this correction, reflecting an ignorance of the law of induced traffic demand (Rule 27), which dictates that increasing the number of outbound lanes at 5 p.m., rather than reducing congestion, tends only to concentrate the rush hour into a shorter stampede.

Given all of its benefits, on-street parking should be a part of all new thoroughfares in locations where it is likely to attract users, and it should be reintroduced to most urban curbs where it is missing. Bringing parking back to a struggling retail street is often the key factor in creating future success.

Curb parking is often found missing in downtowns for the strangest reasons. In Albuquerque, block long fire-lane markings were found along curbs in streets with more than 30 feet clear width for fire trucks. In Tulsa, the City required 20-foot clear-view setbacks around every driveway, creating huge gaps in parking. (More walkable cit-

ies like New York require a curb-cut setback of 0 feet.) In Cedar Rapids, an architect's proposal for a more retail-friendly 3rd Street eliminated all but a handful of parking spaces in order to create deeper sidewalks. . . . Apparently, somebody forgot to consult any retail experts!

In rare instances, it makes sense to eliminate a flank of parking for a bike or transit lane. Except in places like New York, where merchants don't depend on curb parking, this needs to be understood as a tradeoff between a local benefit and a regional benefit. In some cases, the few merchants must suffer so that many commuters can thrive. Such difficult tradeoffs can be justified if made publicly with a full discussion of the costs.

Most often, though, the proper solution is to create the space for bike and transit lanes by removing not parking lanes, but extra driving lanes. As noted in *Walkable City*, "If they are truly to offer an alternative to the automobile, bikes and trolleys must displace moving cars, not parked ones."[203]

RULE 63: Stripe streets to contain parking on both flanks in all locations where that parking is likely to be used, with exceptions only where a bike lane is deemed more necessary.

64 | Design Parallel Parking Properly
Get the details right.

THE PROPER WIDTH: On urban streets with at least moderate traffic, parallel parking spaces should be 7 to 8 feet wide in most locations. Eight feet is the standard, but seven used to be, and there is no reason to consider it inadequate; a Chevrolet Suburban is 6'9" wide. Wider parking spaces are one more thing that contributes to the elbow room that encourages speeding. On thoroughfares with less traffic, especially slow-flow and yield-flow streets (see Rule 50), parking spaces can be marked as narrow as 6 feet if space is tight. This gets people to park closer to the curb.

A 9-foot space alongside a 10-foot driving lane is safer than an 8-foot space alongside an 11-foot driving lane.

In contrast, it sometimes makes sense to widen a parking space to 9 or even 10 feet, if there is too much room in the roadway. A 9-foot space alongside a 10-foot driving lane is safer than an 8-foot space alongside an 11-foot driving lane. Beyond 10 feet, spaces look preposterous, and you can probably find a better use for that extra space, like a bike lane.

The proper length: In the days of tail fins, parking spaces were stretched to 22 feet long. As marvelous as those gas-guzzling boats were, those days are gone. A Chevy Suburban is 18'8" long, and a Honda Accord is 15'9". As with speed, 20' is plenty, and corner spaces can be two feet shorter. Those cities that maintain a 22-foot standard are robbing themselves of valuable parking.

Markings: There is no one proper way to stripe a parking space. Proper solutions range from boxes surrounding each space to little white T's where the spaces meet at the edge of the driving lane. Given the ease of application, the T's make the most sense, but a bolder paint job may help reduce speeding in problem areas. On slow-flow and yield-flow streets in residential areas, the best aesthetic approach is to not stripe spaces at all, but this approach needs changing if nobody is parking in them or if people are speeding.

Optimizing supply: Curb cuts (driveways) don't just ruin sidewalks (see Rule 81); they wreak havoc on parking supply. So do loading zones, which must be kept as

On this new residential street, 9 foot parking spaces visually narrow the driving zone.

short and infrequent as possible, and fire hydrants, which, whenever possible, should be placed near corners, in the area where people aren't allowed to park anyway. This no-parking zone, for corner visibility, should stretch 10 feet from the edge of the crosswalk, and no farther. Some cities require 20 to 30 feet, which they believe to be safer, but more thoughtful consideration of sight triangles would suggest that this is wrong (see Rule 66).

Uber zones: While parking spaces should be marked close to corners, there is a strong logic to marking corner parking spaces as standing-only zones, to handle the onslaught of ride-hailing drivers who need a place to make pickups. Currently, two thirds of all congestion-related traffic citations in San Francisco are going to Uber and Lyft drivers, who continually block driving and cycling lanes.[204] As of this writing, no great momentum seems to have been generated around the obvious solution to this problem, which is to designate a certain number of parking spots at each corner—no more than necessary—for pickups and drop-offs only. Customers would be required to walk to corners, and the app would send drivers there automatically. Where blocks are particularly long—say, more than 400 feet—similar locations would be placed at midblock. Cities could begin to enforce such a rule in their problem areas immediately.

Our autonomous future: We've all heard the stories about how swarming fleets of autonomous vehicles may eventually make curb parking obsolete (see Rule 26). Similarly, AI computing may make humans obsolete. Neither of these futures can be predicted with enough accuracy to be allowed to influence the design of streets today.

RULE 64: Carefully size parking spaces to the circumstances present, with the goal of controlling traffic speeds while optimizing supply; mark spaces boldly where speeding persists; create ride-hailing pickup zones at corners.

65 Provide Angle Parking Where Warranted

Angle parking is a great tool for using up excess pavement.

ONCE A STAPLE OF AMERICAN MAIN STREETS, angle parking is making a comeback. In many cities, it was converted to parallel parking in order to increase the number of driving lanes, to speed up traffic. Now that many streets are being right-sized to meet true travel demand,

When Tucson converted a major thoroughfare from front-angle to rear-angle, it went from roughly one car/bicycle crash per week to none in four years.

and lanes are being narrowed to safer widths, extra pavement is becoming available for better use. In some cases, that use is bike or transit lanes; in others it is to increase the supply of parking. If a street already has parallel parking on both flanks, the next step to adding more parking is to convert one or both flanks to an angled configuration.

Angle parking increases the parking supply and slows traffic, both of which are great for urban retail. It is rare to see people speeding on streets with angled parking, because the opportunities for conflict—and finding a spot—are so high. Like many things that seem dangerous, drivers backing up into heavily-traveled roads is safe precisely because it scares people into proceeding with caution.

While angle parking is most common and useful on retail streets, it is an acceptable configuration on all streets where there is both a demand for parking and extra pavement to use up. Spaces typically sit at an angle of either 45° or 60° to the curb, depending on the amount of roadway available. Traffic engineers are often too conservative in providing room for angle parking, so some rules of thumb are useful: Generally, both 60° and 45° parking require a zone 18 feet deep, but the former should sit against a (wider than standard) 11-foot driving lane, while the latter requires only a 10-foot lane. Beyond that width—once driving plus parking exceeds 30 feet—the parking should sit perpendicular to the curb. As usual, providing more room than needed can be expected to cause speeding.

Rear-angle parking is clearly safer for cyclists, but can cause some confusion.

The biggest challenge with angle parking is the danger that it poses for cyclists; cars backing into the path of bikes is not a good formula for public health. For this reason, angle parking should be avoided along popular cycling corridors, and certainly against bike lanes.

But there is a solution: rear-angle parking. Now proliferating from coast to coast, rear-angle parking reduces risks to all street users, especially cyclists, by allowing drivers to exit the spot in forward gear. It also makes it easier to load and unload your trunk, and creates a safer configuration for getting kids out of the car, since the open rear doors direct them away from traffic rather than into it.

The data surrounding angle parking and cycling are compelling. When Tucson converted a major thoroughfare from front-angle to rear-angle, it went from roughly one car/bicycle crash per week to none in four years.[205] The only problem with rear-angle parking is that people hate it, at least at first, because backing into a tight spot takes a little practice. A few cities have tried and abandoned it, and a large percentage seem unwilling to give it a go.

In these places, the mandate is less to eliminate front-angle parking than to keep cyclists away from it. The street reconfiguration plan for downtown Cedar Rapids—a city that temporarily experimented with rear-angle parking "for the entertainment value if nothing else,"[206] according to one city council member—places cycling facilities and angle parking in alternating streets, making conflicts less likely.

Streets with angle parking are wide, and take a long time to cross. For that reason, angle parking spaces should always be surrounded by "bulb-outs," built curb extensions that narrow crossing distances by effectively bringing the sidewalk to the edge of the driving lanes at crosswalks (see Rule 68). While parking may angle at 45° or 60°, these extensions should be built at 90° to the curb, both for aesthetic reasons and to allow a city to change its mind regarding whether parking is front-angle or rear-angle. Most cities get this one wrong.

RULE 65: Where appropriate, use angle parking to fill up excess street width, being careful to isolate front-angle parking from significant bike routes.

PART XIV

FOCUS ON GEOMETRY

BEYOND THE NUMBER OF LANES, the width of the lanes, and the presence of cycling and parking, one other factor contributes markedly to the speed of drivers and the safety of pedestrians: the shape of the street itself. Is it straight or curved? Does the striping swoop gently like on a highway? Do the curbs help to constrict flow and provide refuge for pedestrians? Are intersections loose or tight, simple or complex? Is there a centerline? Are cars allowed at all? The answers to these questions have dramatic impacts, often counterintuitive, on the safety and success of potentially walkable places.

66 Avoid Swoops, Slip Lanes, and Sight Triangles

Gentle curves and wide-open corners undermine safety.

HERE'S AN INTERESTING TEST: try to think of a successful downtown with gently curving streets. Drawing a blank? That's because walkable urbanism is characterized by straight-line geometries, with the occasional circle or oval thrown in, but no swooping curves. Medieval urbanism is cranky, not curvy, and even Frederick Law Olmsted, the king of curves, got straight as an arrow when he arrived downtown.

Vocabulary counts, and curving streets softly whisper "suburbia," but it's more than that. When presented with a slight curve, drivers tend to speed up; the g forces just feel too good. Interestingly, curves are associated with the traffic engineer's *design speed,* and minimum design speeds—still a factor in many city codes—ensure that they swoop broadly. Tight curves, when allowed, do slow traffic, but they still create cognitive dissonance in urban environments, where they remind drivers and pedestrians alike of the cul-de-sacs and fast-food drive-throughs of sprawl. Aside from pure geometries like the Royal Crescent at Bath, they have no place in new urban plans.

In that vein, one hopes that the 2010 prize for Honesty in Journalism was awarded to the *Las Vegas Sun* for

The auto zone at the heart of Las Vegas' latest "neighborhood."

their caption to the image above: "Some say the entrance to CityCenter is not inviting to pedestrians."[207] Ya think? Whenever a street presents would-be walkers with stream-form geometrics—aerodynamic shapes like "amoebas" and "pork chops"—they make it clear that a place is for cars, not people. Even 10-foot driving lanes cannot save this swoopy moonscape from keeping gamblers at bay.

Before and after: in Atlanta, the Midtown Alliance is replacing slip lanes with tight, landscaped intersections.

The same problem holds with slip lanes, those tidy corner shortcuts that engineers love to insert so that drivers turning right don't need to wait for a green light. "We put in a pedestrian refuge island," they will tell you, but the refuge is only needed thanks to the excessively swoopy corner. Smart neighborhoods like Midtown Atlanta are investing in the elimination of these slip lanes, so that turning vehicles actually have to slow down first. They are highway-era erosions that do not belong in urban places.

In his classic *Boulevard Book,* the urban planner and educator Alan Jacobs includes a section called "Professional and Bureaucratic Constraints," in which he shows the ways that engineering convention and municipal rules often stand in the way of making great streets.[208] Worthy of particular attention is the intersection sight-triangle requirement, which keeps buildings and trees at a distance from street corners, so that cars can see clearly around them while approaching at speed.

In the world of traffic engineering, in which there has historically been a complete refusal to acknowledge that environment influences behavior, we must keep visual obstructions away from intersections because drivers are going to speed through them. In the real world, of course, keeping visual obstructions away from intersections is one thing that *causes* drivers to speed through them.

For this reason, most of the world's most dangerous streets satisfy a sight-triangle requirement, while many of the safest do not. Jacobs demonstrates how applying an American sight-triangle requirement to Barcelona's Passeig de Gràcia would eliminate 41 of 107 trees in a single block.[209] The mandate to cities is clear: any code revision with the goal of making safer and more walkable streets must dispense with the sight-triangle rule.

RULE 66: Other than clear shapes like circles and ovals, do not use curving streets in the design of urban places; also avoid other swooping geometries like "pork chops" and slip lanes. Throw out your city's sight-triangle requirement.

67

Design Left-Turn Lanes Properly.

Don't use a highway standard in urban areas.

MOST OF THE SWOOPING GEOMETRIES to be found in downtown streets are located in those owned by the State DOT, which is in the habit of misapplying design techniques developed for highways to city centers as well. In some places, like Omaha and Kansas City, that same habit can be found in the municipal engineering office where, it would seem, they are hiring their professionals from the DOT.

In urban places, drivers look to the landscape for their cues, so designing in anticipation of illegal speeds makes speeding more common.

Whoever is responsible, the problem stems from a misunderstanding that what is safe on highways is also safe in cities. This could not be more wrong, due to how we determine our speed in each environment (see Rule 34). On highways, most drivers set their speed based on the posted limit, so it is smart to design with forgiveness—wider lanes and longer swoops. In urban places, by contrast, drivers look to the landscape for their cues, so designing in anticipation of illegal speeds makes such speeding more likely.

Probably the most common incursion of highway-style road design into America's downtowns is the high-speed left-turn lane. A proper urban center

An urban left-turn lane should not be a major production.

Highway-style left turns are introduced by swooping medians.

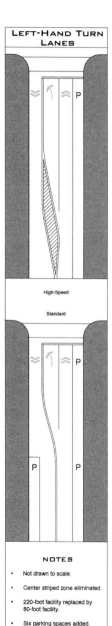

turn lane, seen at left above in Albuquerque, is short and simple. A couple of parallel parking spaces drop off the curb, and a center lane appears. If extra guidance is desired, a dashed line can sweep right to direct through-travel to that lane. Enough said.

A highway-style left-turn lane is quite different. Pictured in part at right above—it's too long to show all at once—the driving lane has swept to the right creating a center no-go zone 160 feet long, in order that no driver going straight at 50 mph ends up in the left-turn lane by accident. In this case, the center zone has eliminated six curb parking spaces unnecessarily (the beer truck is parked illegally).

This is not a state highway, but Water Street in Lancaster, PA, a city that is now trying to remake its streets to encourage safer driving speeds. While most downtown streets are owned by PennDOT, and therefore tough to change, this one is not.

The difference between the two types of facilities is shown at right—although not to scale—because the central no-go zones are often twice as long. The impact on parking provision is clear, as is the fact that one just *feels* like a highway, inviting highway speeds.

There are other examples of high-speed standards inappropriately brought into downtowns, but this one is the most common. Most can be spotted by their swooping curves and wasted asphalt, and many are quite new. Their presence is often a sign that city staff needs some reeducating on the difference between highways and towns.

RULE 67: In urban areas, use an urban left-turn-lane standard, which does not include an anticipatory no-go zone.

68 Place Neckdowns at Wide Crossings

Use pavement extensions to make intersections safer.

A NEW FAVORITE TERM among urban designers is "Sneckdown." It's what happens in northern cities when it snows, and the tire tracks on the street demonstrate how little room vehicles actually need to make it around corners. The remaining snow necks down the intersection, suggesting how far the sidewalk could ideally be expanded without impeding flow. And of course, in this limited area, vehicles move much more slowly and safely.

For new streets three lanes wide or wider, and streets with angle parking, bulb-outs should be considered a must.

Whether persuaded by snowfall or not, cities have been building neckdowns for some time now to make intersections safer, with great outcomes. Neckdowns reduce driving speeds, shorten crossing distances, and give pedestrians a place of refuge to stand safely in antici-pation of the opportunity to cross. Neckdowns fall into two basic categories: *bulb-outs* and *intersection repair*.

Bulb-outs

When building new streets, or making problem intersec-tions safer, it makes sense in all but the narrowest streets to insert bulb-outs. As noted in Rule 65, bulb-outs are pave-ment extensions that occupy the parking lane at corners where the parking stops, ideally beginning about 10 feet beyond the crosswalk.

Bulb-outs are not needed on narrow streets because crossing distances are already small and cars are already moving slowly. Still, there is likely more good than harm in instituting a bulb-out standard for all new free-flow streets that contain curb parking, even if they are only two lanes wide. The challenge in these circumstances, and also in places where a central median limits the road width, is to make sure that buses and trucks can turn the corner without running up on the curb. Toward this end, there are standard engineering templates that must be used. Within the context of keeping curb return radii no larger

In anticipation of repaving, a dangerous intersection in Chicago was reconfigured temporarily with paint and posts.

ment construction can be budgeted. For ease of plowing and cleaning, constructed bulb-outs should be chamfered to approach the main curb at a 45° angle, except for deep bulbouts surrounding angle parking, which are best built at 90° to allow a variety of parking solutions.

Intersection Repair

Beyond bulb-outs, the other type of curb extension emulates the "sneckdown" in its strategy of dieting intersections to hold no more asphalt than they actually need to function. Because so many American places were built with the approach of pave first and ask questions later, a large percentage of intersections—especially main/main intersections—have room for a little nip and tuck. The technique for doing so properly includes right-sizing the number and width of driving lanes (see Rules 45–50), applying the proper truck template to determine turning motions, and then relocating the curbs to the edges of those trajectories.

than necessary (See Rule 51), installing bulb-outs often results in a larger radius that would otherwise be the case.

For new streets three lanes wide or wider, and streets with angle parking, bulb-outs should be considered a must. And at existing intersections where collisions are occurring, they are the first line of defense against further damage and injury. Often, where people are being hit by cars, locals team together and work with their city—or without it (see Tactical Urbanism, Rule 98)—to install temporary bulb-outs with paint and vertical posts until new pave-

Often, projects include both types of curb extension at once. The image at left shows a temporary intervention awaiting an eventual repaving, in which bulb-outs and intersection repair included the elimination of two slip lanes (see Rule 66). Moving curbs can be expensive, so it is often not possible to right-size intersections everywhere. Across the city, these interventions should be prioritized based on where people are most likely to walk, and most likely to get hit.

RULE 68: Surround curb parking at each corner with bulb-outs on all new streets with three or more driving lanes, and potentially on narrower streets. Use curb extensions at existing dangerous intersections to right-size the drivable area to the minimum needed for anticipated vehicle motions.

69 Use Roundabouts with Discretion

They are extremely safe; they're just not all that urban.

THE CITY OF CARMEL, IN, HAS MORE than 100 roundabouts. These have reduced injury accidents in this upscale Indianapolis suburb by more than 80% and do a tremendous job of handling large amounts of traffic. In fact, by acquiring the four-lane Keystone Parkway from the State DOT where it passes through Carmel, and constructing special "peanut" roundabouts at each of its off-ramps, the City was able to stop that road from being widened into a six-lane highway.

> *The modern roundabout is a great tool, as long as the intention is not to create or reinforce a sense of urban vitality.*

Of Carmel's many roundabouts, it is worth noting that only one of them sits on the city's Main Street, and that one at its western edge, where shops mix with single-family homes. Jim Brainard—in his sixth 4-year term as Carmel's mayor, and an international booster for round-

The roundabout at Sarasota's "Five Points" downtown.

abouts—understands that, as effective as they are, roundabouts are not exactly urban. They are great for increasing convenience and reducing car crashes in a largely suburban city, but they are not the ideal intersection for the center of a walkable shopping district.

The same lesson can be learned in Sarasota, FL where the City, not exactly following a downtown plan by DPZ,

Appropriate mostly to suburban settings, roundabouts force pedestrians trying to go straight to walk well off-axis.

vocabulary which is unavoidably *automotive*: they swoop. As discussed in Rule 66, this vocabulary communicates that the intersection is a place for cars more than people, however safe it may be.

The modern roundabout is a tremendous invention, in the right place. When two or more streets come together carrying a significant amount of traffic, and the goal is to process it effectively and safely—even with pedestrians around—they are a great tool, as long as the intention is not to create or reinforce a sense of urban vitality.

In this discussion, these modern roundabouts need to be distinguished from traffic circles and rotaries, which are generally big, threatening vehicle processing machines, and from proper urban circles like Dupont Circle in Washington DC and Monument Circle in Indianapolis, which are made walkable and urban by traditional surrounding intersections.

They are also distinct from a nice feature of Berkeley, Coral Gables, and elsewhere, where tiny planted circles have been dropped in the middle of existing intersections to slow the traffic through them. This feature finds its apotheosis in small southern cities, where a statue sits in the middle of a traditional main/main intersection. These are also good places for walking, as they don't take the pedestrian off axis.

Modern roundabouts are very safe. When there is a crash, you call the tow truck, not the ambulance. It can be said that they are the safest, most pedestrian-friendly *automotive* environment you can build.

keeps placing roundabouts along its Main Street. These are expensively built and lovely, but they do not enhance the downtown's sense of walkability, even as they make it safer. Why is this?

There are a number of features that make roundabouts feel less walkable than traditional intersections. First, they ask people who are trying to walk in a straight line to divert well to the side, and then back again, in order to keep moving across town. Second, while they require cars to slow and yield to pedestrians, vehicles never actually come to a full stop unless something is blocking them; roundabouts feel dynamic, and pedestrians prefer environments that are static. Third, they introduce into urban areas a design

---

RULE 69: Build modern roundabouts according to current best practices to solve problems of safety and/or congestion, but do not locate them in shopping districts and other places where pedestrian vitality is desired.

70 Do Not "Fix" Complexity

The most confusing intersections may be the safest.

IN *SUBURBAN NATION*, we told the story of Confusion Corner in Stuart, FL, a concatenation of seven streets and a railroad track:

> The state Department of Transportation was prepared to spend hundreds of thousands of dollars to reconfigure the entire area because their manuals suggested that it would be dangerous. Local citizens, however, defended their notorious intersection, the community's prime postcard-worthy location. Despite the intersection's reputation, studies revealed that it was among the region's safest major intersections, with only one accident in its multi-decade history. The deadliest local intersections were all the standard D.O.T. models.[210]

Since Confusion Corner, many other similar intersections have been brought to our attention. By now, it should be clear why such complex street configurations are typically safer: they elicit caution, which translates into slower, more attentive driving.

As might be expected, the traffic engineering manuals, with their blind spot toward the relationship between environment and behavior, argue against complexity. Engineering wisdom, translated into many a city's codes and design manuals, outlaws streets that meet at sharp angles, intersections that stagger, and classic five-point junctions. When one is designing new communities, these restrictions can pose a real impediment to creating unique and memorable loca-

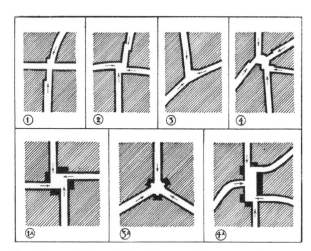

From Raymond Unwin's *Town Planning in Practice*, complex intersections create memorable locations.

Unconventional intersections (in this case, a Y) are useful for creating effectively terminated vistas.

tions, the sort of configurations that improve visitor orientation and establish a spatial hierarchy that awards pride of place to specific sites.

When done properly, as illustrated in Raymond Unwin's *Town Planning in Practice* of 1909, unconventional intersections create honorific sites for honorable buildings, those civic structures housing institutions valued by the community. These are placed at the end of long views—terminated vistas—to be visible from a distance, often on high points. At The Waters, a new community near Montgomery, AL, the designer Steve Mouzon forked a street around a hilltop that was reserved for the community chapel and meeting hall.

Intersection laws also often inhibit new plans from properly responding to a site's topography. When design-

ing the new town of Mount Laurel, outside of Birmingham (also Alabama), the DPZ planning team was initially limited to right-angle intersections on the site's sloping terrain. This County rule ignored the fact that Birmingham's historic hillside neighborhoods managed to avoid regrading by bringing streets together around small triangular greens. When applied to the Mount Laurel site, these forked intersections saved every tree not in the direct path of a road. In contrast, the re-grading required around each of the County's mandated 90° intersections would have led to a half-acre of clear cutting around every single one. Fortunately, many months of difficult negotiations eventually led to the project receiving the necessary variances.

RULE 70: Ensure that city codes and/or staff do not inhibit the construction of unconventional intersections.

71 Remove Centerlines on Neighborhood Streets

When a street loses its centerline, speeds drop approximately 7 mph.

HERE'S A USEFUL LITTLE ITEM. Our friends at the Ministry of Silly Driving (a.k.a. Transport for London) had been suspicious for some time that streets might be safer without a center stripe. The City had already enacted in 2009 a "Better Streets" policy that embraced the Dutch concept of Naked Streets (see Rule 77), and engineers in the department were hopeful that a "less is more" approach might apply to centerlines as well. Holding to the initially counterintuitive logic of Naked Streets, these engineers expected that centerlines are one of many road markings that can make drivers feel more confident, causing them to speed as a result.

The City repaved three two-lane regional roads without centerlines, and compared driver speeds before and after. The results did not disappoint: when adjusted for the not insignificant impact of fresh pavement—which notably

Before and after views of Brighton Road, London, which was repaved with no centerline, resulting in less speeding.

		CORRECTED CHANGE IN AVERAGE SPEED (MPH)
Seven Sisters Road	N/bound	-7.0
	S/bound	-8.6
Wickham Road	E/bound	-7.4
	W/bound	-7.5
Brighton Road	N/bound	-5.6
	S/bound	-5.4

Data from the three roads studied suggested an average nominal speed reduction of 6.9 mph.

tends to encourage speeding—drivers on the reconfigured streets slowed down about 7 mph on average.[211]

In the context of danger to people walking, 7 mph is a huge margin. At the speeds witnessed in this study, around 30 mph, a 7 mph reduction can cut the risk of death almost in half (see Rule 31).

As one considers driver behavior (see Rule 34), this study's outcomes are unsurprising. While making an effort to avoid conjecture, the authors suggest that some drivers "position their vehicles close to a white line regardless of the traffic conditions, believing it is their 'right' to be in that position. Centerline removal introduces an element of uncertainty which is reflected in lower speeds." They also note that the most conspicuous speed reductions occur when drivers see oncoming vehicles approaching.[212]

It turns out that this study was not the first of its kind. The authors note an earlier effort undertaken by the Wilshire County Council between 2003 and 2007, which found that resurfacing streets without centerlines led to not only lower speeds, but also fewer injury crashes. And prior research by the UK's independent Transport Research Laboratory had similar findings.[213]

Based on all this evidence, with no opposing data, it seems safe to conclude that streets without centerlines are safer. Any public works department that insists on keeping them, without substantial evidence to the contrary, is likely valuing convention over human lives.

A few notes deserve elaboration. First, the increased speeds caused by resurfacing are real, averaging 4.5 mph in this study. The implied instruction worth sharing here is that, unless a safer striping configuration is being introduced, it likely hurts safety to resurface a road before mandated by deteriorating pavement.

Second, the study's authors note that "not all roads would be suitable for removing central markings, particularly where the markings highlight a particular hazard." There are exceptions to every rule, but purported exceptions must be reviewed critically.

RULE 71: When repaving a two-lane, two-way street in an area where pedestrians are present, do not include a centerline without a site-specific justification.

72 Create Pedestrian Zones Properly

Start temporary and stay flexible.

MAKE NO MISTAKE: the best main streets, and the best city centers, have no cars. Being able to shop, stroll, dine on the sidewalk, and let your kids loose in an environment free of noise, exhaust, and the constant risk of death is truly a blessing. So is the culture that springs up around the *passegiata,* the early evening see-and-be-seen community stroll that can only take root when given ample space. For these reasons, creating car-free streets and zones in our towns and cities must be a goal and even a priority if we truly value walkability.

Unfortunately, this goal must be weighed against the hard facts presented in Rule 30. Depending on how you measure failure, between 85% and 95% of the roughly two hundred American main streets that were closed to cars in the twentieth century failed in short order. To avoid repeating that experience, we must create new pedestrian zones tentatively and reversibly—as already discussed—and we must take pains to get the details right.

An important first step in any such effort is to investigate what percentage of shoppers are arriving by car, and where they are parking. In places that seem to rely on curb parking in front, make an effort to locate nearby alterna-

tives, and prepare temporary wayfinding to direct people to them. In places where few customers drive, know that you can be much more aggressive, potentially even creating a large pedestrian zone like in Copenhagen. For example, in Manhattan, where curb parking plays almost no role in retail sales, it would be possible to remove cars from entire

Between 85% and 95% of the roughly two hundred American main streets that were closed to cars in the twentieth century failed in short order.

stretches of the city. The best candidate would seem to be the entirety of Broadway from 17th Street to 108th Street, where the street is redundant to the underlying urban grid.[214] Indeed, the only good argument against pedestrianizing these 90 blocks immediately is that they are already too successful.

In the doldrums for decades, Boston's Downtown Crossing has come back to life with a new, flexible streetscape.

The second step to pedestrianizing a street, as noted, is to close it temporarily. This should be done simply and cheaply, with a scattering of potted plants and small trees, and lightweight tables and chairs that people can move around as they please. Yes, a few will be stolen. . . so what?

When the evidence supports making the change more than temporary, focus on programming more than on design. Bring in the community stakeholders to create a shared vision for a "final" but ever-evolving outcome. Identify the institutions and individuals that will give it life. Determine the equipment needed to serve the desired activities, and locate it strategically. Keep the moveable chairs, but add some substantial street furniture and, where possible, more green. But in so doing, be sure not to create immovable barriers to cars, should things eventually not turn out as planned. This sort of layout also allows for easy servicing by trucks off hours.

And as success spreads, look to Europe, where many cities have pedestrian zones of substantial size. There are more than a handful of American cities that are walkable enough to have large pedestrian zones downtown, including Boston, New York, Philadelphia, Washington, Chicago, Portland, Seattle, and San Francisco.

A few other details need mentioning. Pedestrian main streets are more likely to succeed if they are crossed frequently by regular streets that provide them with cars, activity, and lots of corners. Since most city blocks are rectilinear and not square, this means that there is a good orientation (across the grain, like 3rd Street in Santa Monica) and a bad orientation (along the grain, like Main Street in Buffalo, before it failed and was reopened to cars). Once again, small blocks are better.

Finally, the best pedestrian streets are not bikeways or bus malls. Yes, pedestrians, bikes, and buses are all safer without cars around, but that doesn't mean that they are best together. A great pedestrian mall lets you sit down for drinks while the children roam.

RULE 72: Create or expand your downtown pedestrian zone, street by street as circumstances allow, with an eye to comparable models, best practices, and community-led programming.

Part XV

FOCUS ON INTERSECTIONS

AS THE PRINCIPAL PLACE where pedestrians must share the road with vehicles, intersections are at the heart of street safety; their design and management is literally a matter of life and death. Proper crosswalks are essential, with speed tables and other, more emphatic solutions warranted in dangerous locations.

Intersection signalization is a field that seems to have gone badly off-course over the past several decades. American cities tend to be over-signalized, and those signals tend to be overcomplicated. What used to be simple, short timing regimes have often become long, many-phase cycles that result in a lot of stalled walking. Pushbuttons, most of which seem not to trigger any result, compound pedestrian frustration. And many intersections that would be properly served by all-way stop signs have been signalized, resulting in a surprising rise in injuries and death.

These mistakes are not so difficult to reverse, and some cities are doing so. In Europe, many places are also experimenting with an even more ambitious alternative to overzealous signalization: *shared space,* in which slow-speed detailing allows pedestrians, bicycles, and vehicles to all mix safely in the absence of traffic controls. US cities are ready to try this technique as well.

73 | Make Great Crosswalks
Use best practices while also testing artistic solutions.

CROSSWALKS are such an important part of pedestrian safety, it is remarkable how little is known about them. The most influential studies about their safety have been discredited, and a new generation of experimentation worldwide would suggest that it is high time for more concerted review of what works and what doesn't. Here's what we seem to know so far.

Great damage was done to the safety of cities by a now-refuted 1972 study that concluded that pedestrians were less safe in crosswalks than in unmarked intersections.

Speed tables are best: If you can afford it, a built crosswalk is more effective than a painted one. A contrasting or textured surface like brick or cobble designates that a crosswalk belongs more to the realm of the pedestrian than the driver. Better yet is to lift the crosswalk up close to sidewalk height, so that the ramps occur not in the curbs but in the roads. In this case the crosswalk sits on a *speed table,* a raised area with gentle yet significant slopes that encourage drivers to approach them more slowly. An ideal intersection has a single speed table that encompasses all four crosswalks and the central area they surround. Of course, given the cost, this treatment should be reserved for truly special locations, such as a downtown's main/main crossing.

Visible crossings on all legs: Great damage was done to the safety of cities by a now-refuted 1972 study that concluded that pedestrians were less safe in crosswalks than in unmarked intersections.[215] Wrongheaded thinking about pedestrian behavior also led cities to stripe only certain legs of many intersections, on the false assumption that pedestrians would abandon their "desire lines" in order to cross in a more visible spot. After many more years of field observation, NACTO notes that "pedestrians are unlikely to comply with a 3-stage crossing and may put themselves in a dangerous situation as a result."[216] The current best practice standard for crosswalks is to place them on all desire lines across all intersections with significant traffic volume and/or speed.

Fresh and eye-catching: The biggest challenge with crosswalks is probably one of maintenance: to keep them visible. Whatever standard you select is meaningless if you don't repaint it when it fades, so a city's commitment to safety needs to be reflected in its maintenance schedule and paint budget. Beyond that, design is a subject of some controversy. All seem to agree that high-contrast "ladder" markings are the most effective standard treatment, but we have recently seen a foray into more creative solutions, producing a lot of excitement and a predictable backlash. With a number of cities introducing exciting crosswalk art programs, the Federal Highway Administration has cracked down, putting the kibosh on designs that deviate from the monochrome standard, potentially confusing means with ends. While nobody doubts that high-contrast is important, one wonders whether white paint is the only way to attract motorists' attention. It is time to investigate how well unique and artful crosswalks perform, given how much they contribute to a community's sense of place.

Bridges and tunnels don't work: For particularly nasty street crossings, the concept of pedestrian bridges and tunnels is often raised, usually by a DOT representative who would love to see pedestrians removed from the roadway, but occasionally by well-meaning citizens who have little experience with the sordid history of these facilities. Neither bridges nor tunnels have an admirable track

A jaw-dropping crosswalk in Iceland is theoretically not noticeable enough to pass muster in the US.[217]

record, especially in American cities, where they are usually sidestepped by people who would rather risk death than climb twenty-five stairs or submerge themselves in a urine-soaked gantlet of potential crime. The safety of a pedestrian in a street is principally a function of vehicle speed and opportunities for refuge. New York's Park Avenue and Chicago's Michigan Avenue teach us that even six lanes, properly designed, are no impediment to crossing at grade.

RULE 73: Build speed tables at especially important or dangerous intersections, and otherwise paint brightly contrasting ladder crosswalks on all desire lines. Experiment with and test novel artistic crosswalks as well. Do not build pedestrian bridges or tunnels.

74 | Keep Signals Simple

Most intersection signals should be concurrent and quick.

IT CAN BE VERY FRUSTRATING to be a pedestrian in Sydney. Standing at a street corner, you wait while the crossing traffic passes. Then you wait while cars coming at you turn right. Then you wait while cars coming from behind you turn left. Only then do you get the signal to enter the crosswalk, alongside cars traveling parallel to you that are not allowed to turn.

If properly designed, most urban intersections serving streets of reasonable width can and should be served by a simple two-phase signal cycle.

This six-cycle (or more) signalization regime can also be found in the United States. It is becoming more common for the obvious reason that it makes crossing streets safer by removing all opportunities for conflict. Most pedestrian crashes involve cars turning into people in crosswalks, and that theoretically never happens when each direction gets its own phase.

The same logic can be found behind that apotheosis of crossing safety, the *pedestrian scramble* intersection. In a pedestrian scramble, people walking are given free rein over the entire intersection, crossing diagonally if they like, but only after waiting for all cars to go about their business in all directions first.

Under either regime, walking around the city becomes an experience of standing more than walking, as what should be a 3-mph pace is slowed to perhaps half that speed. Walking becomes duller and less convenient, in the name of being safer. But it is really safer?

That is open to question. Is walking safer if pedestrians, frustrated from waiting, dash across the intersection against the light? Is it safer if people do the math, stop walking, and drive instead? And, while safety must remain the highest priority, can we not point out that, if safety makes walking inconvenient, there has been a failure in the street design?

Given all the factors that add up to a safer or less-safe crossing, there is no one-size-fits-all solution for how to

Pedestrian scramble intersections allow people to cross diagonally. . . after a very long wait.

best signalize an intersection. Clearly, there are intersections with extreme pedestrian volumes and diagonal desire lines, where a pedestrian scramble makes sense. There are also intersections that currently invite fast turns, where six-phase signal cycles make sense. But neither of these is common in a walkable city. If properly designed, most urban intersections serving streets of reasonable width can and should be served by a simple two-phase signal cycle. This is called *concurrent signalization.*

Under concurrent signalization, pedestrians get the walk sign when the cars next to them get the green. When you arrive at an intersection, if you can't cross in one direction, you can cross in the other; there is always a way to

walk. If your path across the city is diagonal to the grid—as most are—you may never need to stop. Instead of waiting 90 seconds for a pedestrian scramble, you cross right and then left (or left and then right) without any wait at all.

Current trends have cities installing six-phase signals and pedestrian scrambles in a lot of places where they just aren't necessary. The typical intersection in Boston is starting to feel like Sydney. As a result, a lot of parents in Boston are reluctantly teaching their children when to ignore the signal in order to jaywalk safely. It's a problem.

The ideal crossing signal is concurrent, and the ideal concurrent signal also includes something called an LPI—a Lead Pedestrian Interval. LPIs give crossing pedestrians a few-second head start before the green light, so that they can claim the intersection, causing cars to turn with much greater caution. LPIs are becoming common all across the United States, and have been used in New York City since 1975. A study of fourteen LPIs in New York found that they reduced the number of turning crashes by 28%, while reducing crash severity by 64%.[218] In response to these data, the City has installed more than 1,200 of them.[219]

Finally, signal cycles should be short, almost always 60 seconds or less, and sometimes as short as 30 seconds. Longer greens are more efficient—they move more cars—but they frustrate drivers with long waits, and make walking extremely ineffective.

RULE 74: Use concurrent signalization regimes at most intersections, reserving more complex solutions for unusual circumstances, and keep most signal cycles in the 30- to 60-second range. Apply Lead Pedestrian Intervals system-wide, prioritizing problem areas.

75

Bag the Beg Buttons and Countdown Clocks

Pedestrians shouldn't have to ask for a light.

PEDESTRIAN PUSHBUTTONS at intersections are almost always the wrong solution. How wrong depends on the type. Worst are the ones, often installed by DOTs, where you don't get a walk signal without pushing. The DOT can move more cars if nobody ever crosses, so these are common in places where the State or County has somehow ended up in charge of signals, including more than a few downtowns. Locals eventually get used to them, but visitors are quickly frustrated, and all pedestrians get the message pretty quickly that they are second-class citizens.

A survey of signals in Austin, Gainesville, and Syracuse found only one functioning pushbutton in those three cities.

The more one considers it, the more preposterous and offensive this situation reveals itself to be: people driving are automatically ushered through, while people walking have to beg for passage. Add to that the fact that people driving are generally wealthier than people walking, and that people driving are a great danger to people walking (and not vice versa) and a sad picture of a society's values begins to emerge.

Such signals only make sense in places where pedestrians almost never cross, and where the pedestrian crossing represents an additional phase and therefore can't be concurrent (see Rule 74); for example, at a midblock crossing in a long stretch of suburban highway. They never belong in downtowns.

The next worst type of pedestrian pushbutton is the type that does nothing at all. This would seem to be the vast majority. In New York City, all but 120 of the city's roughly 3,000 pushbuttons do exactly nothing. A survey of signals in Austin, Gainesville, and Syracuse found only one functioning pushbutton in those three cities.[220] Most of these are not placebos, but rather once-functioning buttons that have been deactivated.[221]

These should of course be removed ASAP, but they are probably no more annoying then the third worst type of pushbutton, the one that serves to lengthen a too-short crossing

L.A. conceptual artist Jason Eppink's take on the pedestrian pushbutton.

signal. These are a problem for several reasons. First, they do nothing to make the crossing signal come any faster, so they seem to be inactive, which leads to frustration and jaywalking. Second, because the signal comes no faster, locals tend not to push them, which means that many people cross during the short standard-length phase. This type of pushbutton also seems more preposterous the more one considers it. Why does it ever make sense to have a crossing signal of inadequate length? They, too, must be removed and replaced by simple automatic signals with proper timing to serve all users.

One type of pushbutton serves a purpose in urban places, and that's the kind that functions—instantaneously—to bring up a walk signal in locations where doing so will save lives. These make sense at busy mid-block crossings and other places where no vehicular signal is present, and are most effective if accompanied with a HAWK (High intensity Activated crossWalK) beacon and a raised crosswalk (see Rule 73). They are also a useful precaution at intersections where some outside circumstance invites rampant dangerous jaywalking. For example, in Brookline, MA, where people dash across speedy Beacon Street to catch the MBTA's Green Line trolley, an instantaneous walk signal provides commuters with a safe alternative to playing Frogger to catch the morning train.

A final related note on the unintended outcomes of good intentions pertains to another relatively new technology, pedestrian crossing countdown clocks. Anyone who drives in cities with these signals will tell you what its inventors should have realized: the rapidly ticking-off seconds, in addition to informing pedestrians of remaining crossing time, also encourage drivers to gun it to beat the light. A four-year study of 1,794 intersections in Toronto proved this out: pedestrian crashes dropped very slightly, while vehicular rear-end crashes jumped dramatically.[222] It would seem that the simple flashing orange hand is a safer solution.

RULE 75: Do not install pedestrian pushbuttons except those that are instantaneous and necessary to mitigate a hazard; remove all others. Do not install pedestrian countdown clocks.

76 Replace Signals with All-way Stops

In many places, stop signs are the safest solution.

FOR MANY YEARS, cities inserted traffic signals at their intersections as a matter of pride, with the sentiment that more signals made a place more modern and cosmopolitan. Recently, that dynamic has begun to change, as concerns about road safety have caused many to question whether signals are the best solution for intersections experiencing moderate traffic. Research now suggests that all-way stop signs, which ask motorists to approach each intersection as a negotiation, turn out to be much safer than signals.

Unlike with signals, no law-abiding driver ever passes an all-way stop sign at more than a very low speed, and there is considerable eye contact among users.

This greater safety has multiple causes. Unlike with signals, no law-abiding driver ever passes an all-way stop sign at more than a very low speed, and there is considerable eye contact among users. People walking and biking are generally waved through first. And nobody tries to beat the light.

While it would be useful to have more data, the main study on this subject, from Philadelphia, is compelling.[223] It recounts the 1978 removal of 462 traffic signals due to a 1977 state ruling disallowing signals at intersections with limited traffic. In almost all cases, the signals were replaced by all-way stop signs. The overall reduction in crashes was 24%. Severe injury crashes were reduced 62.5%. Severe pedestrian injury crashes were reduced by 68%.

While some pedestrians and drivers prefer signalized intersections, these data are too conclusive to ignore. Until a contradicting study is completed, cities should be compelled to conduct an audit of current signalization regimes to determine which signals may be eliminated.

When converting signals to stop signs, cities face the choice of two-way and all-way stops. Clearly, if one street contains tremendously more traffic than the other, a two-way stop makes more sense. However, there is no doubt that all-way stops should be used wherever they do not pose an undue burden, as they are 50% to 80% safer

As part of a walkability study, nineteen of Albuquerque's downtown traffic signals were deemed unnecessary. Nine have since been removed.

these reversions is signal reorientation. However, while signals are almost always required where multilane one-ways intersect, they are often not required where two-lane two-ways intersect. Moreover, when two-lane two-ways cross at a four-way stop sign, there is often no need or use for left-turn lanes, and that pavement can be used instead for parking or cycling.

A word is also needed about the driver experience that accompanies the replacement of signals with all-way stops. It is true that, compared to a network of signals, a network of stops signs result in a drive that is interrupted by more pauses. But these pauses are all quite brief. Never does the driver have to sit and wait for a light to turn from red to green. Such waits at signalized intersections are often 30 seconds long or longer, and, across a network, can add up to a lot of time wasted. Surprisingly, more stops can mean a quicker commute.

Finally, some air-quality advocates will argue against new stop signs due to the additional pollution caused by cars stopping and starting. This argument is accurate, but only in isolation, ignoring the smaller carbon footprint of more walkable places. As stop signs make places safer to walk, they can be expected to reduce overall driving, countering this impact.

There is no reason to conduct an expensive study on this subject. For each intersection with traffic that is moderate and fairly balanced, conduct a one-week test of an all-way stop configuration. If problems don't arise, make it permanent.

than two-ways.[224] Additionally, two-way stops hurt walkability, as they require people crossing the major street to dodge traffic. For this reason, it seems wise to leave signals in place in locations where an all-way stop is not justified.

One great byproduct of converting signals to stops is money saved: stop signs are much cheaper to install and maintain than signals. This fact is important to keep in mind as one considers the conversion of a downtown's streets from one-way to two-way. The principal cost of

RULE 76: Replace traffic signals with all-way stops at intersections without heavy traffic, unless mitigating circumstances demand otherwise.

77 | Build Naked Streets and Shared Spaces

The United States is ready for this technology.

COULD IT BE THAT, AFTER DECADES of discussion, Naked Streets and Shared Space may finally be coming to the United States? Washington, DC, is experimenting with them in its new The Wharf development; perhaps this will be the built example that planners can use to bring the concept elsewhere.

The number of collisions dropped from 4–7 serious crashes per year to none.

At is simplest, a naked street is a segment of roadway, ideally including an intersection, in which low-speed geometries are introduced and traffic-control devices removed in order to create an environment in which people, bikes, and motorized vehicles all mix comfortably at low speeds. Its principal inventor was the Dutch engineer, Hans Monderman, who found that he could make intersections safer by removing stripes and signs in order to create a condition of confusion. This initial confusion leads naturally to increased care and even courtesy.

The UK has been a leader in developing this technology. The mayor of London's *Better Streets* Policy, released in 2009, contains a number of suggested interventions to improve the City's streets. One of these is to "declutter," where highway authorities are challenged to:

> Justify each piece of equipment and obstruction with a presumption that it should be removed unless there is a clear case for retention. Look particularly carefully at the need for signs, posts, guard rails, bollards and road markings.[225]

When it comes to making a naked street that works for all users, however, removing clutter may not be enough. Other details are probably needed to ensure driving speeds slow enough to allow cars and pedestrians to mix safely. These include tighter dimensions, textured pavement like cobbles, and ideally the elimination of curbs, so that the street truly feels like a plaza. Instead of curbs and stripes, different colors and patterns of stone are used to indicate distinct areas for driving, walking, and parking. These features turn a naked street into a shared space.

Poynton, UK, before: heavy traffic, high speeds, and collisions.

Poynton, UK, after: smooth flow, low speeds, and safety.

Because of all the stonework, shared spaces don't come cheap. But, in some places, they are clearly worth the investment. In Poynton, UK, the main street was dying, sundered by a busy highway junction characterized by congestion, collisions, and truck exhaust. In the face of tremendous skepticism, local officials presided in 2011 over the first large shared space intervention in England. In the design, by Ben Hamilton-Baillie, signals, signage, and curbs were removed, replaced by a gentle mixing bowl paved like a plaza. The intersection now handles over 25,000 vehicles per day, with almost no congestion or crashes. The number of collisions has dropped from 4–7 serious crashes per year to none.[226]

More noticeably, the town has come back to life. Business has improved in the vast majority of stores.

The cost of reconstruction was £4M (roughly $6M).[227] Is it worth that much to turn a dying city around? Many regularly pay $10M for a new parking deck without batting an eye.

The Poynton story is well documented in the YouTube video *Poynton Regenerated.*[228] Particularly interesting to witness is how, with the new configuration, pedestrians feel free to cross everywhere at all times. As in the best urban places, "jaywalking" is the norm.

Similar reconstructions have been accomplished in Montreal and Mexico City. There are hundreds of main streets in the United States, overwhelmed by traffic, in which shared-space interventions seem worthy of investment.

RULE 77: Ask whether there is an opportunity for a true shared space in your city, and, if so, pursue the Poynton model.

Part XVI

MAKE SIDEWALKS RIGHT

IT MAY SEEM SURPRISING that, in a book about walkable cities, sidewalks only merit five rules. But the fact is that, in most cities, the sidewalks themselves are not a problem, and what most impacts walking is located on either side of them: dangerous roadways and unfriendly or missing buildings. Still, it is possible to screw a sidewalk up, and this section addresses what cities need to get right if that area between the street and the building is to help walkability rather than harm it.

Naturally, then, we begin with street trees, which are almost always central to making sidewalks safe, healthy, comfortable, and sustainable. The exceptions prove the rule: in North America, successful streets need trees, and lots of them. Beyond a tree zone against the curb—also ideal for dining—urban sidewalks must maintain adequate clear zones for walking and rolling, and frontage zones for entering buildings, where book tables and clothing racks are welcome. Curb cuts across sidewalks must be made illegal and, ideally, removed. And when a sidewalk needs more width, a new technology—the parklet—is available to serve that purpose at minimal cost.

78 Put Street Trees Almost Everywhere

There is no better use of public funds.

AMONG ALL THE HUNDREDS of physical assets that American cities do or don't invest in, none is as consistently undervalued as street trees. If our leaders were to understand their true worth, street trees would receive many multiples of their current funding. Communicating this worth has to be central to any campaign to improve walkability and urban vitality.

What makes street trees so valuable, and so essential? *Walkable City* dedicated a full chapter to this topic, and more evidence has been uncovered since.

Street trees protect sidewalks. Like parked cars, mature street trees form a sturdy barrier between moving vehicles and pedestrians. When viewed in perspective, a tight row of trees can almost feel like a wall between the sidewalk and the street.

Street trees reduce crashes. A study along Orlando's Colonial Drive compared a segment of roadway with street trees and other vertical objects along it to a segment without. It found that the segment with no trees experienced 45% more injurious crashes and many more fatal crashes: six vs. zero.[229]

Street trees shape space. As discussed in Rule 83, people are drawn to places with firm edges. Street trees can play a vital role of providing good spatial definition to public spaces that would otherwise feel poorly shaped. Also, people just like being around them.

Street trees absorb stormwater. A typical mature tree absorbs about the first half inch of each rainfall that hits it.[230] Many of our cities' costly and destructive Combined Sewage Overflow problems could have been avoided if we had planted more trees in the 1990s. Avoiding future problems means planting more now.

Street trees absorb UV and pollutants. In addition to keeping ultraviolet rays from reaching the ground, street trees absorb a tremendous amount of airborne carbon dioxide—ten times more than trees located farther from roadways.[231]

Street trees reduce urban heat islands. As the planet warms, heat waves have already begun to claim hundreds of lives daily in major cities. Street trees have been shown to create local temperature reductions as great as 15° Fahrenheit. The federal government reports that a single mature tree has the same cooling impact as "ten room size air conditioners operating 24 hours a day."[232]

Street trees protect the sidewalk in part because their presence causes cars to slow down. Sometimes abruptly.

Street trees improve property value. A study conducted by the Wharton School of Business found that street trees increase home prices by 9%.[233] Such improved valuations translate directly into increased property tax revenue. The City of Portland found that, for this reason, its investment in tree planting and maintenance pays off at a ratio of twelve to one.[234]

Street trees improve retail viability. From Nantucket to Beverly Hills, the most desirable Main Street districts in North America are, with few exceptions, characterized by consistently planted street trees. One study found that shops on streets with good tree cover earn 12% more income.[235] Visibility-seeking merchants who fight for tree removal forget that much main-street shopping is experienced-based. With cheaper prices and better convenience on Amazon, providing a great environment is becoming central to retail viability.

Street trees improve public health. Multiple studies have shown that regular exposure to trees prolongs life, aids mental health, reduces asthma, obesity, stress, and heart disease, and basically just makes us happier.[236] Along with urban cycling facilities, street trees represent a well-justified use of public health funds.

RULE 78: Launch a "Continuous Canopy Campaign" around planting trees citywide. Modify land development codes to require new streets to include not only sidewalks but also street trees along the curb. Allocate funding to tree planting and maintenance from city budgets for stormwater management, sustainability, and public health.

79 Select and Locate Street Trees Properly

It's easy to get street trees wrong; here are some important tips.

The right tree: Given their potential health and environmental impacts, street trees, even in shopping districts, should be selected for their capacity to grow large and hefty. In tight circumstances, taller and narrower, but still substantial, species should be chosen. Smaller flowering trees can be used to create a special experience on a unique street, but should remain an exception to the rule. Most palm trees are merely decorative, and should not find their way onto city tree lists unless your city has Palm in its name. Or you could change the name.

Be consistent: The best streets develop a unique character by containing the same tree planted consistently down their full length. While fear of blights like Dutch elm disease has led some cities away from this approach, the risk can be averted by planting similar-appearing but genetically distinct subspecies side by side.

Proper spacing: The objective with street trees is to achieve "arboring:" canopies that touch at maturity. This means ideally planting the tree at an on-center spacing distance no greater than its anticipated diameter. Tighter spacing works just fine, and even the broadest trees can be happily planted 40 feet apart; any farther is not adequate to line a street. The proper spacing for most urban trees is 30 feet on-center. Narrower species chosen due to a tight fit can be planted as closely as twenty feet on-center, budget permitting. One tree per parking space is a nice solution along a main street. Spacing should be as consistent as possible to create a legible rhythm.

Line 'em up: While not essential, aligning the trees on both sides of the street contributes markedly to the quality of place, as it helps arboring to occur over the roadway. When three or more rows of trees are used, as with a median, alignment becomes even more impactful. In tighter circumstances, an aligned diagonal stagger can be a good solution. The challenge is to design each street's tree cover in a way that imparts the greatest degree of rhythm and order to the street space.

Double allées: When sidewalks are wider than 20 feet, it often makes sense to insert a second row of trees on the inboard side of the walking zone. This solution, which can be seen on New York's Fifth Avenue against Central Park, costs a bit more, but pays off in multiples in creating places of value.

Build to the corner: When designing a block with street trees, the trees closest to the corners should be located

In tight spaces, a vertical species like ginkgo biloba can provide ample cover—and fall color.

about 10 feet from the crosswalk edge. City codes that push them farther away from intersections need to modify their sight-triangle requirements.

No medians without trees: A median with regularly spaced street trees contributes markedly to a street's safety, comfort, and beauty. A median without trees makes a street look and function like a highway. Municipal engineers must sometimes be reminded that the era of referring to trees as FHOs—Fixed and Hazardous Objects—is over.

Structural soil and pervious top: The conventional tree-pit is designed for failure. Best practices have advanced, and the proper foundation for an urban street tree is a continuous trench of structural soil—an engineered, root-friendly, load-bearing substrate of crushed stone and soil—that should sit beneath the entire sidewalk to a depth of about 3 feet.[237] This trench is well drained underneath, and topped with a pavement that, at least within the tree-zone, allows ample infiltration. Pavements built on structural soil cost more, but they allow trees to thrive without creating the sort of root heaves that create accessibility failures and demand expensive replacement.

RULE 79: On most streets, plant trees of a consistent large species in a regular pattern with a spacing distance of 20 to 40 feet, depending on the tree. Use double allées where they fit, and put trees in all medians. Place urban street trees in structural soil following current best practices.

80 Design Sidewalks Properly

It's easy to get sidewalks wrong; here are some important tips.

The right width: Suburban sidewalks should typically be 5 feet wide, 6 feet in places where a lot of walking is anticipated. In urban areas—including suburban shopping districts—this 6-foot measure should be maintained as a minimum clear zone, meaning that width for trees, placards,

> *The walkable city is the rollable city, and when a city works well for people in wheelchairs, it works well for everyone.*

tables, benches, and other furnishings must be provided in addition. As a result, the typical urban sidewalk is 12 feet wide or more, depending on the amount of foot traffic that is expected. In very busy places, like Manhattan's avenues, 20 feet is not even enough, but most city streets do not have enough activity to demand much more than 12 feet. One of the most popular sidewalks in the world, along Ocean Drive in Miami's South Beach, holds trees, tables, chairs, and gangs of strolling tourists in less than 16

feet. Observation might lead one to conclude that people enjoy a tight squeeze.

Sidewalk zones: Beyond the curb, urban sidewalks are properly designed to contain three zones, as follows:

- In the middle is the Clear Zone—what streets guru Dan Burden calls the "walk and talk zone"—at least 6 feet wide, to remain unobstructed for strolling and rolling. While nicer pavement solutions are welcome, this zone is appropriately paved in simple concrete scored into roughly 5-foot squares. (A mica admix can add a nice sparkle.)

- Against the street is the Tree Zone, typically 5 to 8 feet wide, which holds trees in pits (within a structural soil trench) and, between them, bike racks, benches, and other street furniture, as well as sidewalk dining if desired. Light poles and trash cans should be located toward the outside of this zone, about 18 inches from the curb. Benches should be placed perpendicular to the sidewalk, ideally in facing pairs about 6 feet apart. This zone is best surfaced in pervious pavers to admit rainwater into the tree trench, and to contrast with the Clear Zone.

- At the outer edge of the right-of-way is the Frontage Zone, typically 1 to 3 feet deep, understood as a transitional area between building fronts and pavement. It is the place for placards, book tables, clothing racks, more benches, and additional sidewalk dining—and also for leaning and hanging out. Its intention is to blur the distinction between shop and street, so that people feel a greater connection to retail. In Europe, this area is often paved with small cobbles, in part to facilitate changes to building facades. This is a nice touch, but unnecessary, and in most of the United States the scored concrete continues into this zone.

Hard granite curbs: Details matter, and conventional suburban curb details do not belong along urban sidewalks. Integrated curb-and-gutter solutions, where there is no hard angle between curb and street, increase the perception (and the likelihood) that a car may jump up onto the sidewalk. The proper configuration places a roughly 6-inch vertical curb edge directly against the street surface, without a contrasting gutter. And while concrete curbs are cheaper up front, multiple studies demonstrate that, when

With open restaurant fronts and tables on both sides of the "clear zone," Santana Row in San Jose has mastered sidewalk dining.

full lifecycle costs are taken into consideration, true granite curbing is ultimately no more expensive.[238]

ADA compliance: The walkable city is the rollable city, and when a city works well for people in wheelchairs, it works well for everyone. Ostensibly, the Americans with Disabilities Act provides for the needs of rolling walkers, requiring adequate clear zones, passable surfaces, and corner curb ramps on all sidewalks. Unfortunately, its implementation is sporadic, and many city streets still don't welcome wheelchair users, which means that they are also daunting to many elderly walkers as well as parents pushing strollers. Particularly as our population ages, cities that wish to be walkable need to place a higher priority on meeting their ADA obligations.

RULE 80: Provide sidewalks of appropriate width for their anticipated use, properly organized into Tree Zones, Clear Zones, and Frontage zones, and edged with vertical granite curbs. Implement ADA requirements with vigor.

81

Disallow Curb Cuts

Driveways across sidewalks don't belong in walkable districts.

EVERY DRIVEWAY that crosses a sidewalk presents a potential danger to people walking and biking who may be hit by a vehicle crossing their path. This danger makes the sidewalk feel less safe and comfortable, a feeling that is reinforced by the tilt of the driveway skirt and the missing curb. Additionally, curb cuts eliminate on-street parking that would otherwise protect the sidewalk edge, resulting in a visual widening of the street that encourages illegal speeds.

Fast-food and bank drive-throughs have no place in walkable districts.

That's not all. When trying to make a place more walkable, curb cuts threaten to derail many of the needed improvements, for several reasons. Adding curb parking to a street by right-sizing the number and width of driving lanes has little impact if the parking is removed for curb cuts. Bike lanes crossed by curb cuts are not as safe as they would be otherwise. Cycle tracks, where parked cars protect bike lanes from traffic, are especially undermined by curb cuts, which replace the parked car with a wide striped

buffer zone providing little protection. Finally, it is more challenging to plant street trees when the sidewalk is regularly interrupted by driveways.

The first step to addressing the curb cut problem in most cities is simply to stop allowing them, except for key facilities like parking structures. Fast-food and bank drive-throughs have no place in walkable districts. Nor do gas stations, car repair, and other auto-centric uses; put them out on the strip. While smaller hotels should be satisfied with curb drop-off in reserved parking spaces, sometimes developing downtowns cannot land a desired hotel without offering a dedicated porte-cochere; these should be located not at front, but off of an alley at the flank or rear. No other uses merit a dedicated driveway through an urban sidewalk.

New curb cuts should never be allowed for any use if the property is adjacent to a public alley that provides alternative access. When they are (rarely) allowed, curb cuts should be paved to match the sidewalk, and no larger than absolutely necessary. The conventional standard for a curb cut is two 12-foot lanes. These gaping maws invite cars to speed across the sidewalk. New curb cuts should be limited to 20 feet in width for any large parking lots need-

In downtown Tulsa, sidewalks that are continually violated by curb cuts do not feel safe to walk along.

ing two lanes, and 10 feet otherwise. Most cars are only 6 feet wide, after all.

But what do cities do about all the curb cuts they are already living with? No established best practice exists. In cities like Tulsa, where curb cuts were given away like candy for fifty years, it would seem that a dedicated and properly funded government effort is needed to close curb cuts along streets that are considered part of the walkable core.[239]

Such a program to eliminate unnecessary curb cuts would have to be structured in a way that acknowledges the cost to property owners, in time and effort, of closing these access points. Ideally, it would provide the following owner-assistance process:

- The property owner is notified of the upcoming curb replacement, and a meeting is requested. If the owner chooses not to meet, the curb is replaced without the owner's involvement.

- For cooperating owners, the City provides a design for reconfiguring owner's property, and executes the design, modified as necessary, with the owner's approval.

- In some cases, reconfiguring a property such as a parking lot will result in a net loss of interior parking spaces, representing a foregone revenue to the owner. This anticipated revenue would be calculated according to a standard formula as the net present value of future income, and paid in a lump sum to the owner as a subsidy.

If properly executed, this owner-assistance program could be funded principally from the additional revenue that the City would receive from new curb parking installed along the reconstructed curbs. Such a program is under consideration in downtown Tulsa and should be tested in other cities with similar challenges.

RULE 81: In would-be walkable districts, disallow all new curb cuts except for parking structures and hotel drop-offs lacking alley access. Limit curb cuts to 20 feet maximum for large parking lots, 10 feet otherwise, and pave them to match the sidewalk. Where needed, create a municipal program for eliminating existing curb cuts.

82 | Introduce Parklets
Hand-crafted decks are the cheap path to wider sidewalks.

HAVE YOU HEARD ABOUT PARK(ING) DAY?[240] On the third Friday of each September, people around the world reclaim parking spaces for humans, transforming what would normally be automobile storage into places for hanging out. Some are filled with benches and greenery, others become mini-playgrounds, bike corrals, or Astroturf putting greens. At the stroke of midnight, the asphalt creeps back into its rightful place. But must it?

Many cities have busy locations where the sidewalk is just not wide enough for all the uses that sidewalks can and should hold.

Both in response to Park(ing) Day and independently, many cities have begun to experiment with parking-space installations that are less than permanent but certainly more than temporary. Sometimes initiated privately, sometimes by the city itself, parking spaces are being reassigned to other uses, often sidewalk dining. In most cases, a wood

Five parklets installed on 75th St. on the South Side of Chicago have boosted sales and street life throughout a three-block corridor.

(or composite) deck is built level with the sidewalk, taking up one or two parking spaces. Because it is located directly adjacent to moving vehicles, this deck is usually built with thin planters or a solid rail on its outboard edge, which helps to calm traffic and protect people from it.

Many cities have busy locations where the sidewalk is just not wide enough for all the uses that sidewalks can and should hold. Sidewalk dining, street furniture, green-

The City of San Francisco has taken the lead in bringing parklets to its neighborhoods.

Some cities, like Cedar Rapids, IA, have taken on this job themselves. Others, like Boston, Seattle, and San Francisco, have launched programs enabling and expediting private enterprise. Given the limited cost of oversight, there is no reason why every mid-sized or larger city should not have a program like San Francisco's.

One impediment to proper parklets—and to tree-zone sidewalk dining in general—is that some states require sidewalk alcohol sales to be located in fenced-off cattle pens against the building facades. These statutes are based on an interesting theory, which is that if a lush is about to fall off the wagon, a three-foot wrought-iron baluster will keep him sober. Cities need to band together and petition their nanny states to delete preposterous rules of this type.

Finally, some cities charge businesses for the permission to build a parklet, in order to defray the cost of the program. Like charging for sidewalk dining permissions, such fees are foolish, as they create a deterrent to precisely the sort of activity that is likely to increase municipal revenue in the long run.

ery, bike racks, lending libraries—walkable cities want to have all of these things and more. For that reason, many communities consider expensive sidewalk widening projects that require new pavement, curbs, and stormwater facilities. It is no exaggeration to say that hundreds of towns and cities across the United States are currently waiting on federal or state funds for that purpose. Most wait in vain. And because curb parking is extremely valuable (see Rule 63) it is likely a mistake to widen a sidewalk continuously in a way that removes most parked cars. Far better to reassign a few spots and build a few cheap parklets where they can do the most good.

RULE 82: Create a Parklets Program in which businesses are encouraged to build sidewalk extensions and led through an expedited approvals process informed by best practices. Consider building additional parklets at city expense where wider sidewalks are needed.

Part XVII

MAKE COMFORTABLE SPACES

MOST PEOPLE WITH A CHOICE will not choose to walk unless the walk is both useful and safe, the subject of the previous sections. But they will also avoid walking if they do not find their path comfortable, which is a different thing altogether, considerably more subtle, and a bit counterintuitive.

Pedestrian comfort is principally a function of *spatial definition*—how places are shaped—and is also influenced by light, both natural and manmade. While the twin goals of good edges and good lighting occasionally find themselves in conflict, much is known about how to balance them to best effect.

Finally, pedestrians do not feel comfortable in landscapes that have been too obviously hardened against the threat of terror; such measures can be as counterproductive as they are expensive.

83

Make Firm Edges

Design spaces as outdoor living rooms.

PICTURED BELOW IS THE SORT OF SCENE that Europeans put on travel posters to lure us to spend our vacations and our hard-earned dollars in Europe. And it works, because these places satisfy deep-seated unconscious cravings about our physical environment. Evolutionary biologists tell us that all animals—humans among them—simultaneously seek *prospect* and *refuge. Prospect* allows you to see your predators as they approach, while *refuge* protects your flanks from attack. If your flanks are not protected, you do not feel safe, and the space becomes *sociofugal*—you want to flee it.

The desire for refuge is why good plazas need good edges, and why excellent streetwalls allow a space to become a place. Urban designers talk about spatial definition and the goal of creating streets and other public spaces as "outdoor living rooms." Living rooms have walls.

The location of those walls, and their proper height relative to the width of the space, is a subject that has been under discussion for centuries. Until cold and dark become a problem, the larger the height-to-width ratio, the better. As illustrated in DPZ's *Lexicon of the New*

Urbanism (at right), many consider 1:1—the Renaissance ideal—to be the best for streets, while, beyond 1:6, the sense of spatial definition may be lost. [241] Even 5:1 can be lovely; think medieval Salzburg, farther north than Montreal. Also visible in the DPZ diagram is how, in the absence of an adequate ratio, street trees can compensate by necking down the space.

Plazas are only as good as their edges.

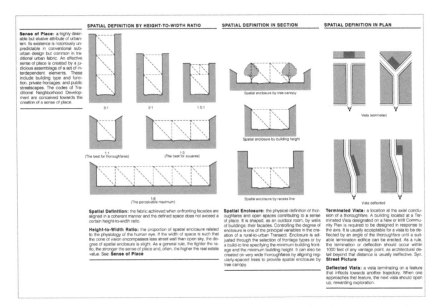

From the Lexicon of New Urbanism: Height-to-width ratio has a profound impact on spatial definition.

But viewing these ratios in cross-section is actually less meaningful than in plan, because the problem to be found in most North American cities is not buildings of inadequate height but streets of inadequate buildings: the "missing teeth" that come from an empty parcel or a surface parking lot. These two are usually one and the same, as property-owners quickly learn that a parking lot is the best way to land-bank at a profit. Whenever an urban streetwall is eroded by such an undeveloped site, its sense of enclosure is lost, and walkability suffers.

After four decades of teardowns—led by the misguided *urban removal* strategies of the 1960s, and eventually stanched by Jane Jacobs and her followers—most cities no longer allow surface parking lots to replace historical buildings in their city centers. Most but not all: as of this writing, Springfield, MA, is poised to allow such a teardown at a key downtown corner, and one can't help but mourn those cities that have not yet learned this lesson. They will get worse before they get better.

For those that have learned, the key question becomes how to fill all the existing missing teeth, and there are a bunch of good answers. Washington, DC, taxes vacant property at a considerably higher rate than the same land with buildings. It also maintains strict height limits that have caused development to spread out onto more land. Rather than towers next to parking lots—historically the Dallas model—midrise buildings fill every block.

And of course, cities can encourage the development of empty lots through expedited permitting, tax increment financing, and other means, including plain old subsidy. The question then becomes which missing teeth deserve filling first, a topic to be covered in Rules 95 and 96.

RULE 83: Approach urban design with an understanding that streets and public spaces generally need good edges to succeed.

84

Never Allow Front Parking

Embrace the sidewalk with building fronts.

ONE OF THE EARLIEST BOOKS to come out of the New Urbanist movement was *City Comforts*, by David Sucher. It begins with three crucial rules for creating community. Rule #1: "Build to the sidewalk."[242] While it takes more than three rules to make great places—how does 101 sound?—it is hard to imagine a better place to start. Because when it comes to destroying walkability, the front parking lot is probably the most common and the most impactful error that cities make.

Front parking lots do five bad things simultaneously.

Case in point, Over-the-Rhine in Cincinnati: 1,200 feet of continuous revitalization along Vine Street after a two-way reversion in 1999 (see Rule 38), stopped in its tracks after three full blocks by a Kroger Deli parking lot. Shoppers and diners stroll north from downtown, hit this beauty—with a mere fifteen spots—and turn on their heels. As of this writing, the buildings to the north, 100 feet from bustling vitality, are still boarded up.

Similar mistakes can be found along more North American main streets than it is possible to count. Some time around 1960, the suburban auto-age Quickie Mart was allowed to invade the downtown, and things went south from there. The ugly, plastic, fluorescent-glowing storefront added insult to injury, but the real culprit was the parking in front.

Front parking lots do five bad things simultaneously. They push buildings back from the street, destroying its spatial definition. They put store windows out of view, making the walk less interesting. They create curb cuts across the sidewalk, undermining its comfort and safety (see Rule 81). They allow patrons to park directly in front of businesses, depopulating sidewalks of strolling shoppers. And they send a not-so-subtle message that the store is meant to serve motorists—who could be from anywhere—rather than locals.

Most cities' planning departments understand that front parking is a blight, but that does not mean it is not allowed. A common struggle is with Walgreens or Rite Aid, whose standard store plans presume front parking, typically right at the corner, where spatial definition is most needed. Happily, these merchants have shown a willing-

The parking lot that stalled redevelopment on Vine Street in Over-the-Rhine.

ness to be flexible—in those cities that insist. The proper solution involves a parking lot that is one bay wide (double head-in in 60 feet) that wraps around the back two sides of a building that sits on the corner.

This result still places gaps in the streetscape while introducing two curb cuts, but it is vastly superior to the alternative. If the curb cuts are paved to match the sidewalk, and the parking lot edged by decorative walls, the impact is limited.

Cities that wish to ensure a positive outcome must be specific in their codes. All good new urban development ordinances outlaw front parking lots. Most also stipulate that stores may have secondary doors facing their rear parking, as long as they have front doors on the sidewalk. But very few remember to require that the front doors be kept open during store hours. This was the problem in Birmingham, MI, which over a decade transformed its downtown from auto-oriented to "walker's paradise" following a DPZ plan. One glitch was a large jeweler who followed the plan to a T but kept their sidewalk doors locked.

Shifting back to urban, walkable development patterns from conventional suburban models has been a struggle, especially in suburbia. The first step has always been—and remains—reorienting buildings to the street.

RULE 84: Do not allow front parking lots, and require businesses with rear or side parking lots to place their primary entrance at front.

85 Build Vancouver Urbanism

Skinny towers on broad bases make great streets and skylines.

THE LARGE CITY WITH THE HIGHEST quality of life on this continent is undisputedly Vancouver. In the 2017 Mercer Quality of Life Ranking, it finished fifth in the world, and ten spots ahead of its closest North American competitor, Toronto. How it achieved this status is a valuable lesson in all the things, large and small, planning can do to make better places.

It all began with a late-1960s citizens' revolt, let by architecture professors, to kill a proposed highway. This success resulted in Vancouver being the only large North American city without a single freeway within its boundaries.[243] Given the devastation wrought by American urban highways, that may have been enough, but the City went on to make a series of additional decisions out of the good-planning handbook, including building great parks, investing heavily in transit and bicycle infrastructure, enforcing mixed use, actively encouraging downtown housing density, removing parking minimums, and establishing tight urban design guidelines. As an outcome of these efforts, fully half of all trips citywide are by foot, bike, or transit.

The last category, urban design, may be the most interesting, because it presents a model that is now almost unique, and of great value. In order to bring high densities of housing downtown in a way that would not destroy view corridors or enshroud city streets in darkness, city planners looked to recent British reforms in Hong Kong and imported a standard that balances prospect and refuge. First introduced in the New York "light and air" codes of 1916—and then forgotten—this standard encourages buildings to fill their blocks, properly shaping city streets, but then step back dramatically above a certain height to rise to the heavens in skinny towers.

The result is remarkable: street after street of great urbanism, ample light, and thousands upon thousands of apartments that can be sold on their views. Because while fat American slabs block sight angles and cast huge shadows, skinny Vancouver towers do something better than having no towers at all: they make a skyline. For most residents, one reason to live on a high floor is to have a better view—of the other towers.

The details can vary. What counts is that the building bases set back from sidewalks only where specific urban places, like plazas and entry courts, are desired, and that the transition to skinny tower happens at a height that is appro-

The remarkable Vancouver skyline arises from some very specific codes.

priate to the width of the street. It would seem wise to aim for a 1:1 height:width ratio, resulting in bases five to eight stories tall on most streets. The skinny towers should then be set toward the middle of the block, and built as tall as possible.

The Vancouver model is beginning to make some headway in New York and San Diego, but it has naturally been slow to arrive in American cites that do not require it. Developers would much rather build fat slabs; conventional suburban office tenants require it, and apartments are cheaper when there are more per floor. Most developers will tell you that a skinny tower requirement would bankrupt them. This is true in the context of what the word "bankrupt" means to developers, which is roughly: "I'll make less money than I promised my investors."

In this regard, Vancouver urbanism is like inclusionary zoning: it is viable, and reasonable, only when it applies to all. If developers want to build towers, and all towers must be skinny, they'll build skinny towers. But if loopholes exist, exceptions abound, or the requirement seems temporary, the result could be an unintentional moratorium or worse.

RULE 85: Limit tall buildings consistently to the Vancouver model: broad, block-filling bases below towers with small footprints.

86 Use Lighting to Support Urbanism
Reject uniform standards for place-based solutions.

AT NIGHT, SPACE IS MADE BY LIGHT. In all cities, especially northern ones, much of the time that people spend in public is after dark. The great success of winter placemaking in cities like Montreal, Edinburgh, and Copenhagen shows us the impact that great exterior lighting can have on the walkability and livability of our communities. Getting it right benefits from paying attention to the criteria that follow.

Only in auto-centric environments should the objective be to maximize coverage per dollar with bright standards and tall poles.

Attraction, not coverage: North American urbanism was struck a blow in the latter twentieth century by a crime-avoidance lighting strategy that insisted the path to safety was a scorched-earth campaign of uniform coverage. Still, many cities control development with guidelines that mandate minimum lighting levels in all locations.

These rules work against the creation of places of distinct character, but may also subvert their own ends by creating unpleasant environments that repel pedestrians. Safety comes not from brightness, but from population, and a place that fails to attract people due to its harsh lighting will become more dangerous. Moreover, the goal of uniform coverage, on a budget, has led to the proliferation of tall street lights spaced far apart, a solution at home on highways but not in character with walkable neighborhoods. In cities, uniform coverage requirements belong in parking lots, not in potentially walkable streets.

A range of solutions based on place: The choice of the light itself (called a "standard"), its placement in a space, and the height and frequency of the light poles are the primary variables that can and should be adjusted to achieve the desired effect. Only in auto-centric environments should the objective be to maximize coverage per dollar with bright standards and tall poles. Otherwise, the solution should respond to two principal conditions: where does the site sit on the rural-to-urban continuum (called the "Transect" by planners), and is it a retail location?

Sustainable, transect-based standards: To minimize energy use and light pollution, all standards used should be LED or MIL with zero uplighting. The spectrum of the light should be close to incandescent, to create a welcoming glow, avoiding a sodium yellow, mercury blue, or fluorescent white effect. The design of the fixture itself should correspond to Transect location; some fixtures have a history of urban use and others, rural use, and that history should be respected.

Light location and frequency: Light poles should almost always be placed about 18 inches from the edge of the roadway. In walkable environments, poles should be between 10 and 14 feet tall, and no taller, to support an intimate feel. While it is difficult to set generic criteria regarding frequency, it is not unusual for rural and truly suburban locations to limit light poles to corners only. As suburban works its way to urban, frequency increases to perhaps every 50 feet. In shopping districts, street lights may even be provided as close as 20 feet apart, to create a more decorative effect. Another attractive solution for urban environments, especially narrow streets and alleys, is to hang lights over the center of the right-of-way on criss-crossing wires.

Alternative lighting: The best sidewalks for shopping are lit primarily by the flanking buildings themselves: spotlights, wall-washers, and decorative lighting make the streetwalls glow, and window displays bathe the sidewalk in colorful light. To the degree that such private lighting can be counted on, street lights themselves become less important. Some main

Denver's Larimer Square didn't get that much attention until the lights went in.

street merchants' associations require stores to keep windows low-lit after hours, to enhance feelings of safety.

Decorative lighting: Do not underestimate the value of decorative lights in contributing to the success of retail or even strictly residential environments. Holiday lights are nice, but many communities have opted for the year-round celebratory feel that comes from strings of mostly white lights arranged creatively around a space. The oldest commercial block in the city, Denver's Larimer Square is a great testament to the power of historic preservation, but most people go there for the canopy of lights that merchants wisely added in the 1990s.

RULE 86: Eliminate minimum-light-coverage requirements in would-be walkable places. Use zero-uplight, low-energy standards placed on moderate-height poles just behind the curb. Determine standard and frequency based on the location's degree of urbanity. Get creative with alternative and decorative light sources.

87 | Don't Let Terrorists Design Your City
The anti-terror landscape is a bad investment.

THE SCENE IS DEVASTATING: a terrorist plows a pickup truck down a Manhattan bike path, killing eight people and injuring almost a dozen more. The public demands a government response, and Mayor De Blasio rises to the occasion, immediately budgeting $50 million for new vehicle barriers around the city, including funding for 1,500 steel bollards costing $30,000 apiece. [244]

While people are still on edge, this commitment is largely met with approval, and a feeling that "our leaders are working to keep us safe." But there remains in the air a general sense that something is amiss. While it is hard to think rationally about terrorism, a cool-headed analysis of the terror threat in our cities leads to some difficult conclusions that could dramatically impact our policies and practices.

A bloody death is a bloody death. Somehow, when a death is intentional, and an "accident" is instead a murder, preventing its recurrence becomes inordinately worthy of public funding—especially if the perpetrators are brown. But those who have personally witnessed a fatal car crash will confirm that the anguish, trauma, and tragic repercussions are no less than what accompanies any other violent death. A rational public safety policy would treat all lives as equal. Remarkably, taxpayers invested less than $22,000 per victim to put an end to the 186 car-crash deaths on Queens Boulevard (see Rule 32), while so far allocating approximately $1.7 billion per victim to avenge 9/11. [245] This discrepancy deserves our attention.

Terrorism is statistically insignificant. There are different ways to do the math, but an objective accounting of several decades of data suggests that you are 568 times less likely to die in a terror attack than a car crash. Fewer people were killed in the New York truck attack than have died in traffic practically every two weeks subsequent. A proper epidemiological approach to public health and safety would allocate resources proportionally to the dangers they address.

There is always a soft target. It is impossible to harden an entire city. This fact is perhaps the greatest source of cognitive dissonance surrounding New York's bollard campaign. For every bike path and sidewalk newly protected, there will remain hundreds exposed. If all public spaces receive bollards—an impossibility—a terrorist need only take an AR-15 to a hotel room window. In this way, we are doomed to be always protecting against the last attack

On Wall Street, aggressive barriers undermine the unifying benefits of a well-designed and embracing public realm.

instead of the next, and misspending millions on what is effectively "security theater."[246]

The anti-terror landscape is terrifying. The purpose of terrorism is not principally to hurt people, but to cause panic and to unravel the social fabric. In that regard, a built environment that loudly proclaims the expectation of attack is in itself a form of terrorism, inciting fear, uncertainty, and suspicion of one's fellow man. Just like subway stop-and-frisks and a constant barrage of "See something, say something" messages, explicitly hardened public spaces are best understood as artifacts of a complicit terror-industrial complex that profits by keeping us scared. The fact that most actors in this drama are well-meaning should not distract us from resisting its grip.

Bollards can be nice. In *Cities for People,* the Danish planner Jan Gehl notes how most people enjoying Siena's Piazza del Campo choose to linger near the large stone bollards that surround the space.[247] Bollards are traditional street furniture and, if designed well, need not participate in a terrorist threat that they may be naively responding to. If De Blasio's bollards are attractive, well crafted, and well-located, they can become a positive feature of the spaces that they inhabit, rather than a permanent emblem of our panic, concrete evidence that the terrorists are winning.

But they are still money wasted. Public safety dollars can instead be spent in a way that has a real impact. With a limited investment, child traffic deaths in the Netherlands went from more than 400 in 1971 to just 14 in 2010.[248] A small fraction of our current anti-terror budgets, transferred to road safety, would save thousands of lives.

RULE 87: Resist the compulsion to throw money away on anti-terror infrastructure, speaking honestly about risk, effectiveness, and proven paths to better public safety. Redirect funding accordingly, to street redesign.

Part XVIII

MAKE INTERESTING PLACES

IF A PLACE IS TO ATTRACT PEDESTRIANS, it must make walking useful, safe, and comfortable. But that is not enough; the walk must also be interesting. Pedestrians demand to be entertained, and a walk that turns out to be boring tends not to be repeated by those who have a choice.

Humans are social primates, and nothing interests us more than other humans. The most interesting spaces are full of people, and those that aren't need to be full of signs of humanity. These signs include windows, balconies, doors, stoops, and porches that might hold or disgorge a human. They also include indications of the human scale and the human touch. A big part of making buildings interesting is to make them less repetitive and, where appropriate, to break them into smaller parts, so that they seem to be the work of many hands. Preserving historic structures can also be essential to keeping places interesting.

It goes without saying—but not without regulating—that exposed parking structures and blank walls must be kept away from would-be walkable areas. Mistakes are made, however, and public artwork can be a great remedial tool for salvaging problem areas from what Jane Jacobs called "the great blight of dullness."

88 Make Sticky Edges

Energize public spaces with active, deep facades.

IN JAN GEHL'S CLASSIC *Cities for People,* the index contains thirty-six distinct entries under the term "edges." Gehl understands—and has helped us to understand—how the quality of a place's perimeter is largely responsible

Codes should require that long facades in would-be walkable areas provide vertical members at their lower stories.

for its success or failure as public space. He uses the term "soft edges" to describe the objective, noting that people almost always linger at the perimeter of a space rather than the center, but that the most successful edges offer more than a blank wall or a sheet of mirror glass.[249] The best do two things well: they are *active,* and they are *thick.*

Active Facades

Active facades provide the street with interest and energy. In terms of what can be written into city codes, these quali-

ties translate into percentage of openings, rhythm, and limited repetition:

- The bluntest instrument for avoiding blank walls is a minimum openings percentage. In its "active facade" zones, the City of Melbourne sets a minimum of 60%,[250] which is appropriate to retail uses. Residential facades can have a minimum closer to 25%, to allow punched openings, but this rule should be tied to a "no blank walls" requirement that demands a window or door every 10 feet or less on each story.

- Rhythm is provided by buildings having vertical rather than horizontal articulation. The ribbon window of early modernism does many things, but it does not support an interesting walk, as it stretches out distances and provides no articulation as you move past. Codes should require that long facades in would-be walkable areas provide vertical members at their lower stories.

- Limited repetition is provided by encouraging small

increments of development and, where that is not possible, breaking up long buildings into distinct segments. This specific practice is described ahead under Rule 90.

Thick Facades

What makes a potential shopper more likely to enter a store? What makes a resident more likely to interact with passers-by? What makes pedestrians more likely to stop and hang out for a while? All these questions have the same answer: robust transition zones between the insides and the outsides of buildings, architectural features that attenuate the path from public to private. In shorthand, these can be called thick facades. Thick facades take the following forms.

Front porches enable neighborly interactions that simply would not happen otherwise.

- *Retail:* Sidewalk dining, benches against facades, placards and merchandise in the frontage zone (see Rule 80), entry alcoves flanked by display windows, roll-up and other wide-open warm-weather facades, arcades, window counters and window bars (the drinking kind), upstairs balconies, and other overhangs abound; most retail facades should have some form of awning. The goal is to blur the distinction between the shop and the sidewalk.

- *Residential:* Short setbacks, front porches and stoops, bay windows, balconies, and active front-yard gardens abound. A new best-practice among skilled multifamily developers is to make first-floor apartments look like rowhouses by giving them stoops and front doors, even though they may still be hallway-served.

- *Office:* First-floor offices in would-be walkable locations are always a challenge. Where possible, they should be given transitional spaces like bay windows and porches against the sidewalk, similar to residential uses. But a better approach, one becoming favored among office tenants, is to forego the large glamorous lobby in favor of leasing out as much space as possible to amenity retail such as restaurants and coffee houses, which can provide proper storefronts instead.

RULE 88: Achieve active and thick facades through requirements and/or incentives for minimum openings, vertical articulation, variety, awnings, stoops, porches, balconies, bay windows, entry alcoves, and other semipublic attachments.

89 Limit Repetition

Break large projects into collections of unique buildings by different architects.

NO MATTER HOW WELCOMING a building facade is, nobody wants to walk past 300 feet of it. That's more than a minute of the exact same thing. Unless the ground floor is made up of shops or individual stoops, more than a few dozen feet of the same facade treatment gets boring. It also suggests a scale of development that is inhuman, a message that, while unfortunately accurate, is best hidden for the sake of walkability.[251]

Modern development practice, with its large infusions of capital, naturally leads to problems of both scale and repetition.

Fast, large-scale development is a sad fact of contemporary real estate practice. When building big projects, most developers find it easier to hire a single architect. Then the trouble begins. Intellectual honesty, ego, and budget all point to the same outcome: a single huge building, or the same smaller building repeated. The hand of the singular architect is visible throughout, so travel along the edges of the building provides no variation or surprise. The walk, unrewarded, is less likely to be taken. As Jane Jacobs noted, "Almost nobody travels willingly from sameness to sameness and repetition to repetition, even if the physical effort required is trivial."[252]

Zaha Hadid's Sky Park in Bratislava creates an artistic statement at the expense of variety.

In Miami Beach's Aqua neighborhood, the design of a collection of rowhouses and midrise buildings was distributed to nine different architects.

Modern development practice, with its large infusions of capital, naturally leads to problems of both scale and repetition. Scale is an easier issue to address: building codes should require developers to break their large projects down into smaller buildings. Avoiding repetition, however, is more difficult to legislate through codes, so it is best perpetrated by city staff on a day-to-day basis, through encouragement and cajoling.

The best approach, by far, is to distribute the buildings to a collection of different architects. It's more work, but developers should be reminded that the most sophisticated builders take this path of their own volition. They understand that architectural variety contributes to a sense of place, which enhances real estate value.

There are other advantages to sharing a project among multiple design firms. A healthy sense of competition prevails, and no one firm becomes overwhelmed with work, or lazy in the confidence of a huge payday. And when an architect makes an error, like choosing the wrong sealant, it impacts one building and not a half dozen.

RULE 89: To create human scale and variety, break large design programs into multiple smaller buildings, and assign each building a different architect.

90 | Break Up Big Buildings

Use demise lines to make big buildings smaller.

DIVVYING UP THE DESIGN of multiple buildings is easy, but what about individual buildings that are too large? Clearly, civic buildings, monumental skyscrapers, and other iconic structures benefit from having a single master architect who imposes a unified vision. But most big buildings are neither civic nor monumental; they're just

At Assembly Row in Somerville, MA, demise lines break a single large building into a collection of smaller ones.

big. Many cities are currently witnessing the construction of block-long buildings—most often housing—on blocks that are as much as 600 feet long. These are especially common in urbanizing suburbs where blocks are intentionally built large in order to hide central parking lots.

For some time now, savvy developers have been taking advantage of a concept called the "demise line" to break up the scale of these larger buildings. A demise line is an artificial vertical boundary that breaks a facade conceptually into several smaller units. There is as yet no theory of demise lines nor literature of demise lines, but they are used often, and most often without much skill. If they are to be effective at reducing scale and creating places of character, demise lines need to follow a number of simple rules. These are roughly as follows:

1. Try to be convincing. The goal is to create a sense of authentic development of distinct buildings designed by different architects.

2. Create a demise line map that reflects the historical sizes of buildings in the area, and places bigger "buildings" facing bigger spaces.

3. Do not repeat similar "buildings" within sight of each other.

4. Make "buildings" that are themselves simple. Each building facade should be made of a limited number of materials, four at most.

5. Cornices, string courses, and other horizontal features should not exactly align.

6. The following things should be clearly different on adjacent "buildings":

   • Wall material or color.

   • Windows: spacing, shape, muntin pattern, and location in wall.

   • Other details like dormers, balconies, and shutters.

Basically, the mandate is to be on the lookout for giveaways.

7. Demise lines should be accompanied by a change in building setback only when doing so makes sense as an urban design (space-making) strategy. Otherwise, unnecessarily wiggling undermines the street space.

8. Very important and often forgotten, each "building" facade should look proper if isolated as a stand-alone structure, without neighbors. This means that the facade is a clear, balanced composition with a proper center and edges.

The ideal way for a developer to achieve a convincing demise-line outcome is to hire different design architects for adjacent facades, and then coordinate them with a single architect of record. However, this work can be avoided if one architect can be found who possesses the rare skill of having different design "hands." In that regard, the burden of proof lies on the architect. Can she make different facades appear to be the work of different designers? If not, that's strike one, and the architect should be asked to distribute the facades to different designers in her firm, who are asked to work independently. If that fails: strike two. There is no strike three; at this point, the architect must give up some or all of the job.

Architects are often uncomfortable with the concept of demise lines, because they are essentially a lie. They misrepresent the huge buildings behind them, and dishonestly reduce the scale of buildings that should be smaller. As such, they can be considered a white lie, necessary to keep people from feeling bad. They should be required on private buildings that otherwise threaten to create a monotonous streetscape.

RULE 90: Design the facades of oversize buildings to look like a collection of smaller structures built independently.

91 | Save Those Buildings
Historic fabric helps more than just walkability.

WHATEVER STYLES OF ARCHITECTURE you may prefer, there is no denying that fine materials, skilled craftsmanship, and detailed handiwork make a place more interesting. These qualities, which can be found in rare pieces of contemporary architecture, are present in most buildings built before World War II. Old buildings also make walking more meaningful by connecting us to our past,

As of this writing, Notre Dame des Canadiens in Worcester, MA, is slated for demolition.

our ancestors, and to the lost institutions that shaped our inherited culture.

As mass production and the spread of corporate chains distributes a collection of identical stores, hotels, and offices everywhere, and as global media quickly transform each new architectural style into an international style, both lowbrow and highbrow design conspire to turn every place into anyplace. Travel loses its reward. More and more, against this landscape of increasing homogeneity, it is principally a community's prewar buildings that serve to distinguish it from everywhere else and make it worth visiting, or perhaps worth calling home.

On these grounds, historic preservation, important for so many reasons, becomes justified on financial terms alone. The economist Donovan Rypkema reminds us that, in market economies, it is the differentiated product that commands a monetary premium. This is why cities like Savannah and Miami Beach can point to historic preservation as the key ingredient in their late twentieth-century recoveries.

In recent years, the preservation community has wisely become less focused on historic buildings and more focused on historic districts. The National Trust for Historic

Preservation, which once kept a list of America's most endangered buildings, now keeps track of "America's 11 most endangered places." They do this both to acknowledge how buildings are principally useful in the way that they contribute to making places, but also to hammer home some powerful findings about how historic districts perform socially, economically, and environmentally.

As Jane Jacobs taught us, new ideas need old buildings.

These findings arose from a Trust study comparing the performance of older and newer sectors of American cites. Starting in Washington, DC, San Francisco, and Seattle, data scientists performed a geospatial statistical regression analysis of comparable mixed-use areas, controlling for mitigating factors like income, investment, and transit. The study found that, compared to newer areas, historic districts demonstrated more jobs per square foot of development, more small business jobs, more "creative" jobs, fewer chain businesses, more new businesses, dramatically more women- and minority-owned businesses, more diversity in housing costs, and more age diversity.[253]

As Jane Jacobs taught us, new ideas need old buildings. So, apparently, does diversity.

Don Rypkema's own research adds more powerful data. He has found that historic districts are much more resilient in economic downturns than newer places, and suffer many fewer foreclosures. Also, despite the rise of green design, a typical structure built before 1920 uses 13% less energy per square foot than one built after 1980.[254]

These facts are not well known. As a society, we seem to appreciate historic buildings from more than a generation ago, but we still witness some heartbreaking teardowns. Federal and state Historic Tax Credit programs, the greatest engine behind building rehabilitation, are constantly under threat, even though they make a profit. One study showed that, of every dollar it spends on preservation, the US government takes in $1.26 in increased tax revenue generated. And, remarkably, preservation grants create 27 times as many jobs per dollar spent as the 2008 economic stimulus did.[255]

Historic buildings can be instrumental in helping a place provide an interesting walk, but they do so much more. It isn't always easy to find a productive use for an empty old building, but tearing it down makes that outcome impossible. In these cases, remember the old adage: "don't just do something, stand there!"

RULE 91: Use social and economic arguments to fight for the preservation of historic buildings, districts, and tax credit programs.

92 Hide the Parking Structures

Exposed parking structures do not belong next to sidewalks.

THE IMAGE BELOW IS FROM GRAND RAPIDS, MI, which, over the last few decades, has achieved a very walkable city center. Unfortunately, very few people want to walk on the street pictured, which connects the front doors of the two best downtown hotels, because when one

A perfect 1:1 street section—the Renaissance ideal—fails to please when it is this dull.

side of the street is an exposed parking deck, and the other side is a conference facility that was apparently designed in admiration for that parking deck, the experience is simply too boring.

The conference facility would benefit from more vertical articulation (see Rule 88); the garage is beyond fixing. While there are many ways to make a parking deck more attractive, there is no way to make it more interesting, except to make it something other than a parking deck. Doing just that—at least at ground level—is a strategy that many cities have been using for decades, with mixed results. A more reliable approach is to hide the parking from the street entirely. Both techniques merit discussion.

Active ground floor: The mid-twentieth century was the era of dropping massive, exposed parking decks into city centers. The late-twentieth century was the era of experiencing the sidewalk blight they caused, and looking for solutions. Two main responses arose. One, common in car-happy Sun Belt cities, was the tower in which a ground-floor lobby sits below a bunch of levels of parking, above which the floors for humans begin. The other was the parking structure with a ground floor of retail.

Both types are viable but not ideal, and rely on super-interesting ground floors to distract passers-by from the utterly inactive parking levels. When that parking forms the base of a taller tower, its success usually depends on how convincingly the parking levels are clad to resemble occupied real estate. The best versions are passable, but they still look like offices with no staff; think Lehmann Brothers circa 2008.

It only takes 20 feet of building to hide 200 feet of parking.

When a parking structure includes a commercial ground floor, the outcomes can vary widely. The two key criteria are a tall ground floor that allows optimal retail, and the location of the garage in a place where the shops can thrive. Some have turned out quite well, but many cities have made the mistake of placing low-ceilinged retail on the ground floor of parking decks in bad retail locations, with sad results.

The lot-liner: For this reason, many cities and developers have moved on to the better solution, which is to set the parking lot back slightly and hide it from view. In the 1990s, Mayor Riley of Charleston, SC, demonstrated that it only takes 20 feet of building to hide 200 feet of parking. That model has since proliferated, even spawning a now-

In Charleston, a little lot-liner building buffers a giant parking deck from its historic neighborhood.

common apartment-house type, the Dallas Donut, in which a ring of apartments hides a large parking lot at its center. Given all the successful versions of this building type across North America, it is fully reasonable for cities to require hidden parking, and to stop allowing buildings to place parking up against would-be walkable streets, however well it is clad.

The other mandate for the twenty-first century is to make parking lots convertible. If ride-hailing services—and eventually AVs—end up drastically reducing the need for parking, as predicted, we will wish that we had built all those parking structures with flat floors, removable ramps, and frames that can support conversion to human uses. Smart developers are doing it now.

RULE 92: Hide all parking structures from abutting streets behind occupied buildings. Design parking structures for eventual conversion to human use.

93

Direct Your Public Art Budget to Blank Walls

Employ artistic talent strategically.

IT WOULD BE NICE to think that the era of "plop art" is behind us. For a few decades, starting in the mid-1960s, the inscrutable sculpture dropped on the plaza was the dominant form of public art. The rise of "1% for Art" programs nationally, while a wonderful trend, unfortunately reinforced this approach, since architects found it so much easier to exile the art to the landscape rather than to involve artists in the building design process. Notable exceptions could be found

Good public art plays a remedial role, lending beauty and interest to places that would otherwise be repellent to pedestrian life.

at the US General Services Administration, which in the past has done a great job of getting architects and artists to collaborate. But, in most places—acknowledging the success of a few Calders and Oldenburgs—these investments, speaking to a small audience of connoisseurs, did little to enliven the places around them.

More recently, some public art programs have made an effort to sponsor artworks that are more universally comprehensible, even interactive. The Bean and the Crown Fountain in Chicago's Millennium Park show what is possible with a good budget and the right attitude. But most cities have fewer resources, and also a preponderance of places where public art is actually necessary to enhance walkability.

Helpful label notwithstanding, this art installation, like most, contributes little to walkability.

Philadelphia's public-art focus on blank walls brings interest to otherwise dull places.

In the same way that good trees provide spatial definition to streets that otherwise lack it, good public art plays a remedial role, lending beauty and interest to places that would otherwise be repellent to pedestrian life. The most common such places are the large blank walls that can be found all over North American cities, especially in neighborhoods that have experienced disinvestment. These walls are at best boring, and more often threatening, as they combine a lack of eyes-on-the-street with a clear emblem of neglect. They are easy to fix, when a city actively targets them as a problem and directs its arts budget that way.

Great examples can be found all over the United States. The best may be in Philadelphia, where the city's Mural Arts program has sponsored the creation of almost 4,000 artworks over thirty years. The program currently employs more than 300 artists each year, about a third of whom are prosecuted graffiti vandals. The typical mural costs less than $15,000 to make.[256]

Every North American city of significant size has within it artists of considerable talent, most of whom are in need of both funding and a prominent place to show their work. Many cities create programs that dedicate empty storefronts to art display, another impactful strategy. But a goal of walkability puts a priority on those places where blank walls interrupt a satisfactory public realm. That is where an art budget can be put to best use.

RULE 93: Create a public art program with the express purpose of placing murals on blank walls, and prioritize those walls that will have the greatest impact on the quality of public spaces.

Part XIX

DO IT NOW

ACHIEVING PALPABLE IMPROVEMENTS in walkability and bikeability is possible in the short run. Some cities, in as little as three years, have dramatically increased their walking and biking populations by implementing the concepts laid out in this volume. But where to begin?

A specific technique, called a *walkability study,* is available to all cities and towns that are ready for change. It uses the structure of the General Theory of Walkability to organize a series of interventions aimed at making walking more useful, safe, comfortable, and interesting. Beyond just recommending changes to street design, it analyzes existing building frontages and anchor locations to direct improvements where they can have the most impact. It also weighs the choice of concentrating funding into new construction or dispersing it among many less-expensive restriping projects.

Becoming more walkable in the long term often means replacing a community's current regulatory framework as well. While wholesale code-reform efforts are needed in most places, stopgap measures, like a one-page zoning overlay, can stop mistakes in the short run.

Almost all of this volume is directed at those places in North America where true walkability is possible, because only true walkability is able to move the needle on walking population. This approach rules out most of our developed land, where the automotive patterns of suburban sprawl foreclose on all but the most localized nodes of walkability. Still, such opportunities are worth pursuing, especially where lives can be saved through better road design.

Finally, because this book is focused on the short term, it does not adequately emphasize the big-picture goals of long-range planning. A final point stresses the parallel need, as we improve walkability, to also dream up dramatic improvements to our cities, especially around open space and transportation.

94 Do a Walkability Study

Identify walkability as a goal and pursue it explicitly.

THIS BOOK lays out a comprehensive strategy for making places more walkable. While its elements can be pursued piecemeal—often with remarkable outcomes—communities that want to make the greatest strides will identify improved walkability as a specific objective and launch a concerted public effort toward achieving it. Such efforts are becoming more common, and are best referred to as *walkability studies.*

A walkability study begins with a simple question: how can an area, typically a downtown, without spending a lot of money, witness in a short amount of time the most palpable increase in the number of people walking and biking? It then uses the categories of the General Theory of Walkability—*the useful walk, the safe walk, the comfortable walk,* and *the interesting walk*—to organize a broad collection of recommendations that arise from studying the facts on the ground. These recommendations necessarily vary from place to place, but generally play out as follows:

The Useful Walk

- The mix of uses in the study area is considered, leading to recommended policy changes, including zoning code reforms, which will incentivize underrepresented activities.
- If the jobs:housing ratio is too high—as is common—specific strategies are offered to increase the housing supply.
- Parking provision and policy is studied, leading to recommendations for leveraging existing supply, reducing or eliminating on-site requirements, and adjusting pricing.
- Understanding that transit requires more detailed planning, general recommendations are given for system reform and the trajectory of downtown circulators.
- Bikeshare provision is reviewed, and suggestions given as needed.

The Safe Walk

- Sector speed limits and enforcement are discussed as appropriate.
- Any one-way streets are considered for reversion to two-way, leading to specific proposals.
- A lane audit (number and width) is completed to determine where road diets are mandated.

- The existing and planned cycling network is studied for improvement in light of the lane audit, resulting in a revised plan.
- Every street within the study area is redesigned to optimize safety, vehicular through-put, cycling, and parking provision.
- Key locations are redesigned to eliminate unsafe conditions and take advantage of opportunities for intersection repair.
- Signalization is studied comprehensively, typically leading to a proposal for replacing certain signals with all-way stop signs.
- Recommendations are made for eliminating pushbuttons, shortening signal timing, and introducing LPIs, HAWKs, and other recent technology.
- Key locations are identified for new or improved tree provision.
- A parklet policy is proposed and candidate sites located.
- Curb cut policy is addressed, and problem areas identified for modification.

The Comfortable and Interesting Walk
- A Frontage Quality Assessment is completed and Anchors are located to help determine the Network of Walkability (see Rule 95).

- The outcomes of these analyses are combined into the Network of Walkability, which is then used to prioritize both street improvements and land redevelopment.
- Missing teeth along the Network of Walkability are considered for specific interventions, including new civic spaces, with specific designs recommended.
- Understanding that development regulations require more detailed planning, general recommendations are given for modifying existing codes and ordinances, possibly including a localized one-page zoning overlay.

Most walkability studies end with a to-do list of *next steps* that incorporates the prioritized improvements already laid out and identifies the parties responsible. In most cases, the leading player is the City engineering or public works department, since it oversees street modifications. For this reason, it is essential that walkability studies, however they are funded, are directed largely by City leadership, as governments rarely implement proposals that they have not commissioned.

About fifteen walkability studies of this type have been completed for American cities over the past decade. The technique is not proprietary, and can be put to use by any planning team experienced in street design and land development, aided by the information contained in this book and the review of past successes. Several can be found online.[257]

RULE 94: Conduct a walkability study, using current best practices, for the would-be-walkable areas of your community.

95

Do a Frontage Quality Assessment and Locate Anchors

Lay a groundwork for determining the Network of Walkability.

ACHIEVING TRUE WALKABILITY IS DIFFICULT, because you have to provide the entire four-part package. If a street is not useful, comfortable, and interesting, people with a choice will not choose to walk on it, even if you make it perfectly safe. Unfortunately, those three catego-

and development decisions, the main way that a city can quickly become more walkable is by making its streets safer. But which streets first? The answer is clear: those streets that, when safer, will provide the whole package. In other words, the ones that are already useful, comfortable, and interesting.

While Frontage Quality explains where people are likely to want to walk, Anchors tell us where people are likely to need to walk—or at least to find the walk most useful.

ries—use, comfort, and interest—are hard to impact in short order, because they are a function primarily of how well the street is lined by attractive buildings. Certainly, through its codes, permitting process, and investments, a city can and should influence what gets built where, but this is a long-term effort that usually begins to have impacts about five years out. Most places would like to see significant change much more quickly than that.

This fact has some serious implications for where cities should invest their walkability dollars in the short run. While not forgetting to pursue better building regulations

The *useful* category, not difficult to measure, is discussed ahead. The *comfortable* and *interesting* categories are also easy to measure, and are basically an outcome of how well the street is lined by buildings with friendly faces. Such a measurement is called a Frontage Quality Assessment.

In a Frontage Quality Assessment, each segment of every street is rated from A to F in terms of comfort and interest. Those ratings are then color coded (usually from brightest to darkest), and patterns emerge that suggest which streets and sectors, independent of their safety characteristics, are most welcoming to pedestrians.

The rating system is necessarily a shifting scale, based upon a study area's relative walkability overall. In most US cities, a street with friendly buildings on both sides is an A. When one side becomes a blank wall, it drops to a B. A blank wall across from a parking structure is perhaps a D. Two trash-strewn lots, an F. What matters is that the system is internally consistent so that pockets of good or bad can be identified.

A Frontage Quality Assessment should not be misconstrued as a wealth test. What matters is whether buildings line the street with sticky edges. Often what is being measured most directly is whether a property was built according to the walkable urban or drivable suburban model. A rickety tenement with a front porch scores well above a shiny new Jiffy Lube.

In terms of determining where people are likely to walk in a study area, the Frontage Quality Assessment presents half the picture. It needs to be merged with another drawing that identifies all the significant anchors in the area. Anchors are defined as sites that are expected to be generators and receivers of pedestrian activity. While Frontage Quality explains where people are likely to want to walk, Anchors tell us where people are likely to need to walk—or at least to find the walk most useful.

The job of Identifying Anchors is part formula and part outreach. Locals may miss some obvious ones, but they will always offer unexpected additions, so it's got to be a team effort. Included in the map should be all significant shops and restaurants, hotels, meeting places, sports facilities, popular night spots, public buildings, civic spaces,

This drawing rates each street segment in downtown Tulsa in terms of its frontage quality and indicates all significant pedestrian anchors.

transportation facilities, parking garages, and large office buildings in the study area.

Combining these Anchors in one drawing with the Frontage Analysis gives us a full picture of where pedestrian activity is likely to happen. This drawing can then serve as a basis for creating another drawing, even more instrumental in the direction of a city's efforts, the Network of Walkability, discussed next.

RULE 95: Conduct a Frontage Quality Assessment and identify Anchors to help determine which streets, if made safer, are poised to attract pedestrian life.

96 | Identify the Network of Walkability
Create a map that prioritizes investment around impact.

TURNING a Frontage Quality Assessment and Anchors diagram into a Network of Walkability is a three-step process. First, the diagram is studied for patterns that emerge, in which certain street segments of higher quality come together to form clear walkable areas. Second, those segments are supplemented by the additional segments that are necessary to connect these different areas together. Finally, that network is expanded yet further to provide the most likely paths among Anchors.

This map of likely pedestrian activity, called the Network of Walkability, is the ultimate goal of this exercise. The Network of Walkability is the place to invest first, both in roadway improvements and in filling missing teeth. It is the place to enforce a higher standard of urban performance, and to supply well with transit options. In short, it is the place to apply all the techniques set forth in this book. While there is still an obligation to improve pedestrian safety wherever it is wanting, the dollars that are going to change a city's very nature will be spent here.

In the United States, even in our most walkable cities, most streets are not particularly walkable. That's okay: the automotive city surrounds and invades the pedestrian city, but, as long as the pedestrian city is thoroughly walkable,

well connected, and large enough to matter, it can provide an urban lifestyle for those who seek it out.

Determining the Network of Walkability is as much an art as a science. There is no one correct answer. The best a planner can do is attempt it multiple times—ideally with multiple team members—reviewing prior efforts, until outcomes start to repeat. This subjective process is imperfect, but would seem necessary. It cannot be accomplished effectively via public participation, because audiences tend to mistake wealthy edges for sticky ones, to the detriment of already struggling areas. It cannot be accomplished effectively via "big data," because it addresses where people might walk under better conditions in the future, not now. Of course, good data can help, but the ultimate process needs to be human-led.

In smaller study areas, the outcome of this effort will be a single Network of Walkability, all of which receives equal priority for short-term improvement. In larger study areas, like downtown Tulsa, the Network of Walkability is often too big to address all at once, and must be broken down hierarchically. As shown in the map at right, three categories are identified: Priority, Primary, and Secondary. These can be defined as follows:

• Street segments in the Priority Network are those that are likely to see a large amount of pedestrian traffic due to their connective nature, but that perform badly in the Frontage Quality Assessment. For this reason, they are the places to prioritize not just street improvements, but also vertical development along streets.

• Street segments in the Primary Network are those that are also most likely to attract walking, but are in less dire need of better edges. They should also be targeted first for street improvements, and second for vertical development alongside.

• Street segments in the Secondary Network are those remaining places where pedestrian activity is anticipated in the near future. Of lower priority, they are still likely to deserve investment sooner than any of the street segments that have not made the cut.

Ideally, the Network of Walkability map becomes a central document for directing city improvement efforts moving forward. Hung prominently in planning and engineering offices, it should also be shared with the development community, and used to direct Tax Increment Financing and other city subsidies of private development.

It must be acknowledged that improving walkability is not the only criterion that should direct the allocation of a city's resources. But, to the degree that a city wishes to become more walkable, the Network of Walkability should be a key tool for guiding its efforts.

Analysis of the Frontage Quality Assessment and Anchors diagram leads to the identification of a Network of Walkability, here ranked by importance.

RULE 96: Based on the Frontage Quality Assessment and identified Anchors, designate a Network of Walkability to guide improvement.

97 | Rebuild. . . or ReStripe?

Before calling in the bulldozers, ask how the same funding can do more with paint.

AS IT BEGAN to consider the walkability of its downtown in 2012, Cedar Rapids, IA, was leaning toward rebuilding five blocks of 3rd Street, an important axis terminating at its convention center. The plan called for a road diet with new, wider sidewalks, and was expected to cost about $3 million. It seemed like a good investment, until a lane audit of the surrounding area found that almost every street was twice the size it needed to be. Most were four-lane, half were one-way, and only one—the State highway—was carrying more than two-lanes worth of traffic.

For the cost of rebuilding a single street, you can restripe a small downtown.

In response to this discovery, the City sponsored a plan for its thirty-block downtown core. The plan right-sized all the streets and distributed the asphalt gained between bike facilities and angle parking, roughly doubling both. It replaced nine of the downtown's thirteen traffic signals with all-way stop signs, a change made possible by the elimination of one-way travel. It added a half-dozen wooden summer parklets in front of restaurants (see Rule 82). The plan's projected cost: about $3 million.

The difference? Moving curbs. Changing the width or location of a sidewalk usually means changing its stormwater system as well, and planting new trees. That's expensive.

Instead of rebuilding 3rd Street, Cedar Rapids restriped it, leaving money on the table for other streets.

Moule & Polyzoides' redesign of this California main street was as transformative as it looks.

Restriping requires new paint and sometimes a new top-coat of asphalt. For the cost of rebuilding a single street, you can restripe a small downtown.

Showing even more frugality—too much?—Cedar Rapids decided not to budget the work at all. Instead, as streets come up for resurfacing due to wear, they restripe them to the new pattern. On this schedule, the work is about half done. But it is getting done, and is having a greater impact than could have been expected from one remade street.

This lesson is not universally applicable. In some places, like Poynton, U.K. (see Rule 77), the reconstruction of a key sidewalk, intersection, or main street can completely turn a place around. When done properly, such work pays for itself in terms of increased tax revenues from abutting properties. In Lancaster, CA, an $11.2 million main street transformation completed in 2010 has created an esti-mated economic impact of $282 million while doubling pedestrian activity, reducing injury crashes by 49% and pedestrian crashes by 78%, and leading to the opening of fifty-seven new businesses, the construction of more than 800 new housing units—most of them affordable—and the estimated creation of 2,000 jobs.[258] Literally hundreds of North American communities would be wise to make a similar investment.

So, rebuild or restripe? The proper design solution can only be found by properly identifying the design prob-lem. If the challenges are localized to one spot or corridor, rebuilding may be smarter than restriping. But most cities suffer from a larger malaise of speeding traffic that needs to be addressed more comprehensively with many streets of new paint.

RULE 97: Consider whether the need for street redesign is localized or more widespread in order to determine whether rebuilding or restriping is the better choice.

98 | Do Some Tactical Urbanism

Be the change you wish to see in your town.

ARE YOU TIRED OF WAITING FOR YOUR CITY to become more walkable? Perhaps you are a citizen, banging you head up against a recalcitrant local government. Or perhaps you are a city official, banging your head up against a recalcitrant public works department. Either way,

This Akron intervention, one of many staged by the Better Block Foundation, included temporary squares, plazas, traffic calming, and the bike lane and beer garden shown here.

you have found that the path to making change in your town is long, winding, and littered with costly red tape. Do not despair, it's tactical urbanism to the rescue!

Tactical urbanism refers to the grassroots, ad-hoc, often temporary, and sometimes unsanctioned efforts that small groups of individuals organize to remake their streets, blocks, and neighborhoods. It has been a factor in the creation of cities for as long as there have been cities, but it is currently experiencing a heyday thanks to the growing walkable cities movement and the productive impatience of today's millennials.

Tactical urbanism interventions cross a wide range of scales, from a few "borrowed" traffic cones in a Hamilton, Ontario, intersection to a three-block transformation of Miami's Biscayne Boulevard, an urban oasis that attracted more than 20,000 visitors over three weeks.

While the movement has many faces, the gurus of Tactical Urbanism are Mike Lydon and Tony Garcia, whose masterwork, *Tactical Urbanism: Short Term Action for Long Term Change,* is part of a five-part series, all available free online.[259] The book's subtitle points to the most obvious goal of these efforts, which is to test walkability improvements quickly, and garner public support for those that deserve to be made permanent.

Such was the case in Hamilton, Ontario, where the aforementioned traffic cones were used to create temporary curb extensions at two corners where residents felt that traffic posed a threat to children crossing the street. Installed in the dead of night, the cones were removed by the City, who called them "illegal, potentially unsafe and adding to the City's cost of maintenance and repair." But then the project organizers stepped forward, a public debate ensued, and, before long, the improvements were made permanent—along with similar changes to more than 100 additional intersections citywide.[260]

An impactful subset of the tactical urbanism movement is *guerilla wayfinding,* represented principally by an effort called *Walk [Your City].* Begun in 2012 by Matt Tomasulo, the *walkyourcity.org* online toolkit provides all you need to quickly and cheaply create a pedestrian-oriented wayfinding system in your downtown. By describing the accessibility of different anchors on foot—"It's a 3 minute walk to the movies"—these attractive signs remind locals and visitors that they don't need to drive.[261]

Top-down planning and large public processes may be needed for big transformations, like a new transit system. For all the rest, consider how you can use tactical urbanism to create local change from the bottom up.

Walk [Your City] campaigns—this one in Charlotte, NC—offer an alternative to typical auto-centric wayfinding.

RULE 98 : Look for opportunities to install desired improvements temporarily. Make good use of the two most powerful words in the English language: "pilot project." Create a Walk [Your City] campaign. And when an official suggests doing an expensive study, ask "can we do a test instead?"

99 | Start Code Reform Now

Introduce stopgap measures while mounting a campaign for true zoning reform.

MUCH HAS BEEN WRITTEN about the failure of twentieth century zoning practice, and how it has been instrumental in creating many of the current problems facing our cities, our country, and our planet (see Rule 9). Thousands of communities have taken half-measures to circumvent their deeply flawed zoning codes and subdivision ordinances, such as eliminating unit size and parking minimums, modifying height limits and setback requirements, and changing street design standards. Every change helps, but many North American cities have reached the conclusion that simple code modifications are not enough. Just as fattening a rat does not make it a cat, conventional land use codes—introduced principally to limit disease and overcrowding, and subsequently developed as a tool for enforcing neighborhood homogeneity—simply lack the DNA to make vibrant, walkable neighborhoods. Particularly as they address the design of private buildings, conventional codes are missing the tools needed to ensure that streets and public spaces end up adequately comfortable and interesting: that edges are firm, parking is hidden, facades are sticky, and repetition is limited. Achieving these objectives requires a code organized around them. Such an instrument is referred to as a form-based code.

The first modern form-based codes were written in the 1980s. As already discussed, close to four hundred have been officially adopted. Some are citywide, but many apply only to areas within cities where walkability is specifically desired. This makes sense, since their rules are largely irrelevant in automotive sprawl.

Cities that want their ordinances to support walkability, rather than undermine it, probably need a form-based code. The problem is that major zoning reform is difficult, expensive, and slow. For that reason, it is smart, while pursing more comprehensive reform, to enact a stopgap overlay for areas where current zoning is allowing mistakes to be made. In Tulsa, fear in the business community over excessive regulation led to the suggestion of a simple one-page code, to be applied in the downtown's Network of Walkability.[262] While it is catered to specific local challenges, one can see how a similar instrument could be useful in many other places.

SEVEN RULES FOR A SUCCESSFUL DOWNTOWN TULSA
A One-Page Zoning Overlay for Private Development

All developments proposed abutting the Network of Walkability shall be reviewed in light of the following criteria by City Planning staff, with exceptions to be granted only in the case of exemplary architectural merit.

1. *Surface parking lots kill vitality.* No surface parking lots may be placed between a building edge and the sidewalk.

2. *Dead walls create dead sidewalks.* Parking structures shall be exposed to sidewalks on the ground floor only at the locations of their car entrances. Entrance drives may be no wider than 11 feet for each lane of travel. The remainder of the parking deck's ground floor (and other floors, if desired) shall be shielded from the sidewalk by a habitable building edge at least 20 feet deep. That edge may be office, retail, residential, and/or vertical circulation, but retail use is not recommended where not adjacent to successful retail, and new retail space must have a minimum ceiling height of 12 feet.

3. *Sidewalks need buildings near them.* With the exception of hotel porte-cocheres (allowed only for hotels with more than 100 guest rooms), all buildings shall place their facades within 10 feet of the sidewalk edge. If retail, any setback shall be paved to match the sidewalk. If residential or office, any setback may include greenery, stoops, patios, and other construction, with the exception that no walls or fences shall exceed three feet in height. Exceptions may be granted for public or semipublic greens, plazas, or courtyards.

4. *Curb cuts endanger people walking.* Curb cuts are not allowed for any buildings other than parking structures and hotels with more than 100 guest rooms. Smaller hotels shall conduct loading against the curb in the parking lane, where several spaces shall be designated for this use. No set of curb cuts shall be more than two lanes in number.

5. *Front doors are essential.* Buildings with sidewalk facades and rear (or side) parking must place a primary entrance on the sidewalk frontage. Said entrance shall be unlocked whenever the secondary entrance is unlocked.

6. *Homes against sidewalks need height.* Residential facades placed within 5 feet of the sidewalk edge must have a ground floor elevation of at least 18 inches. Ground-floor residential units are encouraged to have front porches or stoops along the sidewalk, even where also hallway-served.

7. *Urban buildings need friendly faces.* Facades enfronting sidewalks shall average no less than 18 feet tall and shall have regularly spaced door and window openings on every story, with at least one opening in every 10 linear feet, with rare exceptions granted for special architectural features. The window-to-wall ratio for all facades shall be between 20% and 80%.

RULE 99: Begin the effort now to create a form-based code for the potentially walkable parts of your city. In the meantime, pass a one-page code overlay for key areas.

100 | Don't Give Up on Sprawl

It's where most Americans live.

IN 1999, when the book *Suburban Nation* was still being written, it seemed that stopping the spread of sprawl might actually be possible. Two decades later, it is difficult to harbor such illusions. Most of the subsidies and market perversities that drove the initial suburban outflux are still in place, and too many powerful organizations still benefit from our dependence on cars and roads. Even though polls and price comparisons show that the auto zone is vastly overbuilt, the sprawl machine will continue to churn, sucking in farmland and fossil fuels and spitting out soulless subdivisions and ever more carbon. The data suggest it might kill us all before long. But while we're still here, why can't we just live in the kind of places we want?

This final question, and our collective failure to change the rules of the game, has led to a new mandate—less ambitious but still important: making the walkable lifestyle available to more of the people who want it but can't find or afford it in their cities. As the sprawl bomb continues to slowly detonate, planners and activists can make the biggest difference by bringing more attainable housing to our city and town centers (see Rule 6). But they can also

The farmers' market at Belmar in Lakewood, CO, which replaced the nation's second oldest suburban shopping mall.

have an impact by creating pockets of urbanism where the people already are: in the belly of the sprawl beast.

This work has been going on for decades now, described in such books as *Retrofitting Suburbia,*[263] new mixed-use town centers plopped in the middle of the auto zone. Most of them, like Legacy Town Center in Plano, TX, or Belmar in Lakewood, CO, occupy the sites of dead malls or office parks. When done properly, they seem to be an almost surefire real-estate home run, because the hundreds of thousands of people surrounding them are absolutely starved for urbanism. While their desirability means that all but their smallest apartments quickly become too expensive for most, they still provide a much-needed experience for regional suburbanites, who drive to them in droves to shop, dine, see a movie, or just walk around. Avalon, one such center in Alpharetta, GA, has more than two hundred

Sometimes, a town that appears to be all sprawl, like Tigard, OR, is stealthily concealing a spore of urbanism that is ready to germinate if given the proper care.

public events each year. These are what planners call "park-once environments." And for those who can afford to live there, they provide a happier, lower-carbon lifestyle.

Are such new suburban centers really more sustainable overall? It's hard to say. But they help to alleviate the monotony of sprawl, which is now where most Americans live, including many of the poorest. When suburbia was more wealthy than poor, planners could theoretically hold their noses and confine their design work to city centers; this would no longer seem to be a moral choice. The statistics make it clear that the vast majority of people living in sprawl

don't want to be there: in a recent National Association of Realtors survey, only 10% of respondents want to live in single-use housing subdivisions.[264] This means that perhaps a third of Americans are trapped in the suburbs involuntarily, most because they can't afford real urbanism. Besides giving them cute town centers to stroll around, what can be done?

The answer lies in the type of suburbia they are stuck in. The first and best opportunity, available only in places that experienced real growth before 1950, is to find the old Main Street and bring it back to life. Sometimes, a town that appears to be all sprawl, like Tigard, OR, is stealthily concealing a spore of urbanism that is ready to germinate if given the proper care. As discussed in Rule 10, wise communities will focus their investment there, fix the streets, build new housing, and reinforce a walkable design standard to create a core of walkability that can lift the entire community.

But then there are all the newer places like Chandler, AZ: 250,000 humans doomed to scuttle around perhaps the most utterly placeless landscape in America, 65 square miles of entirely car-dependent nowhere. Without the full-scale insertion of a large, new town center, what can be done to make the denizens of the purest sprawl less isolated? While true walkability is out of the question, the most essential improvements would seem to surround safety for pedestrians, cyclists, and drivers, too. People are dying in these landscapes at an alarming rate, thanks to high-speed road geometrics, inadequate crossings, and rare and dangerous bike lanes. Such places can't really be fixed, but they can—and should—be made safer using many of the techniques contained in this volume.

RULE 100: In sprawl, invest in old main streets where they exist, and otherwise focus on safety for all road users.

101 | Dream Big
Great cities still need great visions.

THIS BOOK IS MOSTLY ABOUT fixing problems and creating short-term wins. Such an approach makes sense when the goal is to impact the day-to-day walkability and livability of a city. But it ignores the fact that North America's most walkable and most livable cities did not turn out that way through fixing problems and creating short-term wins. Rather, most either started with visionary proposals, like Philadelphia and Savannah, or were the beneficiaries of visionary improvements, like New York and Chicago. . . or both. The ordinary fabric of a city can make it very good, but only big dreams make a city great. In attending to the day-to-day, we can't forget to pursue greatness as well.

Founder of the Mayor's Institute on City Design, Joseph P. Riley served as mayor of Charleston, SC, for ten four-year terms. He would often visit Mayors' Institute sessions, at which he would occasionally tell the attending mayors: "You should balance the budget, but nobody is going to remember you for balancing the budget. If you want to be remembered, build a park."[265]

A new park is one of many things that Mayor Riley built in Charleston during a tenure marked by a focus on the physical quality of the public realm. Not trained as a designer, the mayor explained his motivation this way:

> *In America we have citizens who have never been to the Great Lakes, or seen the sun set on the Pacific, or seen the purple mountains' majesty or amber waves of grain. They've never been to Europe. All they have is their city. . . . That fact brings with it a moral imperative, that the city should be a place where every citizen's heart can sing.*[266]

Happily, obeying the moral imperative has practical rewards. Unlike investments in highways, which depress real estate value, investments in public spaces tend to create real estate value—so much that they end up paying for themselves in increased tax revenue, generally pretty quickly.

Chicago is a city that has regularly invested in making itself more spectacular. Mayor Daley was attacked roundly for the City's $270 million contribution to the construction of Millennium Park in the early 2000s. But within ten years—slow years for real estate—the City saw $3 billion invested in new private construction near the park, which now attracts more than five million visitors each year.[267]

Riverfront Park, Charleston, SC.

A summer swing dance in downtown Grand Rapids' redeveloped main plaza, designed by Maya Lin.

Similar stories attend to the other big park projects of this century. The first phase of New York's High Line cost $260 million to build—of which the City paid $50 million—but it has since contributed close to $1 billion to the City's tax revenue.[268]

Like new parks, transit projects can also have outsize effects on long-term returns. From 2000 to 2010, fully 70% of the population growth in Arlington County, VA, occurred in only 6% of the County's land area, that being the corridor of the DC Metro's Orange Line.[269] Yet Metro service declines as the system struggles for funds. Vision, call your office!

In 1974, the City of Grand Rapids wanted to celebrate the new presidency of native son Gerald Ford with a parade downtown. "Not so fast," said the Secret Service: "too many empty windows for snipers." This was a wake-up call to local business leaders, who collectively pledged to move more of their offices downtown, while building a new Arena and Convention Center. A medical school, hotels, and other key institutions followed. Before long, Grand Rapids had one of the healthiest downtowns in the Midwest.

Daniel Burnham was half wrong; small plans are important, too. But they must be pursued in parallel with big ones, especially around open space and transportation, because it is the big plans—the visions and the dreams—that can make a city great.

RULE 101: Parallel with efforts to improve walkability, set ambitious goals for improved transportation, open space, and institutions downtown.

EPILOGUE 1

There's an exception to every rule, but you're probably not it.

THE FACT THAT THE VAST MAJORITY of pedestrian-only zones failed miserably is not invalidated by Lincoln Road Mall or 3rd St. Santa Monica. The fact that most one-way conversions sundered their downtowns is not invalidated by 5th Avenue or Newbury Street. The fact that small increments of development make better streetscapes is not invalidated by Rockefeller Center or Horton Plaza. But these exceptions do exist as rebukes to many of the principles laid out in this volume.

Exceptions deserve our attention, as they are available to teach useful lessons. Why are the multilane one-ways in downtown Philadelphia so walkable? Probably because their lanes are only 9 feet wide. Why is Denver's 16th Street Mall such a hit? Probably because it is surrounded by tremendous mixed-use density. Hidden within each exception is usually another rule.

Any book of rules about something as complex as city planning needs to acknowledge that there are moments when each rule is bound to be wrong. But with that admission must come an acknowledgement that the likelihood of that happening here and now, in the particular instance that concerns you, is very small.

EPILOGUE 2

Your perfect is the enemy of our good.

CITY PLANNING is the art of the possible. The recommendations in this book are not theoretical, but rather are real, buildable, and in fact all built somewhere already. Every one is a compromise, and most are hard won. Many would be different if current laws and conventions carried no sway.

For example: in an ideal world, downtown driving lanes would probably be 9 feet wide, not 10. Similarly, *Level of Service* measures would just go away. Most parking lanes would be replaced by bike lanes. We would stop building parking structures entirely. Whole city centers would go car-free. But such outcomes are impossible in most North American communities, so they are not recommended here.

The good news is that much of what these pages hold would have been considered outlandish as little as a decade ago. The past thirty years of new urban practice have seen compromise become less and less necessary. This is most dramatically true in the case of cycling infrastructure, which is evolving at a remarkable clip. There is no doubt that the cycling part of this book is the section that will become outdated the most quickly. It is already outdated in Europe, and perhaps soon in Seattle.

Still, for most of us, this change is not coming fast enough. We, the dissatisfied, seem to fall into two categories: those who plow on, fighting for every small change, understanding that it represents some improvement to somebody's quality of life; and those who deem those small changes inadequate, and work to discredit the people who make them. A lot can be said about the latter group; the most relevant is that few of them have much experience in the trenches, actually making change in cities. It's easy to say that two-way cycle tracks are crap when you've never had to make the choice between either that solution or a pair of exposed lanes.

This observation is meant as both a defense and an apology. The 101 rules in this volume are an attempt to define achievable best practices in North America, circa 2020. They are not more ambitious because, right now, more ambitious almost always fails. Many will become obsolete eventually, one hopes soon. In the meantime, these rules are offered with the humble conviction that limited, reasonable measures can create dramatic outcomes in our communities.

EPILOGUE 3

Have you identified your model?

CITY PLANNING is not just an art, but also a profession, and like in the professions of law or medicine, its practitioners have a responsibility to learn from past successes and failures. There is nothing new under the sun, and a wide world of examples sits at our fingertips—now more available than ever—for us to emulate. When it comes to successes, we can and should copy with pride.

Most urban designers are trained as architects, which can be a problem. There exists a healthy tension in the practice of architecture between its status as a profession and its status as an art. Most architecture schools function principally like art schools, where creativity and invention are prized above more practical considerations. When this sensibility is brought to urban design, a lot of people can suffer, many more than are victimized by a bad piece of architecture.

This leads up to a fairly simple admonition for urban planners: Stop feeling obliged to invent! People are counting on you not to wreck their lives. The only barrier to finding the right solution to a complex urban problem is not a lack of creativity, but a lack of a broader knowledge of the world's 10,000 great urban places. The answer is there somewhere. It may need to be interpreted to a new population, a new climate, or a new technology, but that's the fun part.

The human species has been around for a long time, and there is a lot to be known about what kind of places make us happy. This fact is not altered by the onset of autonomous vehicles, AI, or *smart city* algorithms. When designing a street, a plaza, a green, a park: find the one that is your model and pin it to the wall. Having multiple models is just fine. What isn't fine is having no model. An urban design with no model manifests either laziness, a death wish, or both.

There is plenty of room for invention in urban design, but beware inventions. Very rarely does a new idea work out as expected—at least not the first time. Remember, the early bird may get the worm, but the second mouse gets the cheese.

ACKNOWLEDGMENTS

Finally: It was stated at the outset, that this system would not be here, and at once, perfected. You cannot but plainly see that I have kept my word. But I now leave [this] standing thus unfinished, even as the great Cathedral of Cologne was left, with the crane still standing upon the top of the uncompleted tower. For small erections may be finished by their first architects; grand ones, true ones, ever leave the copestone to posterity. God keep me from ever completing anything. This whole book has been a draught—nay, but the draught of a draught. Oh, Time, Strength, Cash and Patience!

—Herman Melville, *Moby Dick*

AS OTHERS ARE WELCOME to build upon my crane-topped tower, it must be acknowledged that this draft itself sits on the foundation of many decades of previous efforts, mostly by others. The continuity of my work with my predecessors', and its embeddedness in a massive larger movement—that *great correction* called the New Urbanism—are facts that demand recognition.

When so many people came across *Suburban Nation*, which I wrote with Andres Duany and Elizabeth Plater-Zyberk, kind words and opportunities were offered to all three of us rather equally, with many not aware that those two were the teachers and I was the pupil. With *Walkable City*, I re-gifted these lessons in a shiny new package, surrounded by the wisdom of other key voices from overlapping fields: thought leaders like Chris Leinberger, Dick Jackson, Donald Shoup, and Carol Coletta, and great mayors like Joe Riley, Manny Diaz, and Mick Cornett. I may have decorated this wisdom with a few personal stories of my own, but on the whole I was still more the medium than the message. That circumstance, again, was forgotten by many who enjoyed the book, and I found myself once more reaping the fruit of others' labor. The fact that I have not yet heard a single complaint from these generous people only reminds me that the movement for reclaiming the North American city has always been one of ideas and not of egos.

That said, certain individuals deserve singling out here. As has become habit, I need to thank Andres and Elizabeth first. Fifteen years since leaving their firm, I have not yet reached the point where most of the things I write are not things I learned from them.

More recently, my steepest learning curve has been in transportation: traffic, transit, and cycling. On those topics I am most deeply indebted to Paul Moore of Nelson\Nygaard, Jarrett Walker of *Human Transit*, Angie Schmitt of *Streetsblog* and Janette Sadik-Kahn of NACTO, Bloomberg, and all the other planets over which she benevolently presides.

For financial support, which means time to write, I am grateful to Lionstone Investments, especially Tom Bacon, whose genero sity effectively amounted to a two-year fellowship. Without their help, this volume would have been the product of another decade.

As with *Walkable City,* I began this book in Italy, where I was again hosted by the American Academy in Rome as an artist in residence. I am grateful to Mark Robins and his welcoming staff, especially Gabriele, who organizes the pool tournaments.

One more time, Gayle and Scott Speck served as skilled volunteer editors, and Alice Speck as first listener and prime motivator.

I am especially grateful to Heather Boyer, Sharis Simonian, Maureen Gately, and their colleagues at Island Press, first for their great interest and expertise in this subject matter, and second for the tremendous labor that this book represents, especially all the extra, non-obligatory effort that they put into it. I have never worked with a publisher who did so much to lighten my load.

Many other people provided wisdom, information, and/or images for this book. An incomplete list includes Scott Bernstein, Spencer Boomhower, Beth Bousley, Jim Brainard, Dan Burden, Brian Carr, David Dixon, Doug Farr, Alyson Fletcher, Ben Hamilton-Baillie, Henry Harrell, Alejandro Henao, Xavier Iglesias, Larry James, Gabe Klein, Dan Kostelec, Walter Kulash, Mike Lydon, Alex MacLean, Charles Marohn, Lauren Mattern, Stephanie Meeks, Joe Minicozzi, Steve Mouzon, Andrea Mrzlak, Mark Ostrow, George Proakis, Jason Roberts, Donovan Rypkema, Meg Schneider, Jason Schreiber, Sam Schwartz, Peter Secchia, Patrick Siegman, Seth Solomonow, Sarah Susanka, Galina Tachieva, Brent Toderian, Matt Tomasulo, Mark Toro, Harriet Tregoning, Ruthzaly Weich, and Dar Williams.

Thank you all.

NOTES

1   Leon Batista Alberti, *On the Art of Building in Ten Books* (Cambridge: MIT Press, 1988), 23.

2   Christopher Leinberger, *The Option of Urbanism* (Washington, DC: Island Press, 2007), 98.

3   Joe Cortright, "Walking the Walk: How Walkability Raises Home Values in U.S. Cities," CEOs for Cities (August 2009), 20, http://blog.walkscore.com/wp-content/uploads/2009/08/WalkingTheWalk_CEOsforCities.pdf.

4   Ibid., 24.

5   The Segmentation Company, "Attracting College-Educated Young Adults to Cities," CEOs for Cities (May 8, 2006), 7, https://slidex.tips/download/attracting-college-educated-young-adults-to-cities. Adapted from "Revisiting Donald Appleyard's Livable Streets" by Streetfilms and Bruce Appleyard.

6   Patrick C. Doherty and Christopher B. Leinberger, "The Next Real Estate Boom," Brookings Institution (November 1, 2010), https://www.brookings.edu/articles/the-next-real-estate-boom/.

7   John Greenfield, "If the Future Will Be Walkable, How Do We Make Sure Everyone Benefits," *StreetsBlog Chicago* (May 11, 2017).

8   Heidi Garrett-Peltier, "Estimating the Employment Impacts of Pedestrian, Bicycle, and Road Infrastructure (University of Massachusetts at Amherst, December 2010), 1–2.

9   Christopher E. Leinberger and Michael Rodriguez, *Foot Traffic Ahead: Ranking Walkable Urbanism in America's Largest Metros* (Washington, DC: George Washington School of Business, 2016), 30, https://www.smartgrowthamerica.org/app/legacy/documents/foot-traffic-ahead-2016.pdf.

10 Catherine Lutz and Anne Lutz Fernandez, *Carjacked* (New York: St. Martin's Press, 2010), 80.

11 Elly Blue, "The Free Rider Myth—Who Really Pays for the Roads," *MomentumMag* (March 24, 2016).

12 Howard Frumkin, Lawrence Frank, and Richard Jackson, *Urban Sprawl and Public Health: Designing, Planning, and Building for Healthy Communities* (Washington, DC: Island Press, 2004).

13 Erica Noonan, "A Matter of Size," *Boston Globe* (March 7, 2010).

14 Wikipedia: List of countries by traffic-related death rate, https://en.wikipedia.org/wiki/List_of_countries_by_traffic-related_death_rate.

15 CDC Motor Vehicle Crash Deaths in Metropolitan Areas—United States, (2009), https://www.cdc.gov/mmwr/preview/mmwrhtml/mm6128a2.htm.

16   American Lung Association, "Trends in Asthma Morbidity and Mortality," (September 2012): 1, 5, http://www.lung.org/assets/documents/research/asthma-trend-report.pdf.

17   Fabio Caiazzo, et. al., "Air Pollution and Early Deaths in the United States. Part 1: Quantifying the Impact of Major Sectors in 2005," (MIT 2013).

18   Catherine Lutz, *Carjacked*, 172.

19   David Owen, *Green Metropolis: Why Living Smaller, Living Closer, and Driving Less are the Keys to Sustainability* (New York: Riverhead Books, 2009), 19.

20   Peter Newman, Timothy Beatley, and Heather Boyer, *Resilient Cities: Responding to Peak Oil and Climate Change* (Washington, DC: Island Press, 2009), 88.

21   Ibid., 48, 104.

22   American Public Transport Association, "A Profile of Public Transportation Demographics and Travel Characteristics Reported in On-Board Surveys," (May 2007), 1824, http://www.apta.com/resources/statistics/Documents/transit_passenger_characteristics_text_5_29_2007.pdf.

23   Chad Frederick, *America's Addiction to Automobiles: Why Cities Need to Kick the Habit and How,* (Santa Barbara: Praeger, 2017), 153, 162.

24   Smart Growth America, *Dangerous by Design*, (2016), 17–18, https://smartgrowthamerica.org/dangerous-by-design/.

25   Ibid., 23.

26   Hilary Angus, "Bicycle Equity: Fairness and Justice in Bicycle Planning and Design," *MomentumMag* (October 26, 2016), https://momentummag.com/bicycle-equity-fairness-justice-bicycle-planning-design/.

27   Donald Appleyard, M. Sue Gerson, and Mark Lintell, *Livable Streets* (Berkeley: University of California Press, 1981).

28   Howard Frumkin, *Urban Sprawl and Public Health,* 172. Also, Robert D. Putnam, *Bowling Alone: The Collapse and Revival of American Community* (New York: Simon & Schuster, 2000).

29   Shannon H. Rogers et al., "Examining Walkability and Social Capital as Indicators of Quality of Life at the Municipal and Neighborhood Scales," *Journal of Applied Research in Quality of Life* 6, no. 2 (2011): 2013.

30   Wade Graham. *Dream Cities: Seven Urban Ideas That Shape the World.* New York: 2016, Harper Collins. 99

31   Jane Jacobs, *The Death and Life of Great American Cities,* (New York: Vintage Reissue, 1992), 154.

32   Jeff Speck, *Walkable City: How Downtown Can Save America, One Step at a Time* (New York: Farrar, Straus and Giroux, 2012), 107–8.

33   National Center for Education Studies, "Overview of Public Elementary and Secondary Schools and Districts: School Year 1999–2000," (September 2001), https://nces.ed.gov/pubs2001/overview/table05.asp and https://nces.ed.gov/pubs2011/pesschools09/tables/table_05.asp.

34   Andres Duany, Elizabeth Plater-Zyberk, and Jeff Speck, *Suburban Nation: The Rise of Sprawl and the Decline of the American Dream* (New York: North Point Press, 2000), 191.

35   National Center for Education Statistics, https://nces.ed.gov/fastfacts/display.asp?id=67, and "Education Spending Per Student by State," *Governing*, http://www.governing.com/gov-data/education-data/state-education-spending-per-pupil-data.html.

36   "The Decline of Walking and Bicycling," Pedestrian and Bicycle Information Center (PBIC), http://guide.saferoutesinfo.org/introduction/the_decline_of_walking_and_bicycling.cfm.

37   "Arriving at School by Bicycle," *Bicycle Dutch* (blog), (December 5, 2013), https://bicycledutch.wordpress.com/2013/12/05/arriving-at-school-by-bicycle/.

38   "Choice Without Equity: Charter School Segregation and the Need for Civil Rights Standards," The Civil Rights Project, https://www.civilrightsproject.ucla.edu/research/k-12-education/integration-and-diversity/choice-without-equity-2009-report.

39   Wikipedia: Soccer mom, https://en.wikipedia.org/wiki/Soccer_mom.

40   Conversation with Andres Duany.

41   Andres Duany, *Suburban Nation*, 10.

42   Lecture by George Proakis, currently the chief planner of Somerville, MA, in Lewiston, ME, 2015.

43   "Form-Based Codes? You're Not Alone," The Codes Study, http://www.placemakers.com/how-we-teach/codes-study/. Also visit the Form-Based Codes Institute, http://formbasedcodes.org.

44   Charles Marohn Jr., *Thoughts on Building Strong Towns,* vol. 1, CreateSpace Independent Publishing Platform (2012), 6.

45   Charles Marohn Jr., "The Cost of Auto Orientation, Update," *Strong Towns Journal* (July 22, 2014), https://www.strongtowns.org/journal/2014/7/22/the-cost-of-auto-orientation-update.html.

46   Ibid.

47   Barbara Lipman, "A Heavy Load: The Combined Housing and Transportation Burdens of Working Families," (Washington DC: Center for Housing Policy, 2006), iv.

48   Jane Jacobs, *The Death and Life of Great American Cities,* 448.

49   Nick Brunick, Lauren Goldberg, and Susannah Levine, "Large Cities and Inclusionary Zoning," Business and Professional People for the Public Interest (2003), 5, http://www.wellesleyinstitute.com/wp-content/uploads/2013/01/ResourceUS_BPI_IZLargeCities.pdf.

50   Julián Castro, "Inclusionary Zoning and Mixed-Income Communities," *Evidence Matters*, Office of Policy Development and Research (PD&R), US Department of Housing and Urban Development (Spring 2013), 1, https://www.huduser.gov/portal/periodicals/em/spring13/highlight3.html.

51   Tanza Loudenback, Crazy-High Rent, Record-low Homeownership, and Overcrowding: California Has a Plan to Solve the Housing Crisis, but Not without a Fight," *Business Insider* (March 12, 2017), http://www.businessinsider.com/granny-flat-law-solution-california-affordable-housing-shortage-2017-3.

52   Josie Huang, "Popular Granny Flats Create a Niche Industry in LA," KPCC Radio (December 25, 2017), http://www.scpr.org/news/2017/12/25/79179/la-embracing-granny-flats-more-than-anywhere-else/.

53   City of Seattle. "A Guide to Building a Backyard Cottage" (June 2010), https://www.seattle.gov/Documents/Departments/SeattlePlanningCommission/BackyardCottages/BackyardCottagesGuide-final.pdf.

54   Daniel Kay Hertz, "Chicago's Housing Market is Broken," posted March 21, 2014, https://danielkayhertz.com/2014/03/21/chicagos-housing-market-is-broken/.

55   Adam Hengels, "Only 2 Ways to Fight Gentrification (you're not going to like one of them)," Market Urbanism (January 28, 2015), http://marketurbanism.com/2015/01/28/2-ways-fight-gentrification/.

56   Joe Cortright, "Lost in Place." CityReports (September 12, 2014), http://cityobservatory.org/lost-in-place/.

57   National Community Land Trust Network, http://cltnetwork.org.

58   Wikipedia: Housing First. https://en.wikipedia.org/wiki/Housing_First.

59   State of Utah, Comprehensive Report on Homelessness (2014), 6, https://jobs.utah.gov/housing/scso/documents/homelessness2014.pdf.

60   Thomas Byrne et al., "Predictors of Homelessness among Families and Single Adults after Exit from Homelessness Prevention and Rapid Re-Housing Programs: Evidence from the Department of Veterans Affairs Supportive Services for Veteran Families Program," Housing Policy Debate (September 14, 2015).

61   Ibid.

62   Jennifer Perlman and John Parvensky, "Denver Housing First Collaborative Cost Benefit Analysis and Program Outcomes Report," Colorado Coalition for the Homeless (December 11, 2006), https://shnny.org/uploads/Supportive_Housing_in_Denver.pdf.

63   Mary E. Larimer et al., "Health Care and Public Service Use and Costs Before and After Provision of Housing for Chronically Homeless Persons with Severe Alcohol Problems," JAMA 301, vol.13 (April 1, 2009):1349–57.

64   National Alliance to End Homelessness: Housing First, http://endhomelessness.org/resource/housing-first/.

65   Eric Betz, "The First Nationwide Count of Parking Spaces Demonstrates Their Environmental Cost," Knoxville News Sentinel (December 1, 2010).

66   Donald Shoup, The High Cost of Free Parking, updated ed., (London: Routledge, 2011).

67   Andres Duany, Suburban Nation, 163.

68   Donald Shoup, High Cost of Free Parking, 498.

69   Eric Roper, "Mpls Relaxes Parking Requirements to Reduce Housing Costs," Star Tribune (July 10, 2015), http://www.startribune.com/mpls-relaxes-parking-requirements-to-reduce-housing-costs/313286521/.

70   Donald Shoup, "Instead of Free Parking," Access, no. 15 (Fall 1999), http://shoup.bol.ucla.edu/InsteadOfFreeParking.pdf.

71   Andres Duany, Suburban Nation, 167.

72   Michael Manville and Donald Shoup, "People, Parking, and Cities," Access, no. 25 (Fall 2004), https://web.archive.org/web/20141026062915/http://www.uctc.net/access/25/Access%2025%20-%2002%20-%20People,%20Parking,%20and%20Cities.pdf.

73   Donald Shoup, High Cost of Free Parking, 214.

74   Ibid., 262.

75   Andres Duany and Jeff Speck, with Mike Lydon, The Smart Growth Manual (New York: McGraw-Hill, 2009), point 11.5.

76   This is quoted from memory and may be slightly inaccurate.

77   Jon Geeting, "Ideas Worth Stealing: Parking Benefit Districts," WHYY Radio (March 28, 2016), https://whyy.org/articles/ideas-worth-stealing-parking-benefit-districts/.

78   Julie Beck, "The Decline of the Driver's License," *The Atlantic* (January 22, 2016), https://www.theatlantic.com/technology/archive/2016/01/the-decline-of-the-drivers-license/425169/.

79   Jarrett Walker, *Human Transit: How Clearer Thinking about Public Transit Can Enrich Our Communities and Our Lives* (Washington, DC: Island Press, 2011), 85.

80   Unless noted otherwise, this entire point is sourced from Jarrett Walker, *Human Transit: How Clearer Thinking about Public Transit Can Enrich Our Communities and Our Lives* (Washington, DC: Island Press, 2011). Also, see the *Human Transit* blog, http://humantransit.org.

81   Walker, 217.

82   Unless noted otherwise, this entire point is sourced from *Human Transit* by Jarrett Walker and his *Human Transit* blog.

83   Enrique Peñalosa, "Why Buses Represent Democracy in Action," TEDTalk (September 2013), https://www.ted.com/talks/enrique_penalosa_why_buses_represent_democracy_in_action.

84   Dan Parolek, lecture, Congress for New Urbanism, June 16, 2000.

85   Charlie Hales, lecture, Congress for New Urbanism, June 16, 2000.

86   "Value Capture and Tax-increment Financing Options for Streetcar Construction," The Brookings Institution, HDR, Reconnecting America, RCLCo (June 2009).

87   Charlie Hales, lecture, Congress for New Urbanism, June 16, 2000.

88   "Value Capture and Tax-increment Financing Options for Streetcar Construction," The Brookings Institution, HDR, Reconnecting America, RCLCo (June 2009).

89   Eric D. Lawrence, "QLINE gets credit for $7B Detroit Transformation," *Detroit Free Press* (May 4, 2017), http://www.freep.com/story/money/business/2017/05/04/qline-detroit-streetcar/101294354/.

90   Speck, *Walkable City*, 155.

91   Darrin Nordahl, *My Kind of Transit: Rethinking Public Transportation in America* (Washington, DC: Island Press, 2009), ix.

92   Beyond DC, "Every US Bikeshare System, Ranked by Number of Stations of Hubs" (January 6, 2014), http://beyonddc.com/log/?page_id=6319.

93   Bobby Magill, "Is Bike Sharing Really Climate Friendly?," *Scientific American* (August 19, 2014), https://www.scientificamerican.com/article/is-bike-sharing-really-climate-friendly/.

94   National Association of City Transportation Officials, "Bike Share in the US: 2010–2016" (March 2017), https://nacto.org/bike-share-statistics-2016/.

95   Eltis news editor, "Mexico Abolishes Bike Helmet Law" (August 1, 2014), http://www.eltis.org/discover/news/mexico-city-abolishes-bike-helmet-law-mexico-0.

96   National Association of City Transportation Officials (NACTO), "Bike-Share Station Siting Guide" (2016), https://nacto.org/wp-content/uploads/2016/04/NACTO-Bike-Share-Siting-Guide_FINAL.pdf. Also see NACTO Bike Share Initiative, https://nacto.org/program/bike-share-initiative/. *Zagster* (blog), "The Guide to Running a Small-City Bike Share," (March 16, 2017), https://www.zagster.com/content/blog/the-guide-to-running-a-small-city-bike-share.

97   Jessica Lynn Peck, "Drunk Driving After Uber," CUNY Graduate Center PhD Program in Economics, Working Paper 13 (January 2017), 3.

98   Bruce Schaller, "Turns Out, Uber is Clogging the Streets," *Daily News* (February 27, 2017), http://www.nydailynews.com/opinion/turns-uber-clogging-streets-article-1.2981765.

99   Schaller Consulting, "Unsustainable? The Growth of App-Based Ride Services and Traffic, Travel and the Future of New York City" (February 27, 2017), http://schallerconsult.com/rideservices/unsustainable.htm.

100 Alejandro Henao, "Impacts of Ridesourcing—Lyft and Uber—on Transportation Including VMT, Mode Replacement, Parking, and Travel Behavior," Doctoral Dissertation Defense, Civil Engineering, UC Denver (January 19, 2017), https://media.wix.com/ugd/c7a0b1_68028ed55eff47a1bb18d41b5fba5af4.pdf.

101 Ibid.

102 Jude Cramer and Alan B. Krueger, "Disruptive Change in the Taxi Business in the Case of Uber," NBER Working Papers 22083, National Bureau of Economic Research, Inc., 2016.

103 "Evidence that Uber, Lyft Reduce Car Ownership," *University of Michigan News* (August 10, 2017), http://ns.umich.edu/new/releases/25008-evidence-that-uber-lyft-reduce-car-ownership.

104 Peter Henderson, "Some Uber and Lyft Riders Are Giving Up Their Own Cars: Reuters/Ipsos Poll," Reuters (May 25, 2017), https://www.reuters.com/article/us-autos-rideservices-poll/some-uber-and-lyft-riders-are-giving-up-their-own-cars-reuters-ipsos-poll-idUSKBN18L1DA.

105 Conversation with Alejandro Henao, August 17, 2017.

106 Adam Brinklow, "Lyft, Uber Commit 64 percent of Downtown SF Traffic Violations," *CurbedSF* (September 26, 2017), https://sf.curbed.com/2017/9/26/16367440/lyft-uber-traffic-citations-sfpd-board-supervisors.

107 Also see Jeff Speck, "Autonomous Vehicles: Ten Rules for Mayors," US Conference of Mayors Winter Meeting, 2017. http://jeffspeck.com/assets/autonomousvehicles2_2.mov.

108 Robin Chase, "Will a World of Driverless Cars Be Heaven or Hell?" *CityLab* (April 3, 2014), https://www.citylab.com/transportation/2014/04/will-world-driverless-cars-be-heaven-or-hell/8784/.

109 Also see Bloomberg Aspen Initiative on Cities and Autonomous Vehicles, https://www.bloomberg.org/program/government-innovation/bloomberg-aspen-initiative-cities-autonomous-vehicles/.

110 Emily Thenhaus, "Ford the River? Ways to Survive the L Train Shutdown," *RPA Lab* (November 22, 2016), http://lab.rpa.org/ford-the-river-ways-to-survive-the-l-train-shutdown/.

111 Andrew Boone, "Fantasizing About Self-Driving Cars, Sunnyvale Opposes El Camino Bus Lanes," *StreetsblogSF* (March 10, 2015), https://sf.streetsblog.org/2015/03/10/fantasizing-about-self-driving-cars-sunnyvale-opposes-el-camino-bus-lanes/.

112 Fred Kent, "Streets are People Places," *PPS* (blog), (May 31, 2005), https://www.pps.org/blog/transportationasplace/.

113 Ample evidence behind all of these claims is compiled in Part 1 of Jeff Speck, *Walkable City.*

114 Sam Schwartz, *Street Smart: The Rise of Cities and the Fall of Cars* (New York: Public Affairs, 2015), 104.

115 Randy Salzman, "Build More Highways, Get More Traffic," *The Daily Progress* (December 19, 2010).

116 Ted Chen and Katharine Hafner, "Commute Times Increase One Minute after Freeway Widening Project," NBC Los Angeles (October 8, 2014), http://www.nbclosangeles.com/news/local/Added-405-Carpool-Lane-Was-it-Worth-the-Delays-278600511.html.

117 Joe Cortright, "Reducing Congestion: Katy Didn't," *City Observatory* (December 16, 2015), http://cityobservatory.org/reducing-congestion-katy-didnt/.

118 Susan Handy, "Increasing Highway Capacity Unlikely to Relieve Traffic Congestion," UC Davis Institute of Transportation Studies (October 2015), http://cal.streetsblog.org/wp-content/uploads/sites/13/2015/11/10-12-2015-NCST_Brief_InducedTravel_CS6_v3.pdf.

119 Melanie Curry, "Caltrans Admits Building Roads Induces More Driving, But Admitting a Problem Is Just the First Step," *StreetsblogCAL* (November 18, 2015), http://cal.streetsblog.org/2015/11/18/caltrans-admits-building-roads-induces-congestion-but-admitting-a-problem-is-just-the-first-step/.

120 Jill Kruse, "Remove It and They Will Disappear: Why Building New Roads Isn't Always the Answer," *Surface Transportation Policy Progress,* vol.2 (March 1998): 5.

121 Jeff Speck, *Walkable City*, 94.

122 Kamala Rao, "Seoul Tears Down an Urban Highway and the City Can Breathe Again" *Grist*, (November 4, 2011).

123 Congress for the New Urbanism, Freeways Without Futures, 2017, https://www.cnu.org/highways-boulevards/freeways-without-futures/2017.

124 Ibid.

125 Stanley Hart and Alvin Spivak, *The Elephant in the Bedroom: Automobile Dependence and Denial,* Pasadena, CA: New Paradigm Books, 1993), 2.

126 Data taken alternately from two sources: 2004 World Technology Winners and Finalists Winner commentary by Ken Livingstone, mayor of London, World Technology Network; and Wikipedia: London Congestion Charge, https://en.wikipedia.org/wiki/London_congestion_charge.

127 Jan Gehl, *Cities for People* (Washington, DC: Island Press, 2010), 13.

128 Winnie Hu, "No Longer New York City's 'Boulevard of Death,'" *New York Times* (December 3, 2017), https://www.nytimes.com/2017/12/03/nyregion/queens-boulevard-of-death.html.

129 Wikipedia, List of countries by traffic-related death rate, https://en.wikipedia.org/wiki/List_of_countries_by_traffic-related_death_rate.

130 Nicole Gelinas, "What Stockholm Can Teach L.A. When It Comes to Reducing Traffic Fatalities," *LA Times* (June 21, 2014), http://www.latimes.com/opinion/op-ed/la-oe-gelinas-traffic-deaths-20140622-story.html. And City Data, "Fatal car crashes and road traffic accidents in Phoenix, Arizona," http://www.city-data.com/accidents/acc-Phoenix-Arizona.html.

131 Vision Zero Three Year Report, New York City Mayor's Office of Operations (February 2017), https://www1.nyc.gov/assets/visionzero/downloads/pdf/vision-zero-year-3-report.pdf. See also the Vision Zero Initiative, http://www.visionzeroinitiative.com, and the Vision Zero Network, http://visionzeronetwork.org.

132 City of New York Official Website, "Vision Zero: Mayor de Blasio Announces Pedestrian Fatalities Dropped 32% Last Year, Making 2017 Safest Year on Record" (January 8, 2018), http://www1.nyc.gov/office-of-the-mayor/news/016-18/vision-zero-mayor-de-blasio-pedestrian-fatalities-dropped-32-last-year-making-2017#/0.

133 Terry Smith, "Talk Show Host Pays Speeding Ticket," Idaho Mountain Express and Guide (September 3, 2014), http://archives.mtexpress.com/index2.php?ID=2007153544#.WWh2QzN7Hq0.

134 20's Plenty for Us campaign, http://www.20splenty.org.

135 David Williams, "One in Three Londoners to Live on Streets with 20mph Speed Limits by Summer," *Evening Standard* (March 18, 2015), http://www.standard.co.uk/news/transport/one-in-three-londoners-to-live-on-streets-with-20mph-limits-by-summer-10115181.html.

136 Hayley Birch, "Do 20mph Speed Limits Actually Work," *Guardian Cities* (May 29, 2015), https://www.theguardian.com/cities/2015/may/29/do-20mph-speed-limits-actually-work-london-brighton.

137 Brighton and Hove City Council, Travel, Transport and Road Safety, http://www.brighton-hove.gov.uk/content/parking-and-travel/travel-transport-and-road-safety/safer-streets-better-places.

138 UK Department of Transport Circular, *Setting Local Speed Limits* (January 2013), https://www.gov.uk/government/uploads/system/uploads/attachment_data/file/63975/circular-01-2013.pdf.

139 Rachel Dovey, "70 Percent of Portland City Streets Get New Speed Limit" *Next City* (January 18, 2018), https://nextcity.org/daily/entry/70-percent-of-portland-city-streets-get-new-speed-limit?utm_source=Next%20City%20Newsletter&utm_campaign=9a8a3541e4-Daily_790&utm_medium=email&utm_term=0_fcee5bf7a0-9a8a3541e4-43848085.

140 Insurance Institute for Highway Safety (IIHS), The Highway Loss Data Institute, http://www.iihs.org/iihs/topics/laws/automated_enforcement/enforcementtable?topicName=speed.

141 Ibid., 10.

142 Vision Zero Three Year Report, New York City Mayor's Office of Operations (February 2017), https://www1.nyc.gov/assets/visionzero/downloads/pdf/vision-zero-year-3-report.pdf.

143 New York City DOT, "Automated Speed Enforcement Program Report, 2014–2016," June 2017, 12, http://www.nyc.gov/html/dot/downloads/pdf/speed-camera-report-june2017.pdf.

144 Danielle Furfaro and Kristin Conley, "Bill for More Speed Cameras Stops in Senate," *New York Post* (June 22, 2017), http://nypost.com/2017/06/22/legislators-vote-to-double-the-citys-number-of-speed-cameras/.

145 City of Seattle, "Vision Zero 2017 Progress Report," http://www.seattle.gov/Documents/Departments/beSuperSafe/VZ_2017_Progress_Report.pdf.

146 Wen Hu and Anne T. McCartt, "Effects of Automated Speed Enforcement in Montgomery County, Maryland, on Vehicle Speeds, Public Opinion, and Crashes," Insurance Institute for Highway Safety (August 2015), 6, https://nacto.org/wp-content/uploads/2016/04/4-2_Hu-McCartt-Effects-of-Automated-Speed-Enforcement-in-Montgomery-County-Maryland-on-Vehicle-Speeds-Public-Opinion-and-Crashes_2015.pdf.

147 Jonathan Becher, "The Curse of the Cul-de-Sac," *Forbes Business* (April 9, 2012), https://www.forbes.com/sites/sap/2012/04/09/the-curse-of-the-cul-de-sac/#5efaf2947e8e.

148 Andres Duany, *Suburban Nation*, 64.

149 Lecture by Andres Duany, 1987.

150 Laurence Aurbach, "The Power of Intersection Density," *PedShed* (blog) (May 27, 2010), http://pedshed.net/?p=574.

151 Ibid.

152 Wesley E. Marshall, Norman W. Garrick, "Street Network Types and Road Safety: A Study of 24 California Cities," *Urban Design International, Basingstoke*, vol.15, no.3 (Autumn 2010): 133–47.

153 Alan Ehrenhalt, "The Return of the Two-Way Street," *Governing* (December 2009), http://www.governing.com/topics/transportation-infrastructure/The-Return-of-the.html.

154 *Traverse City Record Eagle* (MI), Editorial (February, 2, 1967).

155 William Riggs and John Gilderbloom, "Two-Way Street Conversion Evidence of Increased Livability in Louisville," *Journal of Planning Education and Research* (July 15, 2015), http://journals.sagepub.com/doi/abs/10.1177/0739456X15593147.

156 Ibid.

157 Jaffe, "The Case Against the One-Way Street.

158 Jeff Speck, *Walkable City*, chapters 1–3.

159 Schwartz, *Street Smart*, 41.

160 Schmitt, "Beyond 'Level of Service'—New Methods for Evaluating Streets" *StreetsblogUSA*, (October 23, 2013), http://usa.streetsblog.org/2013/10/23/the-problem-with-multi-modal-level-of-service/.

161 The article is no longer online. It is referenced here: https://www.communitycommons.org/2016/04/americas-worst-city-for-walking-gets-back-on-its-feet/.

162 Project 3-72, Relationship of Lane Width to Safety for Urban and Suburban Arterials, NCHRP 330, Effective Utilization of Street Width on Urban Arterials.

163 Dewan Masud Karim, "Narrower Lanes, Safer Streets," Conference Paper, Canadian Institute of Transportation Engineers, Regina (2015), https://www.researchgate.net/publication/277590178_Narrower_Lanes_Safer_Streets.

164 FDOT *Conserve by Bike Program Study*, 2007.

165 National Association of City Transportation Officials, *Urban Street Design Guide*, (Washington, DC: Island Press, 2013), https://nacto.org/publication/urban-street-design-guide/street-design-elements/lane-width/. (The entire Guide is a valuable resource.)

166 Elisabeth Presutti, personal communication, Des Moines Area Regional Transit Authority.

167 Walter Kulash, *Residential Streets* (Washington, DC: Urban Land Institute, 2001), https://uli.bookstore.ipgbook.com/residential-streets-products-9780874208795.php.

168 Luke Kerr-Dineen, "Beaufort's New Fire Trucks Hailed for a 6-figure Savings," *The Digitel* (May 7, 2011), http://www.thedigitel.com/s/beaufort/news/beauforts-new-fire-trucks-hailed-6-figure-savings-110507-74112/.

169 Jason Gill and Carlos Celis-Morales, "We All Know Biking Makes Us Healthier. But It's Even Better Than We Thought," *Yes* (May 19, 2017), http://www.yesmagazine.org/happiness/we-all-know-biking-makes-us-healthier-but-its-even-better-than-we-thought-20170619?utm_source=YTW&utm_medium=Email&utm_campaign=20170519>.

170 Speck, *Walkable City*, 107–8.

171 Schmitt, "Cycling Is Getting a Lot Safer in American Cities Adding a Lot of Bike Lanes," *Streetsblog* (November 16, 2016), http://usa.streetsblog.org/2016/11/16/cycling-is-getting-a-lot-safer-in-american-cities-adding-a-lot-of-bike-lanes/.

172 Atlanta Bicycle Coalition, https://lasesana.com/2012/10/12/bikeonomics-the-economics-of-riding-your-bike/.

173 Maggie L. Grabow et al., "Air Quality and Exercise-Related Health Benefits from Reduced Car Travel in the Midwestern United States," *Environmental Health Perspectives* vol.120 no.1 (2012), 68–76. PMC. Web. 29, March 2018. https://www.ncbi.nlm.nih.gov/pmc/articles/PMC3261937/.

174 Charlie Sorrel, "Bike Lanes May Be The Most Cost-Effective Way To Improve Public Health," *Fast Company* (November 14, 2016), https://www.fastcompany.com/3065591/bike-lanes-may-be-the-most-cost-effective-way-to-improve-public-health.

175 Angie Schmitt, "Less Affluent Americans More Likely to Bike for Transportation," *StreetsblogUSA* (January 24, 2014), http://usa.streetsblog.org/2014/01/24/less-affluent-americans-more-likely-to-bike-for-transportation/.

176 Michael Andersen, *PeopleforBikes* (blog) (October 31, 2013), http://peopleforbikes.org/blog/denver-tech-companies-the-no-1-thing-they-want-is-bike-lanes/.

177 Speck, *Walkable City*, 31n.

178 Lasesana, "Bikeonomics: The Economics of Riding Your Bike" (October 12, 2012), https://lasesana.com/2012/10/12/bikeonomics-the-economics-of-riding-your-bike/.

179 Gwynne Hogan, "Property Sales Jump 16 percent Along Bike Lanes in Bushwick, Study Says, DNAinfo (July, 2017), https://www.dnainfo.com/new-york/20170713/bushwick/bike-lane-property-bushwick-gentrification-lane-bikes-rent-sales-price.

180 New York City DOT, "Measuring the Street: New Metrics for the 21st Century Street"(2012), http://www.nyc.gov/html/dot/downloads/pdf/2012-10-measuring-the-street.pdf.

181 Portland Bureau of Transportation, "Bicycles in Portland Fact Sheet," https://www.portlandoregon.gov/transportation/article/407660.

182 Wikipedia, Cycling in the Netherlands, https://en.wikipedia.org/wiki/Cycling_in_the_Netherlands.

183 Mikael Colville-Andersen, "The 20 Most Bike-Friendly Cities in the World, From Malmö to Montreal." *Wired* (June 14, 2017), https://www.wired.com/story/world-best-cycling-cities-copenhagenize/>

184 John Pucher and Ralph Buehler, "Why Canadians Cycle More than Americans: A Comparative Analysis of Bicycling Trends and Policies," Institute of Transport and Logistics Studies, University of Sydney, Newtown, NSW, Transport Policy 13 (2006), 265–79.

185 League of American Bicyclists, "The Growth in Bike Commuting" (2015), http://www.bikeleague.org/sites/default/files/Bike_Commuting_Growth_2015_final.pdf.

186 Angie Schmitt, "Macon, Georgia, Striped a Good Network of Temporary Bike Lanes and Cycling Soared," *StreetsblogUSA* (June 28, 2017), https://usa.streetsblog.org/2017/06/28/macon-georgia-striped-a-good-network-of-temporary-bike-lanes-and-cycling-soared/.

187 Adele Peters, "New York City's Protected Bike Lanes Have Actually Sped Up Its Car Traffic," *Fast Company* (September 12, 2014), https://www.fastcompany.com/3035580/new-york-citys-protected-bike-lanes-have-actually-sped-up-its-car-traffic.

188 Jason Rodrigues, "Five Things More Likely to Kill You Than a Shark," *The Guardian* (December 7, 2010), https://www.theguardian.com/theguardian/2010/dec/07/things-likely-kill-than-shark.

189 Peter Walker, "How Bike Helmet Laws Do More Harm Than Good," *CityLab* (April 5, 2017), https://www.citylab.com/transportation/2017/04/how-effective-are-bike-helmet-laws/521997/.

190 Cyclists Rights Action Group, "How to Escape Bicycle Helmet Fines in Australia" (January 6, 2017), https://crag.asn.au.

191 Speck, *Walkable City*, 208.

192 For greater detail on each type of bike facility see *The Urban Bikeway Design Guide* by the National Association of City Transportation Officials, https://nacto.org/publication/urban-bikeway-design-guide/.

193 David P. Racca and Amardeep Dhanju, "Property Value/Desirability Effects of Bike Paths Adjacent to Residential Areas," Center for Applied Demography and Research University of Delaware (November 2006), 23, http://headwaterseconomics.org/wp-content/uploads/Trail_Study_51-property-value-bike-paths-residential-areas.pdf..

194 Tim Eling, "Crime, Property Values, Trail Opposition & Liability Issues," Presentation at the Lexington Big Sandy Workshop (April 1, 2006), http://atfiles.org/files/pdf/CrimeOppLiability.pdf.

195 Noah Kazis, "New PPW Results: More New Yorkers Use It, Without Clogging the Street," *StreetsblogNYC* (December 8, 2010); https://nyc.streetsblog.org/2010/12/08/new-ppw-results-more-new-yorkers-use-it-without-clogging-the-street/ And Gary Buiso, "Safety First! Prospect Park West Bike Lane Working," *Brooklyn Paper* (January 20, 2011). https://www.brooklynpaper.com/stories/34/3/ps_bikelanesurvey_2011_1_28_bk.html

196 Max Rivlin-Nadler, "Bike-Hating NIMBY Trolls Grudgingly Surrender to Reality," *Village Voice* (September 21, 2016), https://www.villagevoice.com/2016/09/21/bike-hating-nimby-trolls-grudgingly-surrender-to-reality/.

197 Mikael Colville-Andersen, "Explaining the Bi-directional Cycle Track Folly," *Copenhagenize* (blog) (June 3, 2014), http://www.copenhagenize.com/2014/06/explaining-bi-directional-cycle-track.html.

198 Noah Kazis, "New PPW Results: More New Yorkers Use It, Without Clogging the Street," *StreetsblogNYC* (December 8, 2010). https://nyc.streetsblog.org/2010/12/08/new-ppw-results-more-new-yorkers-use-it-without-clogging-the-street/

199 Robert Hurst, *The Cyclists Manifesto: The Case For Riding on Two Wheels Instead of Four* (Guilford, CT: Falcon Guides, 2009), 176.

200 Angie Schmitt, "Study: Sharrows Don't Make Streets Safer for Cycling," *StreetsblogUSA* (January 14, 2016), https://usa.streetsblog.org/2016/01/14/study-sharrows-dont-make-streets-safer-for-cycling/.

201 Andres Duany, *Smart Growth Manual*, point 8.5.

202 Jeff Speck, *Walkable City*, 182.

203 Ibid.

204 Joe Fitzgerald Rodriguez, "SFPD: Uber, Lyft Account for Two-Thirds of Congestion-Related Traffic Violations Downtown," *San Francisco Examiner* (September 25, 2017), http://www.sfexaminer.com/sfpd-uber-lyft-account-two-thirds-congestion-related-traffic-violations-downtown/.

205 Jeff Speck, *Walkable City,* 183n.

206 Ibid., 184n.

207 Liz Benston, "Design Challenges Leave Passers-by Passing CityCenter By," *Las Vegas Sun* (November 28, 2010), https://lasvegassun.com/news/2010/nov/28/passers—are-passing-citycenter/.

208 Alan Jacobs, Elizabeth MacDonald, and Yodan Rofe, *The Boulevard Book: History, Evolution, Design of Multiway Boulevards* (Cambridge: MIT Press, 2001), 112–21.

209 Ibid., 118.

210 Andres Duany, *Suburban Nation,* 36.

211 Ryan Cooper and Sam Wright, "Centerline Removal Trial," Outcomes Design Engineering, Transport for London (August 2014), http://content.tfl.gov.uk/centre-line-removal-trial.pdf.

212 Ibid.

213 Ibid.

214 Jeff Speck, "The Great Green Way," *New York Daily News* (April 14, 2013), http://www.nydailynews.com/opinion/great-green-article-1.1309203.*

215 Angie Schmitt, "Traffic Engineers Still Rely on a Flawed 1970s Study to Reject Crosswalks," *StreetsblogUSA* (February 12, 2016), https://usa.streetsblog.org/2016/02/12/traffic-engineers-still-rely-on-a-flawed-1970s-study-to-refuse-crosswalks/.

216 National Association of City Transportation Officials, *Urban Street Design Guide.*

217 Angie Schmitt, Why Can't We Have Traffic-Calming "3-D" Crosswalks Like Iceland? *StreetsblogUSA* (October 31, 2017), https://usa.streetsblog.org/2017/10/31/why-cant-we-have-traffic-calming-3-d-crosswalks-like-iceland/.

218 Dona Sauerburger, with input from Michael King, "Leading Pedestrian Interval—A Solution We've Been Waiting For!" *Metropolitan Washington Orientation and Mobility Association* (WOMA), Newsletter (March 1999), http://www.sauerburger.org/dona/lpi.htm.

219 Jen Kirby, "New York City Recorded Its Lowest Number of Traffic Fatalities in 2016," *New York Magazine* (February 24, 2017), http://nymag.com/daily/intelligencer/2017/02/nyc-recorded-its-lowest-number-of-traffic-deaths-in-2016.html.

220 Christopher Meleoct, "Pushing That Crosswalk Button May Make You Feel Better, but . . . ", *New York Times* (October 27, 2016), https://www.nytimes.com/2016/10/28/us/placebo-buttons-elevators-crosswalks.html?_r=0.

221 Vicky Gan, "Ask *CityLab*: Do "WALK" Buttons Actually Do Anything?" *CityLab* (September 2, 2015), https://www.citylab.com/life/2015/09/ask-citylab-do-walk-buttons-actually-do-anything/400760/.

222 CTVNews staff, "Countdown Crosswalk Signals Leading to More Crashes: Study" (April 11, 2013), http://www.ctvnews.ca/autos/countdown-crosswalk-signals-leading-to-more-crashes-study-1.1233782.

223 Bhagwant Persaud et al., "Crash Reductions Related to Traffic Signal Removal in Philadelphia," *Accident Analysis & Prevention*, Elsevier (November 1997), https://doi.org/10.1016/S0001-4575(97)00049-3.

224 Jane Lovell and Ezra Hauer, "The Safety Effect of Conversion to All-Way Stop-Control," *Transportation Research Record*, vol. 1068 (1986): 103–7.

225 Ryan Cooper and Sam Wright, "Centerline Removal Trial," Outcomes Design Engineering, Transport for London (August 2014), http://content.tfl.gov.uk/centre-line-removal-trial.pdf.

226 Wikipedia: Shared Space, https://en.wikipedia.org/wiki/Shared_space.

227 *Poynton Regenerated,* https://www.youtube.com/watch?v=-vzDDMzq7d0.

228 Ibid.

229 Eric Dumbaugh and J. L. Gattis, "Safe Streets, Livable Streets," *Journal of the American Planning Association*, vol. 72 (2005), 285–90.

230 See "Rainfall Interception of Trees," in Benefits of Trees in Urban Areas,"coloradotrees.org. Also see Dan Burden, "Urban Street Trees: 22 Benefits, Specific Applications" (Summer 2006), http://www.walkable.org/download/22_benefits.pdf.

231 Henry F. Arnold, *Trees in Urban Design,* 2nd ed., (Hoboken: John Wiley and Sons, 1992), 149.

232 US Department of Agriculture, Forest Service Pamphlet #FS-363.

233 Anthony S. Twyman, "Greening Up Fertilizes Home Prices, Study Says." *Philadelphia Inquirer* (January 10, 2005).

234 Geoffrey Donovan and David Butry, "The Effect of Urban Trees on the Rental Price of Single-Family Homes in Portland, Oregon," *Urban Forestry & Urban Greening* (2011), 163–8.

235 Don Burden, "Urban Street Trees." Henry F. Arnold, *Trees in Urban Design*, 149.

236 Rob McDonald et al., "Funding Trees for Health," *Nature Conservancy* (2017), https://thought-leadership-production.s3.amazonaws.com/2017/09/19/15/24/13/b408e102-561f-4116-822c-2265b4fdc079/Trees4Health_FINAL.pdf.

237 Nina Bassuk et al., "Structural Soil: An Innovative Medium Under Pavement that Improves Street Tree Vigor," Urban Horticulture Institute, Cornell University, Presentation at 1998 Conference of the American Society of Landscape Architects, http://www.hort.cornell.edu/uhi/outreach/csc/article.html.

238 Mohamed Elkordy and Faizal S. Enu, "Granite and Concrete Curbing: A Cost Comparison," New York State DOT (September 1998), http://www.williamsstone.com/documents/NYS-DOT.pdf. Also John Collura, "Life Cycle Cost Comparison."

239 This entire section is adapted from the 2017 Tulsa, Oklahoma, Downtown Walkability Study by Speck & Associates.

240 Park(ing) Day, http://parkingday.org.

241 Duany, Plater-Zyberk & Co., "Lexicon of the New Urbanism"(2014), 7.2, http://www.dpz.com/uploads/Books/Lexicon-2014.pdf.

242 David Sucher, *City Comforts: How to Build an Urban Village,* rev. ed., City Comforts, Inc. (2003), 12.

243 Trevor Boddy, "New Urbanism: The Vancouver Model," Places 16.2, https://designobserver.com/media/pdf/New_Urbanism:__%22.pdf.

244 Jake Offenhartz, "City to Spend $30,000 Apiece on Anti-Terror Bollards," *Village Voice* (January 3, 2018). https://www.villagevoice.com/2018/01/03/city-to-spend-30000-apiece-on-anti-terror-bollards/.

245 Linda J. Bilmes, "The Financial Legacy of Iraq and Afghanistan: How Wartime Spending Decisions Will Constrain Future National Security Budgets," HKS Faculty Research Working Paper Series RWP13-006 (March 2013), https://research.hks.harvard.edu/publications/workingpapers/citation.aspx?PubId=8956&type=WPN.

246 Jake Offenhartz, "Anti-Terror Bollards."

247 Jan Gehl, *Cities for People*, 137.

248 "How the Dutch Got Their Cycle Paths," https://www.youtube.com/watch?v=XuBdf9jYj7o&feature=youtu.be&t=2m3s.

249 Gehl, *Cities for People*, 75.

250 Ibid., 151.

251 Speck, *Walkable City*, 246–9.

252 Jacobs, *The Death and Life of Great American Cities*, 129.

253 Stephanie Meeks with Kevin Murphy, *The Past and Future City: How Historic Preservation is Reviving America's Communities*, (Washington, DC: Island Press, 2016), 43–48.

254 Don Rypkema, lecture, Akron, OH, (October 17, 2017).

255 Ibid.

256 Wikipedia: Mural Arts Program, https://en.wikipedia.org/wiki/Mural_Arts_Program. Also see also see https://www.muralarts.org.

257 See Speck & Associates, 2017 Tulsa, Oklahoma, Walkability Study, http://www.jeffspeck.com/assets/tulsa_walkability_analysis.pdf. Speck & Associates, 2015 Lancaster, Pennsylvania, Walkability Study, http://cityoflancasterpa.com/sites/default/files/documents/WALKABILITYANALYSIS.pdf. City of 2014 Albuquerque, New Mexico, Walkability Study, https://www.cabq.gov/council/find-your-councilor/district-2/projects-planning-efforts-district-2/downtown-walkability-study. Speck & Associates, 2014 West Palm Beach, Florida, Walkability Study, http://walkablewpb.com/reference-documents/downtown-walkability-study/.

258 Robert Steuteville, "From Car-Oriented Thoroughfare to Community Center," *CNU Public Square* (December 14, 2017), https://www.cnu.org/publicsquare/2017/12/14/car-oriented-thoroughfare-community-center.

259 Mike Lydon and Tony Garcia, *Tactical Urbanist's Guide to Getting it Done*, http://tacticalurbanismguide.com.

260 Sarah Goodyear, "What 'Tactical Urbanism' Can (and Can't) Do for Your City," *CityLab* (March 20, 2015), https://www.citylab.com/design/2015/03/what-tactical-urbanism-can-and-cant-do-for-your-city/388342/; updated based on conversation with Mike Lydon.

261 https://walkyourcity.org.

262 Excerpted from the 2017 Tulsa Downtown Walkability Analysis, Speck & Associates.

263 Ellen Dunham-Jones and June Williamson, *Retrofitting Suburbia: Urban Design Solutions for Redesigning Suburbia*, updated ed. (Hoboken: John Wiley and Sons, 2011). Also see Galina Tachieva, *The Sprawl Repair Manual* (Washington, DC: Island Press, 2010).

264 Beldon, Russonello & Stewart, "What Americans are looking for when deciding where to live," The 2011 Community Preference Survey, (March 2011), 2.

265 Overheard at Mayor's Institute sessions, confirmed with Mayor Riley.

266 Ibid.

267 Blair Kamin, "Millennium Park:10 Years Old and a Boon for Art, Commerce and the Cityscape," *Chicago Tribune* (July 12, 2014), http://www.chicagotribune.com/news/columnists/ct-millennium-park-at-10-kamin-0713-met-20140712-column.html.

268 John Rainey, "New York's High Line Park: An Example of Successful Economic Development," *Leading Edge Newsletter* (Fall/Winter 2014), http://greenplayllc.com/wp-content/uploads/2014/11/Highline.pdf.

269 Yonah Freemark, "The Interdependence of Land Use and Transportation" (February 5, 2011), thetransportpolitic.com. https://www.thetransportpolitic.com/2011/02/05/the-interdependence-of-land-use-and-transportation/

WORKS CITED

Recommended key resources are marked with an asterisk (*).

Alberti, Leon Batista. *On the Art of Building in Ten Books*. Cambridge: MIT Press, 1988.

American Lung Association. "Trends in Asthma Morbidity and Mortality" (September 2012).
http://www.lung.org/assets/documents/research/asthma-trend-report.pdf.

American Public Transport Association. "A Profile of Public Transportation Demographics and Travel Characteristics Reported in On-Board Surveys" (May 2007).
http://www.apta.com/resources/statistics/Documents/transit_passenger_characteristics_text_5_29_2007.pdf.

Andersen, Michael. *PeopleforBikes* (blog), October 31, 2013.
http://peopleforbikes.org/blog/denver-tech-companies-the-no-1-thing-they-want-is-bike-lanes/.

Angus, Hilary. "Bicycle Equity: Fairness and Justice in Bicycle Planning and Design," *MomentumMag*, October 26, 2016.*
https://momentummag.com/bicycle-equity-fairness-justice-bicycle-planning-design/.

Appleyard, Donald M., Sue Gerson, and Mark Lintell. *Livable Streets*. Berkeley: University of California Press, 1981.*

Arnold, Henry F. *Trees in Urban Design*, 2nd ed. Hoboken: John Wiley and Sons, 1992, 149.

"Arriving at School by Bicycle." *Bicycle Dutch* (blog), December 5, 2013.
https://bicycledutch.wordpress.com/2013/12/05/arriving-at-school-by-bicycle/.

Bassuk, Nina, Jason Grabosky, Peter Trowbridge, and James Urban. "Structural Soil: An Innovative Medium Under Pavement that Improves Street Tree Vigor." Urban Horticulture Institute, Cornell University. Presentation at 1998 Conference of the American Society of Landscape Architects.
http://www.hort.cornell.edu/uhi/outreach/csc/article.html.

Becher, Jonathan. "The Curse of the Cul-de-Sac." *Forbes Business*, April 9, 2012.
https://www.forbes.com/sites/sap/2012/04/09/the-curse-of-the-cul-de-sac/#5efaf2947e8e.

Beck, Julie. "The Decline of the Driver's License." *The Atlantic*, January 22, 2016.
https://www.theatlantic.com/technology/archive/2016/01/the-decline-of-the-drivers-license/425169/.

Beldon, Russonello & Stewart. "What Americans are looking for when deciding where to live." The 2011 Community Preference Survey, (March 2011).

Benston, Liz. "Design Challenges Leave Passers-by Passing CityCenter By." *Las Vegas Sun*, November 28, 2010. *https://lasvegassun.com/news/2010/nov/28/passers--are-passing-citycenter/.*

Betz, Eric. "The First Nationwide Count of Parking Spaces Demonstrates Their Environmental Cost." *Knoxville News Sentinel*, December 1, 2010.

Beyond DC. "Every US Bikeshare System, Ranked by Number of Stations of Hubs" (January 6, 2014). http://beyonddc.com/log/?page_id=6319.

Bilmes, Linda J. "The Financial Legacy of Iraq and Afghanistan: How Wartime Spending Decisions Will Constrain Future National Security Budgets." HKS Faculty Research Working Paper, Series RWP13-006March 2013. https://research.hks.harvard.edu/publications/workingpapers/citation.aspx?PubId=8956&type=WPN.

Birch, Hayley. "Do 20mph Speed Limits Actually Work?" *Guardian Cities*, May 29, 2015. https://www.theguardian.com/cities/2015/may/29/do-20mph-speed-limits-actually-work-london-brighton.

Bloomberg Aspen Initiative on Cities and Autonomous Vehicles.* https://www.bloomberg.org/program/government-innovation/bloomberg-aspen-initiative-cities-autonomous-vehicles/.

Blue, Elly. "The Free Rider Myth—Who Really Pays for the Roads." *MomentumMag*, March 24, 2016.

Boddy, Trevor. "New Urbanism: The Vancouver Model," *Places Journal*, v. 16 no. 2, 2004, 14–21. https://designobserver.com/media/pdf/New_Urbanism:__%22.pdf.

Boone, Andrew. "Fantasizing About Self-Driving Cars, Sunnyvale Opposes El Camino Bus Lanes." *StreetsblogSF*, March 10, 2015. https://sf.streetsblog.org/2015/03/10/fantasizing-about-self-driving-cars-sunnyvale-opposes-el-camino-bus-lanes/.

Brighton & Hove City Council. "Travel, Transport and Road Safety." http://www.brighton-hove.gov.uk/content/parking-and-travel/travel-transport-and-road-safety/safer-streets-better-places.

Brinklow, Adam. "Lyft, Uber Commit 64 percent of Downtown SF Traffic Violations." *CurbedSF*, September 26, 2017. https://sf.curbed.com/2017/9/26/16367440/lyft-uber-traffic-citations-sfpd-board-supervisors.

Brookings Institution. HDR, Reconnecting America, RCLCo. "Value Capture and Tax-increment Financing Options for Streetcar Construction," June 2009.*

Brunick, Nick, Lauren Goldberg, and Susannah Levine. "Large Cities and Inclusionary Zoning." Business and Professional People for the Public Interest, 2003.

Buiso, Gary. "Safety First! Prospect Park West Bike Lane Working." *Brooklyn Paper*, January 20, 2011.

Burden, Dan. "Urban Street Trees: 22 Benefits, Specific Applications." Summer 2006. http://www.walkable.org/download/22_benefits.pdf.

Byrne, Thomas, Dan Treglia, Dennis P. Culhane, John Kuhn and VincentKane. "Predictors of Homelessness among Families and Single Adults after Exit from Homelessness Prevention and Rapid Re-Housing Programs: Evidence from the Department of Veterans Affairs Supportive Services for Veteran Families Program." *Housing Policy Debate*, September 14, 2015. https://www.tandfonline.com/doi/abs/10.1080/10511482.2015.1060249.

Caiazzo, Fabio et al. "Air Pollution and Early Deaths in the United States. Part 1: Quantifying the Impact of Major Sectors in 2005." MIT (2013).

Castro, Julián. "Inclusionary Zoning and Mixed-Income Communities." *Evidence Matters*, Spring 2013. Office of Policy Development and Research (PD&R), US Department of Housing and Urban Development.

CDC Motor Vehicle Crash Deaths in Metropolitan Areas—United States, 2009. https://www.cdc.gov/mmwr/preview/mmwrhtml/mm6128a2.htm.

Chase, Robin. "Will a World of Driverless Cars Be Heaven or Hell?" *CityLab*, April 3, 2014. https://www.citylab.com/transportation/2014/04/will-world-driverless-cars-be-heaven-or-hell/8784/.

Chen, Ted, and Katharine Hafner. "Commute Times Increase One Minute after Freeway Widening Project." NBC Los Angeles, October 8, 2014. http://www.nbclosangeles.com/news/local/Added-405-Carpool-Lane-Was-it-Worth-the-Delays-278600511.html.

City of New York Official Website. "Vision Zero: Mayor de Blasio Announces Pedestrian Fatalities Dropped 32% Last Year, Making 2017 Safest Year on Record," January 8, 2018. https://www1.nyc.gov/office-of-the-mayor/news/016-18/vision-zero-mayor-de-blasio-pedestrian-fatalities-dropped-32-last-year-making-2017#/0.

City of Seattle. "A Guide to Building a Backyard Cottage," June 2010.* https://www.seattle.gov/Documents/Departments/SeattlePlanningCommission/BackyardCottages/BackyardCottagesGuide-final.pdf.

———. "Vision Zero 2017 Progress Report." http://www.seattle.gov/Documents/Departments/beSuperSafe/VZ_2017_Progress_Report.pdf.

Civil Rights Project. "Choice Without Equity: Charter School Segregation and the Need for Civil Rights Standards," 2009. https://www.civilrightsproject.ucla.edu/research/k-12-education/integration-and-diversity/choice-without-equity-2009-report.

Collura, John. "Life Cycle Cost Comparison." American Granite Curb Producers, November 2006. http://www.williamsstone.com/documents/11-06-Life-Cycle-Cost.pdf.

Colville-Andersen, Mikael. "Explaining the Bi-directional Cycle Track Folly." *Copenhagenize* (blog), June 3, 2014. http://www.copenhagenize.com/2014/06/explaining-bi-directional-cycle-track.html.

———. "The 20 Most Bike-Friendly Cities in the World, From Malmö to Montreal." *Wired*, June 14, 2017.* https://www.wired.com/story/world-best-cycling-cities-copenhagenize/.

Congress for the New Urbanism. "Freeways without Futures,"2017.* https://www.cnu.org/highways-boulevards/freeways-without-futures/2017.

Cooper, Ryan, and Sam Wright, "Centerline Removal Trial." Outcomes Design Engineering, Transport for London, August 2014.* http://content.tfl.gov.uk/centre-line-removal-trial.pdf.

Cortright, Joe. "Walking the Walk: How Walkability Raises Home Values in U.S. Cities." CEOs for Cities, August 2009.*

———. "Lost in Place." *CityReports*, September 12, 2014. http://cityobservatory.org/lost-in-place/.

———. "Reducing Congestion: Katy Didn't." *City Observatory*, December 16, 2015. http://cityobservatory.org/reducing-congestion-katy-didnt/.

Cramer, Jude, and Alan B. Krueger. "Disruptive Change in the Taxi Business in the Case of Uber." NBER Working Papers 22083, National Bureau of Economic Research, Inc. (2016).

CTVNews Staff. "Countdown Crosswalk Signals Leading to More Crashes: Study," April 11, 2013. http://www.ctvnews.ca/autos/countdown-crosswalk-signals-leading-to-more-crashes-study-1.1233782.

Curry, Melanie. "Caltrans Admits Building Roads Induces More Driving, But Admitting a Problem Is Just the First Step." *StreetsblogCAL,* November 18, 2015. http://cal.streetsblog.org/2015/11/18/caltrans-admits-building-roads-induces-congestion-but-admitting-a-problem-is-just-the-first-step/.

Cyclists Rights Action Group. "How to Escape Bicycle Helmet Fines in Australia," January 6, 2017. https://crag.asn.au.

Doherty, Patrick C., and Christopher B. Leinberger. "The Next Real Estate Boom." Brookings Institution, November 1, 2010.

Donovan, Geoffrey, and David Butry. "The Effect of Urban Trees on the Rental Price of Single-Family Homes in Portland, Oregon." *Urban Forestry & Urban Greening*, vol. 10 (2011): 163–8.

Dovey, Rachel. "70 Percent of Portland City Streets Get New Speed Limit." *Next City*, January 18, 2018. https://nextcity.org/daily/entry/70-percent-of-portland-city-streets-get-new-speed-limit?utm_source=Next%20City%20 Newsletter&utm_campaign=9a8a3541e4-Daily_790&utm_medium=email&utm_term=0_fcee5bf7a0-9a8a3541e4-43848085.

Duany, Andres, Elizabeth Plater-Zyberk, and Jeff Speck. *Suburban Nation: The Rise of Sprawl and the Decline of the American Dream*. New York: North Point Press, 2000.*

Duany, Plater-Zyberk & Co. "Lexicon of the New Urbanism," 2014.* http://www.dpz.com/uploads/Books/Lexicon-2014.pdf.

Duany, Andres, and Jeff Speck, with Mike Lydon. *The Smart Growth Manual*. New York: McGraw-Hill, 2009.*

Dumbaugh, Eric, and J. L. Gattis. "Safe Streets, Livable Streets." *Journal of the American Planning Association*, vol. 72 (2005): 285–90.

Dunham-Jones, Ellen, and June Williamson. *Retrofitting Suburbia: Urban Design Solutions for Redesigning Suburbia*, updated ed. Hoboken: John Wiley and Sons, 2011.*

Eling, Tim. "Crime, Property Values, Trail Opposition & Liability Issues." Presentation at the Lexington Big Sandy Workshop, April 1, 2006. http://atfiles.org/files/pdf/CrimeOppLiability.pdf.

Elkordy, Mohamed, and Faizal S. Enu. "Granite and Concrete Curbing: A Cost Comparison." New York State DOT, September 1998.

Eltis News Editor. "Mexico Abolishes Bike Helmet Law," August 1, 2014. http://www.eltis.org/discover/news/mexico-city-abolishes-bike-helmet-law-mexico-0.

"Fatal car crashes and road traffic accidents in Phoenix, Arizona." http://www.city-data.com/accidents/acc-Phoenix-Arizona. html#ixzz5B0Pg7lphhttp://www.city-data.com/accidents/acc-Phoenix-Arizona.html.

Frederick, Chad. *America's Addiction to Automobiles: Why Cities Need to Kick the Habit and How*. Santa Barbara: Praeger, 2017.

Freemark, Yonah. "The Interdependence of Land Use and Transportation." February 5, 2011. thetransportpolitic.com.

Frumkin, Howard, Lawrence Frank, and Richard Jackson. *Urban Sprawl and Public Health: Designing, Planning, and Building for Healthy Communities*. Washington, DC: Island Press, 2004.*

Furfaro, Danielle, and Kristin Conley. "Bill for More Speed Cameras Stops in Senate." *New York Post*, June 22, 2017. http://nypost.com/2017/06/22/legislators-vote-to-double-the-citys-number-of-speed-cameras/.

Gan, Vicky. "Ask *CityLab*: Do "WALK" Buttons Actually Do Anything?" *CityLab*, September 2, 2015. https://www.citylab.com/life/2015/09/ask-citylab-do-walk-buttons-actually-do-anything/400760/.

Garrett-Peltier, Heidi. "Pedestrian and Bicycle Infrastructure: A National Study of Employment Impacts." Political Economy Research Institute, University of Massachusetts, Amherst, June 2011.

Geeting, Jon. "Ideas Worth Stealing: Parking Benefit Districts." WHYY Radio, March 28, 2016. https://whyy.org/articles/ideas-worth-stealing-parking-benefit-districts/.

Gehl, Jan. *Cities for People.* Washington, DC: Island Press, 2010.*

Gelinas, Nicole. "What Stockholm Can Teach L.A. When It Comes to Reducing Traffic Fatalities." *LA Times*, June 21, 2014.

Gill, Jason, and Carlos Celis-Morales. "We All Know Biking Makes Us Healthier. But It's Even Better than We Thought." *Yes*, May 19, 2017. http://www.yesmagazine.org/happiness/we-all-know-biking-makes-us-healthier-but-its-even-better-than-we-thought-20170619?utm_source=YTW&utm_medium=Email&utm_campaign=20170519.

Goodyear, Sarah. "What 'Tactical Urbanism' Can (and Can't) Do for Your City." *CityLab*, March 20, 2015. https://www.citylab.com/design/2015/03/what-tactical-urbanism-can-and-cant-do-for-your-city/388342/.

Governing. "Education Spending Per Student by State." http://www.governing.com/gov-data/education-data/state-education-spending-per-pupil-data.html.

Grabow, Maggie L. et al. "Air Quality and Exercise-Related Health Benefits from Reduced Car Travel in the Midwestern United States." *Environmental Health Perspectives* 120.1 (2012): 68– 76. PMC. Web. 29, March 2018. https://www.ncbi.nlm.nih.gov/pmc/articles/PMC3261937/.

Greenfield, John. "If the Future Will Be Walkable, How Do We Make Sure Everyone Benefits." *StreetsBlog Chicago*, May 11, 2017. https://chi.streetsblog.org/2017/05/11/if-the-future-will-be-walkable-how-do-we-make-sure-everyone-benefits/.

Handy, Susan. "Increasing Highway Capacity Unlikely to Relieve Traffic Congestion." UC Davis Institute of Transportation Studies, October 2015. http://cal.streetsblog.org/wp-content/uploads/sites/13/2015/11/10-12-2015-NCST_Brief_InducedTravel_CS6_v3.pdf.

Hart, Stanley, and Alvin Spivak. *The Elephant in the Bedroom: Automobile Dependence and Denial.* Hope Publishing House, 1993.*

Henao, Alejandro. "Impacts of Ridesourcing—Lyft and Uber—on Transportation Including VMT, Mode Replacement, Parking, and Travel Behavior." Doctoral Dissertation Defense, Civil Engineering, UC Denver, January 19, 2017.* https://media.wix.com/ugd/c7a0b1_68028ed55eff47a1bb18d41b5fba5af4.pdf.*

Henderson, Peter. "Some Uber and Lyft Riders Are Giving Up Their Own Cars: Reuters/Ipsos Poll." Reuters, May 25, 2017. https://www.reuters.com/article/us-autos-rideservices-poll/some-uber-and-lyft-riders-are-giving-up-their-own-cars-reuters-ipsos-poll-idUSKBN18L1DA.

Hengels, Adam. "Only 2 Ways to Fight Gentrification (You're Not Going to Like One of Them)." Market Urbanism, January 28, 2015. http://marketurbanism.com/2015/01/28/2-ways-fight-gentrification/.

Hu, Wen, and Anne T. McCartt. "Effects of Automated Speed Enforcement in Montgomery County, Maryland, on Vehicle Speeds, Public Opinion, and Crashes." Insurance Institute for Highway Safety, August 2015. https://nacto.org/wp-content/uploads/2016/04/4-2_Hu-McCartt-Effects-of-Automated-Speed-Enforcement-in-Montgomery-County-Maryland-on-Vehicle-Speeds-Public-Opinion-and-Crashes_2015.pdf

Hu, Winnie. "No Longer New York City's 'Boulevard of Death.'" *New York Times*, December 3, 2017. https://www.nytimes.com/2017/12/03/nyregion/queens-boulevard-of-death.html.

Huang, Josie. "Popular Granny Flats Create a Niche Industry in LA." KPCC Radio, December 25, 2017. http://www.scpr.org/news/2017/12/25/79179/la-embracing-granny-flats-more-than-anywhere-else/.

Hurst, Robert. *The Cyclists Manifesto: The Case for Riding on Two Wheels Instead of Four.* Guilford, CT: Falcon Guides, 2009.*

The Insurance Institute for Highway Safety (IIHS), The Highway Loss Data Institute. http://www.iihs.org/iihs/topics/laws/automated_enforcement/enforcementtable?topicName=speed.

Jacobs, Alan, Elizabeth MacDonald, and Yodan Rofe, *The Boulevard Book*: *History, Evolution, Design of Multiway Boulevards.* Cambridge: MIT Press, 2001.*

Jacobs, Jane. *The Death and Life of Great American Cities.* New York: Vintage Reissue, 1992.*

Kamin, Blair. "Millennium Park: 10 Years Old and a Boon for Art, Commerce and the Cityscape." *Chicago Tribune*, July 12, 2014. http://www.chicagotribune.com/news/columnists/ct-millennium-park-at-10-kamin-0713-met-20140712-column.html.

Karim, Dewan Masud. "Narrower Lanes, Safer Streets." Conference Paper, Canadian Institute of Transportation Engineers, Regina, 2015. https://www.researchgate.net/publication/277590178_Narrower_Lanes_Safer_Streets.

Kazis, Noah. "New PPW Results: More New Yorkers Use It, without Clogging the Street." *StreetsblogNYC*, December 8, 2010. https://nyc.streetsblog.org/2010/12/08/new-ppw-results-more-new-yorkers-use-it-without-clogging-the-street/.

Kay Hertz, Daniel, "Chicago's Housing Market is Broken," March 21, 2014. https://danielkayhertz.com/2014/03/21/chicagos-housing-market-is-broken/.

Kent, Fred. "Streets are People Places." *PPS* (blog), May 31, 2005. https://www.pps.org/blog/transportationasplace/.

Kerr-Dineen, Luke. "Beaufort's New Fire Trucks Hailed for a 6-figure Savings." *The Digitel*, May 7, 2011. http://www.thedigitel.com/s/beaufort/news/beauforts-new-fire-trucks-hailed-6-figure-savings-110507-74112/.

Kirby, Jen. "New York City Recorded Its Lowest Number of Traffic Fatalities in 2016." *New York Magazine*, February 24, 2017. http://nymag.com/daily/intelligencer/2017/02/nyc-recorded-its-lowest-number-of-traffic-deaths-in-2016.html.

Kruse, Jill. "Remove It and They Will Disappear: Why Building New Roads Isn't Always the Answer." *Surface Transportation Policy Progress,* vol. 7.2 (March 1998): 5.

Kulash, Walter. *Residential Streets.* Washington, DC: Urban Land Institute, 2001.* https://uli.bookstore.ipgbook.com/residential-streets-products-9780874208795.php.

Larimer, Mary E., Daniel K. Malone, Michelle D. Garner, David C. Atkins, Bonnie Burlingham, Heather S. Lonczak, Kenneth Tanzer et al. "Health Care and Public Service Use and Costs Before and After Provision of Housing for Chronically Homeless Persons with Severe Alcohol Problems." *JAMA* 301, no. 13 (April 1, 2009): 1349–57.

Lasesana. "Bikeonomics: The Economics of Riding Your Bike," October 12, 2012. https://lasesana.com/2012/10/12/bikeonomics-the-economics-of-riding-your-bike/.

Lawrence, Eric D. "QLINE Gets Credit for $7B Detroit Transformation." *Detroit Free Press*, May 4, 2017. http://www.freep.com/story/money/business/2017/05/04/qline-detroit-streetcar/101294354/.

League of American Bicyclists. "The Growth in Bike Commuting," 2015. http://www.bikeleague.org/sites/default/files/Bike_Commuting_Growth_2015_final.pdf.

Leinberger, Christopher. *The Option of Urbanism.* Washington, DC: Island Press, 2008.*

Leinber ger, Christopher B., and Michael Rodriguez. *Foot Traffic Ahead: Ranking Walkable Urbanism in America's Largest Metros*. Washington, DC: George Washington School of Business, 2016.

Lipman, Barbara. *A Heavy Load: The Combined Housing and Transportation Burdens of Working Families*. Washington DC: Center for Housing Policy, 2006.

Littman, Todd Alexander. "The Economic Value of Walkability." Vancouver. Victoria Transport Policy Institute, April 20, 2017.* http://www.vtpi.org/walkability.pdf.

Loudenback, Tanza. "Crazy-High Rent, Record-Low Homeownership, and Overcrowding: California has a Plan to Solve the Housing Crisis, but Not without a Fight." *Business Insider*, March 12, 2017. http://www.businessinsider.com/granny-flat-law-solution-california-affordable-housing-shortage-2017-3.

Lovell, Jane, and Ezra Hauer. "The Safety Effect of Conversion to All-Way Stop-Control." *Transportation Research Record*, vol. 1068 (1986): 103–7.

Lutz, Catherine, and Anne Lutz Fernandez. *Carjacked: The Culture of the Automobile and Its Effect on Our Lives*. New York: St. Martin's Press, 2010.*

Magill, Bobby. "Is Bike Sharing Really Climate Friendly?" *Scientific American*, August 19, 2014. https://www.scientificamerican.com/article/is-bike-sharing-really-climate-friendly/.

Manville, Michael, and Donald Shoup. "People, Parking, and Cities." *Access*, no. 25 (Fall 2004). https://web.archive.org/web/20141026062915/http://www.uctc.net/access/25/Access%2025%20-%2002%20-%20People,%20 Parking,%20and%20Cities.pdf.

Marohn Jr., Charles. *Thoughts on Building Strong Towns*, vol. 1. CreateSpace Independent Publishing Platform, 2012.*

———. "The Cost of Auto Orientation, Update." *Strong Towns Journal*, July 22, 2014. https://www.strongtowns.org/journal/2014/7/22/the-cost-of-auto-orientation-update.html.

McDonald, Rob et al. "Funding Trees for Health." The Nature Conservancy, 2017. https://thought-leadership-production.s3.amazonaws.com/2017/09/19/15/24/13/b408e102-561f-4116-822c-2265b4fdc079 /Trees4Health_FINAL.pdf.*

Meeks, Stephanie, with Kevin Murphy. *The Past and Future City: How Historic Preservation Is Reviving America's Communities*. Washington, DC: Island Press, 2016.*

Meleoct, Christopher. "Pushing That Crosswalk Button May Make You Feel Better, but . . ." *New York Times*, October 27, 2016. https://www.nytimes.com/2016/10/28/us/placebo-buttons-elevators-crosswalks.html?_r=0.

National Alliance to End Homelessness: Housing First. (April 20, 2016).* http://endhomelessness.org/resource/housing-first/.

NACTO Bike-Share Initiative.* https://nacto.org/program/bike-share-initiative/.

National Association of City Transportation Officials. *Urban Street Design Guide*. Washington, DC: Island Press, 2013.*

———.*Urban Bikeway Design Guide*. Washington, DC: Island Press, 2014.*

———. "Bike-Share Station Siting Guide." 2016. https://nacto.org/wp-content/uploads/2016/04/NACTO-Bike-Share-Siting-Guide_FINAL.pdf.

———. "Bike Share in the US: 2010–2016," released March 2017. https://nacto.org/bike-share-statistics-2016/.

National Center for Education Statistics. "Education Spending Per Student by State." https://nces.ed.gov/fastfacts/display.asp?id=67.

National Center for Education Studies. "Overview of Public Elementary and Secondary Schools and Districts: School Year 1999–2000," September 2001. https://nces.ed.gov/pubs2001/overview/table05.asp, and https://nces.ed.gov/pubs2011/pesschools09/tables/table_05.asp.

National Community Land Trust Network.* http://cltnetwork.org.

Newman, Peter, Timothy Beatley, and Heather Boyer. *Resilient Cities: Responding to Peak Oil and Climate Change.* Washington, DC: Island Press, 2009.*

New York City DOT. "Measuring the Street: New Metrics for the 21st Century Street," 2012. http://www.nyc.gov/html/dot/downloads/pdf/2012-10-measuring-the-street.pdf.

———. "Automated Speed Enforcement Program Report, 2014–2016." June 2017, 12.* http://www.nyc.gov/html/dot/downloads/pdf/speed-camera-report-june2017.pdf.

Noonan, Erica. "A Matter of Size." *Boston Globe*, March 7, 2010.

Nordahl, Darrin. *My Kind of Transit: Rethinking Public Transportation in America.* Washington, DC: Island Press, 2009.*

Offenhartz, Jake, "City to Spend $30,000 Apiece on Anti-Terror Bollards." *Village Voice*, January 3, 2018. https://www.villagevoice.com/2018/01/03/city-to-spend-30000-apiece-on-anti-terror-bollards/.

Owen, David. *Green Metropolis: Why Living Smaller, Living Closer, and Driving Less Are the Keys to Sustainability.* New York: Riverhead Books, 2010.

Park(ing) Day. http://parkingday.org.*

Peck, Jessica Lynn. "Drunk Driving after Uber." CUNY Graduate Center PhD Program in Economics, Working Paper 13, January 2017.

Pedestrian and Bicycle Information Center (PBIC). "The Decline of Walking and Bicycling." http://guide.saferoutesinfo.org/introduction/the_decline_of_walking_and_bicycling.cfm.

Peñalosa, Enrique. "Why Buses Represent Democracy in Action." TEDTalk, September 2013. https://www.ted.com/talks/enrique_penalosa_why_buses_represent_democracy_in_action.

Perlman, Jennifer, and John Parvensky. "Denver Housing First Collaborative Cost Benefit Analysis and Program Outcomes Report." Colorado Coalition for the Homeless, December 11, 2006. https://shnny.org/uploads/Supportive_Housing_in_Denver.pdf.

Persaud, Bhagwant et al. "Crash Reductions Related to Traffic Signal Removal in Philadelphia."*Accident Analysis & Prevention*, Elsevier, November 1997. https://doi.org/10.1016/S0001-4575(97)00049-3.

Peters, Adele. "New York City's Protected Bike Lanes Have Actually Sped up Its Car Traffic." *Fast Company*, September 12, 2014. https://www.fastcompany.com/3035580/new-york-citys-protected-bike-lanes-have-actually-sped-up-its-car-traffic.

Portland Bureau of Transportation. "Bicycles in Portland Fact Sheet." https://www.portlandoregon.gov/transportation/article/407660. Updated 2016,

Poynton Regenerated. https://www.youtube.com/watch?v=-vzDDMzq7d0.

Project 3-72. Relationship of Lane Width to Safety for Urban and Suburban Arterials. NCHRP 330. Effective Utilization of Street Width on Urban Arterials. http://onlinepubs.trb.org/Onlinepubs/nchrp/nchrp_rpt_330.pdf.

Pucher, John, and Ralph Buehler. "Why Canadians Cycle More than Americans: A Comparative Analysis of Bicycling Trends and Policies." Institute of Transport and Logistics Studies, University of Sydney, Newtown, NSW. *Transport Policy* 13 (2006): 265–79.

Putnam, Robert D. *Bowling Alone: The Collapse and Revival of American Community.* New York: Simon & Schuster, 2000.*

Racca, David P. and Amardeep Dhanju. "Property Value/Desirability Effects of Bike Paths Adjacent to Residential Areas." Center for Applied Demography and Research University of Delaware, November 2006. http://headwaterseconomics.org/wp-content/uploads/Trail_Study_51-property-value-bike-paths-residential-areas.pdf.

Rainey, John. "New York's High Line Park: An Example of Successful Economic Development." *Leading Edge Newsletter*, Fall/Winter 2014. http://greenplayllc.com/wp-content/uploads/2014/11/Highline.pdf.

Rao, Kamala. "Seoul Tears Down an Urban Highway and the City Can Breathe Again." *Grist*, November 4, 2011. https://grist.org/infrastructure/2011-04-04-seoul-korea-tears-down-an-urban-highway-life-goes-on.

Rivlin-Nadler, Max. "Bike-Hating NIMBY Trolls Grudgingly Surrender to Reality." *Village Voice*, September 21, 2016. https://www.villagevoice.com/2016/09/21/bike-hating-nimby-trolls-grudgingly-surrender-to-reality/.

Rodrigues, Jason. "Five Things More Likely to Kill You than a Shark." *The Guardian*, December 7, 2010. https://www.theguardian.com/theguardian/2010/dec/07/things-likely-kill-than-shark.

Rodriguez, Joe Fitzgerald. "SFPD: Uber, Lyft Account for Two-Thirds of Congestion-Related Traffic Violations Downtown." *San Francisco Examiner*, September 25, 2017. http://www.sfexaminer.com/sfpd-uber-lyft-account-two-thirds-congestion-related-traffic-violations-downtown/.

Rogers, Shannon H., J. Halstead, K.H. Gardner, C. Carlson. "Examining Walkability and Social Capital as Indicators of Quality of Life at the Municipal and Neighborhood Scales." *Journal of Applied Research in Quality of Life* 6, no. 2 (2011): 201–213.

Rypkema, Don. Lecture. Akron, OH, October 17, 2017.

Salzman, Randy. "Build More Highways, Get More Traffic." *The Daily Progress*, December 19, 2010.

Sauerburger, Dona, with input from Michael King. "Leading Pedestrian Interval—A Solution We've Been Waiting For!" *Metropolitan Washington Orientation and Mobility Association* (WOMA), March 1999 Newsletter. http://www.sauerburger.org/dona/lpi.htm.

Schaller, Bruce. "Turns Out, Uber Is Clogging the Streets." *Daily News*, February 27, 2017. http://www.nydailynews.com/opinion/turns-uber-clogging-streets-article-1.2981765.

Schaller Consulting. "Unsustainable? The Growth of App-Based Ride Services and Traffic, Travel and the Future of New York City." February 27, 2017. http://schallerconsult.com/rideservices/unsustainable.htm.

Schmitt, Angie. "Beyond 'Level of Service'— New Methods for Evaluating Streets." *StreetsblogUSA*, October 23, 2013. http://usa.streetsblog.org/2013/10/23/the-problem-with-multi-modal-level-of-service/.

———. "Less Affluent Americans More Likely to Bike for Transportation." *StreetsblogUSA*, January 24, 2014. http://usa.streetsblog.org/2014/01/24/less-affluent-americans-more-likely-to-bike-for-transportation/.

———. "Study: Sharrows Don't Make Streets Safer for Cycling." *StreetsblogUSA*, January 14, 2016. https://usa.streetsblog.org/2016/01/14/study-sharrows-dont-make-streets-safer-for-cycling/.

———. "Traffic Engineers Still Rely on a Flawed 1970s Study to Reject Crosswalks." *StreetsblogUSA*, February 12, 2016. https://usa.streetsblog.org/2016/02/12/traffic-engineers-still-rely-on-a-flawed-1970s-study-to-refuse-crosswalks/.

———. "Cycling Is Getting a Lot Safer in American Cities Adding a Lot of Bike Lanes." *StreetsblogUSA*, November 16, 2016. http://usa.streetsblog.org/2016/11/16/cycling-is-getting-a-lot-safer-in-american-cities-adding-a-lot-of-bike-lanes/.

———. "Macon, Georgia Striped a Good Network of Temporary Bike Lanes and Cycling Soared." *StreetsblogUSA*, June 28, 2017. https://usa.streetsblog.org/2017/06/28/macon-georgia-striped-a-good-network-of-temporary-bike-lanes-and-cycling-soared/.

———. "Why Can't We Have Traffic-Calming '3-D' Crosswalks Like Iceland?" *StreetsblogUSA*, October 31, 2017. https://usa.streetsblog.org/2017/10/31/why-cant-we-have-traffic-calming-3-d-crosswalks-like-iceland/.

Schwartz, Sam. *Street Smart: The Rise of Cities and the Fall of Cars.* New York: Public Affairs, 2015.

Segmentation Company. "Attracting College-Educated Young Adults to Cities." CEOs for Cities, May 8, 2006.

Shoup, Donald. "Instead of Free Parking." *Access*, no.15 (Fall 1999). http://shoup.bol.ucla.edu/InsteadOfFreeParking.pdf.

———. *The High Cost of Free Parking,* updated ed. London: Routledge, 2011.*

Smart Growth America. *Dangerous by Design, 201*: 17–18.* https://smartgrowthamerica.org/dangerous-by-design/.

Smith, Terry. "Talk Show Host Pays Speeding Ticket." *Idaho Mountain Express and Guide*, September 3, 2014. http://archives.mtexpress.com/index2.php?ID=2007153544#.WWh2QzN7Hq0.

Sorrel, Charlie. "Bike Lanes May Be the Most Cost-Effective Way to Improve Public Health." *Fast Company*, November 14, 2016. https://www.fastcompany.com/3065591/bike-lanes-may-be-the-most-cost-effective-way-to-improve-public-health.

Speck, Jeff. *Walkable City: How Downtown Can Save America, One Step at a Time.* New York: Farrar, Straus and Giroux, 2012.

———. "The Great Green Way." *New York Daily News*, April 14, 2013. http://www.nydailynews.com/opinion/great-green-article-1.1309203.

———. "Autonomous Vehicles: Ten Rules for Mayors." US Conference of Mayors Winter Meeting, 2017.* http://jeffspeck.com/assets/autonomousvehicles2_2.mov.

Speck & Associates. 2014 Albuquerque, New Mexico, Walkability Study. https://www.cabq.gov/council/find-your-councilor/district-2/projects-planning-efforts-district-2/downtown-walkability-study.

———. 2014 West Palm Beach, Florida, Walkability Study. http://walkablewpb.com/reference-documents/downtown-walkability-study/.

———. 2015 Lancaster, Pennsylvania, Walkability Study. http://cityoflancasterpa.com/sites/default/files/documents/WALKABILITYANALYSIS.pdf.

———. 2017 Tulsa, Oklahoma, Walkability Study.* http://www.jeffspeck.com/assets/tulsa_walkability_analysis.pdf.

State of Utah. Comprehensive Report on Homelessness, 2014: 6.* https://jobs.utah.gov/housing/scso/documents/homelessness2014.pdf.

Steuteville, Robert "From Car-Oriented Thoroughfare to Community Center." CNU Public Square, December 14, 2017. https://www.cnu.org/publicsquare/2017/12/14/car-oriented-thoroughfare-community-center.

Sucher, David. *City Comforts: How to Build an Urban Village*, rev. ed. City Comforts. Inc. 2003.

Tachieva, Galina. *The Sprawl Repair Manual.* Washington, DC: Island Press, 2010.*

The Street Plans Collaborative. "Tactical Urbanist's Guide to Getting it Done."* http://tacticalurbanismguide.com.

Thenhaus, Emily. "Ford the River? Ways to Survive the L Train Shutdown." *RPA Lab*, November 22, 2016. http://lab.rpa.org/ford-the-river-ways-to-survive-the-l-train-shutdown/.

"20's Plenty for Us" campaign.* http://www.20splenty.org.

Twyman, Anthony S. "Greening Up Fertilizes Home Prices, Study Says." *The Philadelphia Enquirer*, January 10, 2005. UK Department of Transport Circular. "Setting Local Speed Limits," January 2013. https://www.gov.uk/government/uploads/system/uploads/attachment_data/file/63975/circular-01-2013.pdf.

University of Michigan News. "Evidence that Uber, Lyft Reduce Car Ownership," August 10, 2017. http://ns.umich.edu/new/releases/25008-evidence-that-uber-lyft-reduce-car-ownership.

US Department of Agriculture. "Benefits of Trees in Urban Areas." Forest Service Pamphlet #FS-363.

Vision Zero Initiative.* http://www.visionzeroinitiative.com.

Vision Zero Network.* http://visionzeronetwork.org.

Vision Zero Three Year Report. New York City Mayor's Office of Operations, February 2017.* https://www1.nyc.gov/assets/visionzero/downloads/pdf/vision-zero-year-3-report.pdf.

Walker, Jarrett. *Human Transit: How Clearer Thinking about Public Transit Can Enrich Our Communities and Our Lives.* Washington, DC: Island Press, 2011.*

———. *Human Transit* (blog). http://humantransit.org.*

Walker, Peter. "How Bike Helmet Laws Do More Harm Than Good." *CityLab*, April 5, 2017. https://www.citylab.com/transportation/2017/04/how-effective-are-bike-helmet-laws/521997/.

Williams, David. "One in Three Londoners to Live on Streets with 20mph Speed Limits by Summer." *Evening Standard*, March 18, 2015. http://www.standard.co.uk/news/transport/one-in-three-londoners-to-live-on-streets-with-20mph-limits-by-summer-10115181.html.

Zagster (blog). "The Guide to Running a Small-City Bike Share," March 16, 2017.* https://www.zagster.com/content/blog/the-guide-to-running-a-small-city-bike-share.

IMAGE CREDITS

[0-1] Jeff Speck

[1] Produced by Discourse Media, data from George Poulos.

[2] Source unknown.

[3a and b] Peter Haas, Center for Neighborhood Technology

[4] US Census Bureau, American Community Survey, 2008–2012

[5] *Livable Streets*, Donald Appleyard and Bruce Appleyard, Elsevier, 2019.

[6] Jake Boyd Photography, c/o Hubbel Realty Company

[7] Bing Maps

[8a] Google Maps

[8b] "Community" mural, © 2002 Anne Marchand

[9a] Source unknown.

[9b] New York City Department of Planning

[10] Urban3

[11] Torti Gallas + Partners

[12] Jeff Speck

[13] Bing Maps

[14] Champlain Housing Trust

[15] REUTERS/Lucas Jackson

[16] Google Maps

[17] Bing Maps

[18] Center for Applied Transect Studies

[19] City of Redwood City, California

[20] TransLink

[21 Spokane Transit

[22] Wikimedia Commons

[23] Darrin Nordahl

[24] Greater Greater Washington and Dan Malouff, Beyond DC

[25] San Francisco Police Department and SFGovTV

[26] © Rinspeed

[27a and b] Walter Kulash

[28] ROCC Buffalo

[29] Holger Ellgaard via Wikicommons

[30] Jeff Speck

[31a] D. C. Richards Transport Research Laboratory, Road Safety Web Publication No. 16, "Relationship between Speed and Risk of Fatal Injury: Pedestrians and Car Occupants," September 2010, Department for Transport: London.

[31b] Source unknown.

[32a and b] Nelson\Nygaard Consulting Associates

[33] Leah Finnegan

[34a] Elie Z. Perler/Bowery Boogie

[34b] Jeff Speck

[35] Jeff Cohn, PhotoEnforced.com

[36] Alex S. MacLean, Landslides Aerial Photography

[37] Google Maps

[38] Jeff Speck

[39] Speck & Associates LLC

[40] Google Maps

[41a and b] Google Maps

[42] George Kirkland

[43] Transportation Research Board, *Highway Congestion Manual*, Third Edition, 1994, Courtesy of the National Academies Press, Washington, D.C.

[44] Jeff Speck

[45a] Jeff Speck

[45b and c] City of Oklahoma City

[46] Nelson\Nygaard Consulting Associates

[47] Jeff Speck

[48a] Richard White aka Everyday Tourist

[48b] From Fitzpatrick, K., P. Carlson, M. Brewer, and M. Wooldridge. Design Factors That Affect Driver Speed on Suburban Streets. *Transportation Research Record: Journal of the Transportation Research Board*, no. 1751, figure 1, 24, 2001. Reproduced with permission of the Transportation Research Board.

[49a and b] Cupola Media

[50] Dan Burden

[51] City of Beaufort/Town of Port Royal Fire Department and Spartan Fire & Emergency Apparatus Inc.

[52] PeopleForBikes, extrapolated from 2006–2010 U.S. Census Transportation Planning Products (most recent available) via AASHTO.

[53a] Jeff Speck

[53b] 2012 Benchmarking Report on Bicycling & Walking in the United States, updated biennial reports available at bikeleague.org.

[54] Original drawing and data analysis by Chris Gillham, http://www.cycle-helmets.com/zealand_helmets.htm. Sources: University of Otago Injury Prevention Research Unit, https://blogs.otago.ac.nz/ipru/statistic. Land Ministry of Transport, https://www.transport.govt.nz/research/travelsurvey/reportsandfactsheets/).

[55] Speck & Associates LLC

[56] JJR/Detroit RiverFront Conservancy

[57] Carrie Cizauskas

[58 a and b] New York City Department of Transportation

[59] Nick Falbo

[60a] Elijah Boyer Moore and Alice Boyer Moore

[60b] Janet Lafleur

[61] Tucson Department of Transportation

[62a] Dan Kostelec

[62b] Mark Ostrow of Queen Anne Greenways

[63a] Jeff Speck

[63b and c] Jeff Speck

[64] Jeff Speck

[65] Boulder *Daily Camera*, Cliff Grassmick

[66a] Steve Marcus/*Las Vegas Sun*/Greenspun Media Group.

[66b and c] Midtown Alliance

[67a] Jeff Speck

[67b] Jeff Speck

[67c] Jeff Speck

[68] Sarah Jindra, WGN-TV

[69a] Google Maps

[69b] Ken Sides, PE

[70a] Raymond Unwin, *Town Planning in Practice*, Public domain.

[70b] Steve Mouzon

[71a, b, c] Transport for London

[72] Keith Bedford/*Boston Globe*/Getty Images

[73] Linda Bjork

[74] Jeff Speck

[75] Jason Eppink and Tyler Menzel

[76] Speck & Associates LLC

[77a and b] Photos from Poynton Regenerated by Martin Cassini, Equality Streets.

[78] Tobias Titz, Getty Images

[79] Jeff Speck

[80] Jeff Speck

[81] Google Maps

[82a] Aly Andrews, Farr Associates

[82b] San Francisco Planning Department

[83a] Galina Tachieva

[83b] DPZ Co-DESIGN

[84] Google Earth

[85] Peak Aerials

[86] VISIT DENVER

[87] *Chicago Tribune*, Getty Images.

[88] Lexey Swall/GRAIN

[89a] Image courtesy of Penta Investment.

[89b] Aerial Photography Inc. c/o DPZ Co-DESIGN

[90] Jeff Speck

[91] Worcester Telegram & Gazette/Rick Cinclair

[92a] Jeff Speck

[92b] Jeff Speck

[93a] Source unknown.

[93b] Our House, ©2015 City of Philadelphia Mural Arts Program / Odili Donald Odita. Brandywine Workshop and Archives, 728 S. Broad Street, Philadelphia, PA. Photo by Steve Weinik for the City of Philadelphia Mural Arts Program. Reprinted by permission.

[95] Speck & Associates LLC

[96] Speck & Associates LLC

[97a] Jeff Speck

[97b and c] City of Lancaster/CNU

[98a] The Better Block Foundation

[98b] Matt Tomasulo / walkyourcity.org

[100] Belmar, Lakewood, CO

[101a] Mark VanDyke Photography

[101b] Jeff Speck

INDEX

Note: Figures are indicated by the letter "f" following the page number.

Island Press | Board of Directors

Pamela Murphy
(Chair)

Terry Gamble Boyer
(Vice Chair)
Author

Tony Everett
(Treasurer)
Founder, Hamill, Thursam
   & Everett

Deborah Wiley
(Secretary)
Chair, Wiley Foundation, Inc.

Decker Anstrom
Board of Directors,
Discovery Communications

Melissa Shackleton Dann
Managing Director,
Endurance Consulting

Margot Ernst

Alison Greenberg
Executive Director,
Georgetown Heritage

Marsha Maytum
Principal,
Leddy Maytum Stacy Architects

David Miller
President, Island Press

Georgia Nassikas
Artist

Alison Sant
Co-Founder and Partner,
Studio for Urban Projects

Ron Sims
Former Deputy Secretary,
U.S. Department of Housing
   and Urban Development

Sandra E. Taylor
CEO, Sustainable Business
   International LLC

Anthony A. Williams
CEO & Executive Director,
Federal City Council